CATHOLIC IDENTITY
AND THE LAITY

CATHOLIC IDENTITY
AND THE LAITY

Tim Muldoon
Editor

THE ANNUAL PUBLICATION
OF THE COLLEGE THEOLOGY SOCIETY
2008
VOLUME 54

ORBIS BOOKS

Maryknoll, New York 10545

Founded in 1970, Orbis Books endeavors to publish works that enlighten the mind, nourish the spirit, and challenge the conscience. The publishing arm of the Maryknoll Fathers and Brothers, Orbis seeks to explore the global dimensions of the Christian faith and mission, to invite dialogue with diverse cultures and religious traditions, and to serve the cause of reconciliation and peace. The books published reflect the views of their authors and do not represent the official position of the Maryknoll Society. To learn more about Maryknoll and Orbis Books, please visit our website at www. maryknollsociety.org.

Published by Orbis Books, Maryknoll, New York 10545-0308.
Manufactured in the United States of America.

Library of Congress Cataloging-in-Publication Data

Catholic identity and the laity / Tim Muldoon, editor.
    p. cm.—(The annual publication of the College Theology Society ; v. 54)
    ISBN 978-1-57075-821-8 (pbk.)
    1. Laity—Catholic Church—Congresses.   2. Catholics—Religious identity—Congresses.   I. Muldoon, Tim.
    BX1920.C42 2009
    262'.152—dc22

                                                    2008053808

Contents

PART III
THE NATURE OF AUTHORITY IN THE CHURCH

PART IV
THE FUTURE CHALLENGES FOR THE LAITY

Introduction: Catholic Identity and the Laity

Tim Muldoon

In July 1859, the British journal *The Rambler* featured an essay by the distinguished Oxford don John Henry Newman entitled "On Consulting the Faithful in Matters of Doctrine." His radical proposal, based on his studies of the Arian controversy of the fourth and fifth centuries, was that Christian teaching had to be measured not solely by the exercise of episcopal authority, but also by the extent to which the Christian faithful—the *laos* in Greek, the laity—accepted that authority as reflective of their shared faith. Newman was mindful of the fact that many bishops themselves were Arian, and that their teachings were defections from the robust Trinitarian faith expressed in the creeds that emerged from the great christological councils. He wrote, "The body of the faithful is one of the witnesses to the fact of the tradition of revealed doctrine, and because their *consensus* through Christendom is the voice of the Infallible Church."[1] Identifying different offices in the church—distinctions similar to Saint Paul's image of the body with its many parts—Newman suggested that no single office holds the authority of what he called the *consensus fidelium* or the "shared feeling of the faithful."

Newman's argument incited such antipathy among certain influential readers that he was forced to resign his post as editor of *The Rambler*, and he subsequently ceased writing for five years. He had put his finger on an emerging controversy within the church as a whole: the proper understanding of the church's authority.

In stark contrast to Newman's was the position of Monsignor George Talbot, who saw in Newman's proposition a threat to ecclesiastical authority itself. Writing from Rome to Edward

Cardinal Manning of England, Talbot expressed his dismay at Newman's agitation of the English laity.

> If a check be not placed upon the laity of England they will be the rulers of the Catholic Church in England instead of the Holy See and the Episcopate.... They are beginning to show the cloven hoof.... They are only putting into practice the doctrine taught by Dr. Newman in his article in the *Rambler*.

Later in his letter, Talbot raised an oft-quoted question: "What is the province of the laity? To hunt, to shoot, to entertain. These matters they understand, but to meddle with ecclesiastical matters they have no right at all, and this affair of Newman is a matter purely ecclesiastical."[2]

From Newman's perspective, part of the issue lay in the way that "consultation" was understood in the context of Christian doctrines. Contrasting differing uses of the term in English, Newman suggested that one might consult the faithful in the way one might consult a barometer for knowledge of the weather, or a sundial for the time of day. Talbot, on the other hand, emphasized the apostolic authority of the bishops in communion with the Holy See, and saw even the suggestion of lay consultation as potentially corrosive of that authority. According to Talbot, the bishops teach, the laity learn.

Around the same time as the disputes between Newman and Talbot, Pope Pius IX released his *Lamentabili Sane*, also known as the Syllabus of Errors (Condemning the Errors of the Modernists), in 1864. Among the positions the pope condemned were two that addressed the relationships between and among the members of the church:

- The "Church learning" and the "Church teaching" collaborate in such a way in defining truths that it only remains for the "Church teaching" to sanction the opinions of the "Church learning." (6)
- In proscribing errors, the Church cannot demand any internal assent from the faithful by which the judgments she issues are to be embraced. (7)[3]

While it is unclear whether the pope was responding directly to Newman, still the first of these condemnations echoed a point that Newman had addressed in his *Rambler* essay. Writing of the different offices in the church, Newman had suggested that "the gift of discerning, discriminating, defining, promulgating, and enforcing any portion of that tradition resides solely in the *Ecclesia docens* [Church teaching]." Even though, according to Newman, the laity may at times be the most authentic manifestation of apostolic tradition, it is still the role of "Church teaching" to subject that tradition to holy order. To put it differently, what Pius condemned was the opinion that sacred doctrine emerged from the ground up, and that the laity, by their common consent, could persuade bishops of the rightness of their understanding of the workings of the Holy Spirit.

The second condemnation noted above is about the apostolic authority of the episcopate, and is best understood by reframing it as an exhortation: "In proscribing errors, the Church must demand the internal assent from the faithful by which the judgments she issues are to be embraced." Nearly a century later, the Second Vatican Council reaffirmed this basic idea in *Lumen Gentium*, its Dogmatic Constitution on the Church: "In matters of faith and morals, the bishops speak in the name of Christ and the faithful are to accept their teaching and adhere to it with a religious assent."[4] Doctrinally speaking, the bishops are the teachers of Catholic faith and "the faithful"—meaning those not ordained to the ranks of the clergy—are obligated to receive it. The role of the laity is, in this framework, fundamentally passive and receptive.

In the latter half of the nineteenth century, the identity of the laity, while acknowledged as distinct from that of the clergy, was still undefined. Hence, as Edward P. Hahnenberg points out in his essay in this volume, the 1891 edition of Wetzer and Welte's *Kirchenlexikon* reflected this lack of clarity: the encyclopedia's entry on "Laity" read simply: "See clergy." For nearly a century there was no extended magisterial treatment of the laity. Are vowed religious and clergy the only authentic or actualized Christians? Is there truly a vocation to lay life? Is the ecclesial role of the lay person a passive and receptive one, or might lay people exercise leadership in the church? Might lay people eventually exercise juridical authority in the church? It was not until the Second Vatican Council that the church's magisterium gave explicit attention to some of these questions, laying the groundwork for attention to others.

The Laity and the Legacy of Vatican II

If the First Vatican Council represented the culmination of extended reflection on the roles of bishops and of the pope in particular, the Second Vatican Council represented the culmination of extended reflection on the laity. Most significant is the document *Apostolicam Actuositatem*, the Decree on the Apostolate of Lay People (1965). The opening of this document is worth quoting at some length.

> Our own times require of the laity no less zeal: in fact, modern conditions demand that their apostolate be broadened and intensified. With a constantly increasing population, continual progress in science and technology, and closer interpersonal relationships, the areas for the lay apostolate have been immensely widened particularly in fields that have been for the most part open to the laity alone. These factors have also occasioned new problems which demand their expert attention and study. This apostolate becomes more imperative in view of the fact that many areas of human life have become increasingly autonomous. This is as it should be, but it sometimes involves a degree of departure from the ethical and religious order and a serious danger to Christian life. Besides, in many places where priests are very few or, in some instances, deprived of due freedom for priestly work, the Church could scarcely exist and function without the activity of the laity.[5]

What Newman discerned in 1859 was the coming of an age in which "the faithful" would represent an important locus for theological reflection. *Apostolicam Actuositatem* articulated what had been evident to Newman: namely, that the Catholic laity, who constitute the vast majority of the body of Christ, manifest in their shared faith life the sacramental work of the Holy Spirit in the world. Lay people, the document insists, must broaden their apostolate precisely because only lay people have the necessary expertise to bring the light of the gospel to bear on the increasingly differentiated areas of science, technology, communications, and so on. To put it differently, lay people possess sufficient knowledge in their areas of expertise such that their apostolate is critical for the church to be a presence in an increasingly fragmented world. To be sure, the role of the bishop as "overseer" (Greek *episkopos*) remains, as *Lumen Gentium* asserts, in teaching the faith. But in view of the fact that lay people are positioned to contribute to the church's discernment of key issues, it is not a stretch to suggest that episcopal authority itself becomes less about an individual bishop's opinion and more about his wise appropriation of the conclusions of authoritative voices of both clergy and laity. The bishop of 1859 was more like the teacher in a one-room schoolhouse; the bishop of today must be more like the provost of a university.

Pope John Paul II highlighted the emerging apostolate of the laity in his 1988 exhortation *Christifideles Laici* (On the Lay Faithful in the Church and the World). The image he uses throughout the exhortation is that of the parable of the laborers in the vineyard, and the master's call to the laborers that "you go into my vineyard too." Picking up the theme from *Apostolicam Actuositatem*, he suggested that the laity were an integral part of the church's mission in the world.

In looking over the years following the Council the Synod Fathers have been able to verify how the Holy Spirit continues to renew the youth of the Church and how he has inspired new aspirations towards holiness and the participation of so many lay faithful. This is witnessed, among other ways, in the new manner of active collaboration among priests, religious and the lay faithful; the active participation in the Liturgy, in the proclamation of the Word of God and catechesis; the multiplicity of services and tasks entrusted to the lay faithful and fulfilled by them; the flourishing of groups, associations and spiritual movements as well as a lay commitment in the life of the Church; and in the fuller and meaningful participation of women in the development of society.[6]

The key word in this excerpt is "collaboration," with its felicitous parallel to the gospel image of "working together" in the vineyard. Anyone familiar with the emergence of lay ecclesial ministry in the United States will at once recognize that the same image is used in the title of the U.S. bishops' 2005 document *Co-Workers in the Vineyard of the Lord*, which gives the most extended theological and pastoral treatment of lay people at work in the local church to date. The essays in this volume by Zeni Fox, Edward P. Hahnenberg, and William H. Johnston explore lay ecclesial ministry from historical, theological, and formational perspectives. What the pope pointed to in his exhortation was a maturation of the ecclesial role of lay people, from the passive and receptive role that one finds in the Syllabus of Errors to a much more active and (we might say) "evangelical" or even "missionary" role, a role that is integral to the very mission of Christ and his church today.

Reflecting on the twentieth anniversary of *Christifideles Laici*, Cardinal Angelo Scola remarked that "the appropriate way to understand the lay dimension of the Church is that of an encounter with Christ which transcends all realms of human existence."[7] His comment suggests a new way forward in reflecting theologically on the laity in the church today. The term "lay person" need no longer be defined using the term "not," as in "not the clergy." The lay person is the person who has encountered the risen Christ and who has responded to the invitation issued to all disciples: "Come, follow me." All Christians begin their pilgrimage with Christ as members of the laity. Some lay persons are called to specific service within the church (as lay ecclesial ministers, as teachers, as prophets, as healers, and so on), some to specific communities of shared prayer (as members of religious orders of women or men), some to sacramental presidency (as deacons, priests, and bishops). But all are members of the church, described so expansively in *Lumen Gentium* as "the people of God."

A Practical Theology of the Laity

If Prosper of Aquitaine's famous dictum *lex orandi, lex credendi* ("worship gives rise to belief") is true, then what we have seen over the past several decades is a development of both ecclesiality and ecclesiology. Paul Lakeland explores this distinction further in his essay in this volume; here, it is sufficient to suggest that the former term refers to the way that a community worships together, while the latter represents theological reflection on that experience of shared worship.

Between the late nineteenth century and the early twenty-first century, there has been dramatic growth in the interrelationships between and among lay people, members of religious orders, deacons, priests, and bishops. Perhaps the most significant factor that has driven this growth is the emergence of a truly educated laity, who, for the first time in ever larger numbers, are capable of exercising careful reflection on the scriptures and the church's traditions. In many cases, lay people are better trained than clergy in the study of theology, scripture, church history, canon law, and ethics. Of note in particular is the College Theology Society (CTS), comprised of mostly Catholic, mostly Ph.D.-holding professors of lay students at mostly Catholic colleges and universities. Over its five-plus decades of existence in the United States, the CTS has become increasingly lay, and increasingly female.[8]

The analogy that emerges as appropriate for the rise of the laity over the past century and a half is that of the family. Pope John XXIII described the church as "Mother and Teacher," in his encyclical of the same name, *Mater et Magistra*. He wrote, "To her was entrusted by her holy Founder the twofold task of giving life to her children and of teaching them and guiding them—both as individuals and as nations—with maternal care."[9] It is a tender image, albeit one that suggests that those she teaches are all children. Today, lay people have assumed adult roles in the church; perhaps they and the clergy must renegotiate their roles in ways not unlike adult children and their parents.

Beyond suggesting the kind of ongoing negotiations that laity and clergy must undertake, the family analogy offers insight into methods, liabilities, and promises in the ongoing development of new ways of being in communion.[10] The maturation of adult children brings new dynamics to a family's life, creating new responsibilities, hazards, and opportunities. It can be difficult for parents to cede responsibility to children, but over time it is necessary and appropriate. Without doubt, the children's assumption of new responsibilities will sometimes involve problems; the parents, especially, will likely be nostalgic for an earlier time. The children are likely to find points over which they rebel against the parents, even as, over time, they mature into an adult way of dealing with differences. Eventually, the great hope is that parents and children can cultivate rich new ways of relating as a family.

For the laity, maturity in faith requires intentionality. Unlike previous generations of Catholics, at least in the West, younger

Catholics cannot rely on the formative influences of strong ethnic communities. Their growth in faith must proceed by making explicit decisions to seek out resources, mentors, and opportunities to cultivate their spiritual lives in communion with those willing to show them how to proceed.[11] There are very few opportunities for systematic lay formation parallel to the kinds of formative opportunities that clergy and religious men and women undergo. Over the past century and a half, lay people have availed themselves of opportunities for remarkable intellectual and social growth through university education and any number of peer organizations, Catholic and non-Catholic. But a relatively small number of lay people can claim understanding of the Catholic faith tradition proportionate to their understanding of (for example) the stock market or politics. The church today faces the challenge of how to devote itself to formation as a people dedicated to advancing a civilization of love rooted in Christ. This volume serves as a contribution to meeting that challenge.

Part 1 of this volume is entitled "Shaping the Catholic Identity of the Laity." Dolores R. Leckey's essay offers a narrative of some of the changes that she has seen over the last several decades. Her perspective as a lay woman entrusted with leadership within the U.S. Conference of Catholic Bishops illustrates the kind of shift that the church in the United States has undergone to embrace more fully the role of lay people and women in particular. While it is clear that the documents of Vatican II have provided the architecture for this shift, still her essay suggests that the church's theology and pastoral ministry are "catching up" to the lived reality of many Catholics. The hunger for spirituality, the renewed emphasis on marriage, the new leadership roles that women are assuming, the attention to the theology of work, the development of new lay communities, and the entrance of lay people into ministry within the church—all these, Leckey writes, are ways that laity are "stirring" the church toward new life.

Accordingly, it is no surprise that the new ecclesial space carved out by contemporary lay people calls for corresponding reflection from the biblical and spiritual traditions. Carol J. Dempsey's essay traces the theme of holiness as applied to the laity, using a text from 1 Peter as a point of departure. Thomas F. Burke's essay attends to the tradition of Ignatian spirituality as a resource for lay formation. This tradition, articulated by Saint Ignatius of Loyola when he was still a lay person, started as an invitation to other lay people to engage in spiritual formation. Burke suggests that the same opportunity is available to us today, and further suggests that it has a particular relevance for the sake of encouraging careful discernment in a time when questions of accountability in leadership are at stake.

Laurie Johnston, a member of the Community of Sant'Egidio, has written an essay that explores that lay community's engagement with the influential French theologian Yves Congar. Influenced by Newman's writings on the laity, Congar is the figure credited with shaping the theology of the laity that so impacted the writings of the Second Vatican Council. As Johnston illustrates, his work influenced the development of Sant'Egidio as a lay apostolate in the areas of international peace mediation and outreach to the poor. In 2004, the Pontifical Council for the Laity published a list of international movements of lay faithful that included the Community of Sant'Egidio. It is clear from this document, as well as from earlier gatherings of new ecclesial movements under Vatican auspices, that the church hierarchy recognizes that these movements offer the beginnings of a new call to lay people to undertake the missionary activity of the church.

Part 2 of this collection, entitled "The Laity in the Modern World," echoes themes from the Vatican II document *Gaudium et Spes*, the Pastoral Constitution on the Church in the Modern World. This section explores questions related to lay mission, arising from what the document calls the "signs of the times." Ann M. Michaud's essay focuses on one area of theological reflection that has grown considerably because of the contributions of lay theologians, beginning in the early twentieth century and continuing to the present day. Her topic is the vocation of marriage, and in particular the place of sexuality and love in a contemporary understanding of the vocation. James T. Cross's essay on Archbishop Raymond Hunthausen's pastoral letter on marriage further explores the relationship between marriage and lay witness in the world, particularly for justice.

Jonathan Malesic pays attention to the question of the public nature of witness, raising the question of whether explicit public acknowledgment of faith serves to advance the mission of lay people today. John Sniegocki's essay then examines the social teaching of Pope Benedict XVI and, in particular, asks how the current pope envisions lay mission for justice. In the final essay in this section Tobias Winright focuses on the liturgy, where most lay people encounter and celebrate their faith, exploring how the liturgy shapes lay people's understanding of war.

Part 3 is entitled "The Nature of Authority in the Church." It is abundantly clear, even from a cursory glance at the fact that over thirty thousand lay people have assumed roles in the church as lay ecclesial ministers, that the laity embrace both a "secular" ministry in the world of work and an "ecclesial" ministry within the church itself. Yet at present there are no ecclesial structures (canonical, doctrinal, disciplinary) that support the laity in ecclesial roles. Lay ecclesial ministers do their work, the data tell us, because they feel that God is calling them there, even in the absence of institutional support.

Carolyn Weir Herman writes about the theological basis for such roles, namely the *sensus fidei* or "sense of the faithful," pioneered by Newman and others. She pays particular attention to the lay group Voice of the Faithful. Next, Angela Senander critiques attempts by the U.S. bishops and different groups of lay Catholics to persuade the Catholic electorate, a topic that received a good deal of attention during the 2008 presidential election, in part because of the fact that Catholics have in recent decades represented an important swing vote. William A. Clark goes on to explore an altogether different exercise of lay authority: namely, the phenomenon of lay people occupying closed parishes in the Archdiocese of Boston. Theirs is a tenacious, albeit boundary-crossing example of leadership. The final three essays in this section, mentioned above, by Zeni Fox, Edward P. Hahnenberg, and William H. Johnston, directly address the phenomenon of lay ecclesial ministry in the U.S. Catholic Church.

Paul Lakeland's essay appears in the final section, "Future Challenges for the Church." It is clear to any observer of the Catholic Church in the United States that the growth of the laity has involved the re-negotiation of many older assumptions; Lakeland is sober about the scope of the challenges.

These essays are a representative sample of the papers presented at the 2008 annual meeting of the CTS; many more could have been included. The members of the CTS spend much of their time in classrooms populated by young people whose experiences of church are, according to the best data, fragmented. Yet a great many of these same young people are attracted to questions about how to cultivate lives of meaning and purpose and often turn to the church and its multivalent symbolic architecture. At the root of their questioning, and consequently at the root of the essays presented in this volume lie passions for discerning the whispers of God, amidst an institution whose history is alternately an anchor and a heavy weight.

Conclusion: Lay Theology, Lay Spirituality

The history of Christian spirituality can be described as a history of movements, and the first was apostolic and evangelical. It issued from encounter with the risen Christ and spread from Jerusalem to the surrounding regions and into the gentile world, giving rise to churches all over the Roman Empire and into Asia and Africa. This movement represents the story of Christian conversion, *metanoia*, a change of heart. The second movement, the monastic period, was a renunciation of the trappings of life in the empire for the sake of direct encounter with God in the sparseness of the (sometimes literal, sometimes metaphorical) desert. This movement yielded spiritual practices like *lectio divina*, meditation, and the liturgy of the hours.

The third movement was mendicant and was practiced especially by the Franciscans and the Dominicans. It was a movement out of the monasteries into the world, especially of the poor, and it is felt today in its emphasis on conformity to Christ's compassion. The fourth movement was missionary. It is exemplified by the Jesuits, whose evangelical travels were modeled on Jerónimo Nadal's well-known maxim "the world is our house."[12] Its humanism and its awe before the mystery of everything human as rooted in God's grace has impacted our appreciation of the sacramentality of the world and everyone in it.

Ours is the age of the fifth movement, which draws from all four previous ones, because it is primarily a lay-led movement of engagement with the secular world. The roots of this movement can be traced to many sources: the development of the "third order" of lay Franciscans in the thirteenth century; the primarily lay *Devotio Moderna* in the Netherlands beginning in the late fourteenth century; the age of exploration in the sixteenth and seventeenth centuries; the formation of women's orders in the seventeenth through the nineteenth centuries; and the formation of lay associations, from the medieval guilds to the Christian Brothers to sodalities and Catholic fraternities. These roots have flowered in contemporary expressions of lay spirituality, from on-the-ground ecumenism and interreligious dialogue (often fueled by interchurch and interfaith marriages) to spiritualities of sex, love, and the family; to the development of myriad lay ecclesial communities, associations, third orders and oblates; to theologies and spiritualities seeking to help lay people sanctify everyday life.

Many lay people today find themselves in the position of having to pioneer their own spiritual pilgrimages, doing their best to find reliable guides along the way. Some draw from charismatic or Pentecostal elements in the tradition, reminiscent of the first movement of Christian spirituality. Many Asian churches, for example, have grown through appealing to these elements.[13] Others learn from the monastic practices of the second movement; several recent books have introduced lay people to the use of such monastic practices in everyday life.[14] The third movement is well represented by those Catholics dedicated to direct work with the poor, for example, the members of the Catholic Worker communities. Those educated at Jesuit schools, colleges, and universities are immersed in the fruits of the fourth movement, and many continue to be fed by the many writers on Ignatian spirituality.[15]

Publishers recognize that the market in spirituality is a remarkable phenomenon of recent decades. Representing some 24 percent of the U.S. population, Catholics no doubt are a significant part of that trend. It is no surprise that many lay Catholics today seek out books to help them in their spiritual development:

> Books are an essential tool because the life of faith is less shaped today by institutions and is more individualized, cut-and-pasted from a variety of convenient sources. Books are better organized than the information free-for-all of the Internet, allowing focus and providing depth.[16]

Today's Catholic laity are hungry for guidance in the life of faith. When they encounter their local pastor or the religious sister who teaches theology at the local college, they may recognize that the church has embraced the various traditions of spiritual formation. They have the sense that perhaps their own lives might be enhanced by greater intentionality, even as they wonder how to balance the desire for spiritual growth against the many other commitments they have to themselves, their work, and their families. Their stories are shaping this fifth movement, and promise to contribute in remarkable ways to the life of the church in coming years.

In closing, let us consider a recent literary example of a young layman wishing to develop a spirituality that will enable him to respond with authenticity to the invitations of God. The setting is, perhaps paradoxically, a Cistercian monastery, yet the story is applicable to any number of other settings, for it is the story of a human being learning spiritual discernment and seeking out a way of life to which God is calling him. Perhaps even more paradoxically, the story was written by a French layman, a banker-turned-novelist, Pierre de Calan, who had no direct experience of monastic life. He wrote *Côme ou le Désir de Dieu* in 1977, which Peter Hebblethwaite translated into English in 1980 with the title *Cosmas or the Love of God*.[17]

Narrated by the novice master of the Cistercian Abbey of La Trappe, the story is about the eponymous postulant, who appears at first to be perfectly suited for the strict observance of the Rule of St. Benedict practiced by the brothers there. Cosmas gives himself fully to monastic life, embracing with great joy the singing of the divine office and the many hours of prayer. Yet eventually problems develop:

> He poured out his troubles conscientiously, almost painstakingly.... He described the gulf between the monastic life as he had previously imagined it and its day-to-day reality; he spoke of the contrast between time spent in prayer in the church and the other activities, which all seemed so remote from any religious ideal.[18]

Cosmas's understanding of the spiritual life is naïve, for it has no room for ordinary humanness. The novice master attempts to help Cosmas find the root of his problems, describing the way that "secular" activities are yet opportunities for encounter with God:

> Driving animals to the fields or to the abattoir, plowing a field, eating, sleeping—these are all forms of prayer that are

just as good as liturgical prayers, the Gloria, or the psalms, provided that all these tasks, even the humblest and most material, are carried out in a spirit of obedience to the Rule and to superiors and, through them, to the will of God.[19]

The novice master's wisdom is in recognizing the integrity of a life lived in obedience to the will of God. Lay people today, in their many professions, avocations, relationships, and desires to serve God's people, are beginning to come to terms with the same struggle that Cosmas faced. For if theirs is primarily a secular vocation, it means that they live out their salvation in the context of the *saeculum*, the time created by God within which they are called to build his kingdom. They will, by necessity, struggle with questions about how to best build that kingdom among the many competing commitments of home, work, and family. *Apostolicam Actuositatem* echoes this struggle:

> Neither family concerns nor other secular affairs should be irrelevant to their spiritual life, in keeping with the words of the Apostle, "Whatever you do in word or work, do all in the name of the Lord Jesus Christ, giving thanks to God the Father through Him" (Col. 3:17).

The holy life is one shot through with desire to love God in the persons and work entrusted to us during our earthly pilgrimage. Such a desire represents the cornerstone of the developing Catholic mission and identity of lay people today.

Notes

[1] John Henry Newman, "On Consulting the Faithful in Matters of Christian Doctrine," sec. 2, online at http://www.fordham.edu/halsall/mod/newman-faithful.html.

[2] A history of the relationships between and among Cardinal Manning, Monsignor Talbot, and Newman can be found in Lytton Strachey, *Eminent Victorians* (1918; Whitefish, MT: Kessinger Publishing, 2004). For these specific quotes by Talbot, see also *Blackwoods' Edinburgh Magazine* 159 (January-June 1896), 824-25, and John Coulson's introduction to Newman's *On Consulting the Faithful in Matters of Doctrine* (Kansas City: Sheed & Ward, 1985).

[3] Pius IX, Encyclical *Lamentabili Sane*, online at http://www.papalencyclicals.net/Pius10/p10lamen.htm.

[4]*Lumen Gentium* 25, online at www.vatican.va.

[5]*Apostolicam Actuositatem* 1, online at www.vatican.va.

[6]Pope John Paul II, *Christifideles Laici* (1988), 2, online at www.vatican. va.

[7]Cardinal Angelo Scola, address to the Pontifical Council for the Laity, in "Cardinal Points to 'Essential' Lay Vocation," *Zenit*, November 18, 2008, online at http://www.zenit.org/article-24290?l=english.

[8]For a history of the College Theology Society, see Sandra Yocum Mize, *Joining the Revolution in Theology: The College Theology Society, 1954-2004* (Lanhan, MD: Rowman & Littlefield, 2007).

[9]Pope John XXIII, *Mater et Magistra* (1961), 1, online at www.vatican. va.

[10]It is worth observing parenthetically that the fourth commandment takes on new relevance with this analogy, in part because of the promise attached to it: "Honor your father and your mother, so that your days may be long in the land that the Lord your God is giving you" (Ex 20:12, see also Dt 5:16). If laity are becoming the adult children of Holy Mother Church, their relationship to the hierarchy can be conceived as a covenantal one.

[11]On the challenges and opportunities facing young Catholics in the United States, see Tim Muldoon, *Seeds of Hope: Young Adults and the Catholic Church in the United States* (Mahwah, NJ: Paulist Press, 2008).

[12]For the early history of the Jesuits, see John W. O'Malley, *The First Jesuits* (Cambridge: Harvard University Press, 1993).

[13]Thomas C. Fox, *Pentecost in Asia: A New Way of Being Church* (Maryknoll, NY: Orbis Books, 2003).

[14]The books by Thomas Merton and more recently by Kathleen Norris are examples.

[15]Recent authors include Timothy Gallagher, Joseph Tetlow, Margaret Silf, William Barry, David Fleming, and many others.

[16]Marcia Z. Nelson, "High Times for Books on Faith," *Publishers Weekly*, August 23, 2004, online at http://www.publishersweekly.com/article/ CA445911.html.

[17]Pierre de Calan, *Cosmas or the Love of God*, trans. Peter Hebblethwaite (Chicago: Loyola Press, 2006.)

[18]Ibid., 87.

[19]Ibid., 90.

PART I

SHAPING THE CATHOLIC IDENTITY OF THE LAITY

From Baptismal Font to Ministry

The Surprising Story of Laity Stirring the Church

Dolores R. Leckey

I have a memory of being baptized on April 30, which, in the old liturgical calendar, was the feast of St. Catherine of Siena. That confluence of saint and baptismal water is something I always believed to be influential. The baptism site was St. Mary Magdalene Church in Queens, New York, with the pastor, Father John Tinney, officiating. He was from the same place in Ireland as my grandparents, an important fact in our family lore. The washbasket in which I slept as an infant had been lined with white linen and trimmed with white satin bows for the occasion. A band played mostly Irish music during the baptismal party, which my mother was preparing (with help) during my time at the baptismal font. The help was not provided by my father because he was at the church. I feel quite certain about these details. Why? Because I heard about them all through my childhood; I was the recipient of the memories of others, which over the years came to feel like my own. I carry within me this communal memory.

In 1958 my first child was born and baptized two weeks after birth. Like my mother before me, I was not present at the sacrament; my husband, however, went to the church in South Bend, Indiana, with two Notre Dame friends who served as proxies for the real godparents, who were in New York.

In 1959, my second child was born in Washington, D.C., baptized a month later in the Bronx in a church across the street from the home of her paternal grandparents. My eighth-grade teacher, a Sparkill Dominican nun who was a close friend, told me she

Previously published in *Origins*, 38, no. 9 (2008).

would be at the baptism (unknown to her superiors) because she had never seen a baptism although she taught the sacrament year after year. She and a companion took a cab to the church and this time I did not stay at home but walked across the street to see her. In doing so, of course I witnessed my second daughter's baptism. My nun friend also expressed surprise that I traveled from Virginia to New York with an unbaptized baby. My presence at that baptism was a break with a long-established tradition.

Child number three was born and baptized in 1961. A month before, the prospective godfather announced that he had left the church and so could not serve in that capacity. His wife, who was to be the godmother, while still a Catholic, was upset enough not to come. I went to the church with my husband, and this time I held my son during the ceremony, which recorded only one godparent (all that is required by canon law).

One other unusual thing about that particular ceremony was that several Mormons who were in a study group with my husband and me came to the church to observe every detail of the ritual and then came to our home to argue the deficiencies in our theology. My in-laws were totally mystified by this turn of events. When that son was nearing the age of confirmation, he announced that he wanted a godfather just like everyone else. He chose a surrogate godfather, a joyful, prayerful member of our parish who also served as his confirmation sponsor.

We celebrated the addition of this surrogate with a home mass during which our parish priest, expressing some confusion, said he would have to make up a ritual for this "different relationship."

In 1963, one year into the Second Vatican Council, our fourth child was baptized, and there was no question of whether I would be there. Indeed, following the ceremony the celebrant blessed the parents (several babies were baptized) one couple at a time. There was no "churching" of women by that time.

All of these baptisms were on Sunday afternoons.

Fast forward to 2008. In my small parish in Arlington, Virginia, about twenty men and women were received into the Catholic Church at the Easter Vigil. Some of them had never been baptized, and some of them were baptized in another Christian community; some of them were never confirmed. During Lent, these men and women from various ethnic backgrounds who had been diligently involved in the Rite of Christian Initiation of Adults presented themselves to the parish not only through various public ceremonies at Sunday mass but through their own words published in the parish newsletter. All of them mentioned the effect that the parish's diversity of persons and ministry had on their decision. They also mentioned the affect, the emotional bonding that occurred when they witnessed infants and small children being baptized during mass. They were impressed with the public nature of the sacrament and its dimension of community.

Today this baptismal community is not comprised of the small private band of godparents and fathers—the preconciliar setting—but of a parish committed to the church's mission. The adult members of this one RCIA program, a program repeated in churches around the world, are not only different in age from the infants whose fathers and godparents took them to church for baptism forty-five years ago, their state of consciousness is different.

What happened? To begin with, the Second Vatican Council put laity at the center by insisting on the foundational character of baptism. This was expressed in different languages with different cultural twists.

The seminal work of Dominican theologian Yves Congar, who reclaimed the power of baptism as the primary sacrament of evangelization and mission, was critical in shaping this different way of thinking about Christian life. Father Congar's conviction that the laity participate in the priesthood of Christ through baptism can be found throughout the documents of the council.

The Canadian bishops also made a huge contribution by forcefully stating that the sacraments of baptism and confirmation were the real basis for the lay apostolate and that they affirmed the dual vocation of the laity: to build the world and to build the church. This affirmation has been most important as postconciliar debates developed and continue over the use of the term "ministry."

By the 1960s I had experienced different styles of baptism and was aware of the developing theology of baptism rising in the council and finding its way to America's shores. As a Catholic laywoman of that time, I wondered what it would mean for the church "that could not change" (because that was thought to be the will of Christ), and for me personally as change gathered force in creating a new horizon.

In the mid-1960s what I knew about change was coming from *Commonweal, Jubilee,* and Xavier Rynne's *New Yorker* stories.

It was also coming from the young priests and seminarians who acted as if their shackles had been loosened. One result was that intentional communities of faith were being formed—my family was on the ground floor of one. The priests who presided at our sacraments were like our rabbis, teaching us about the latest revelations, with a small "r." A new element entered church life—priests and laity together planned liturgies, a step in collaboration. And a new awareness surfaced in many that church could be fun.

It was reminiscent of the W. B. Yeats poem "The Fiddler of Dooney." You may recall that the fiddler begins by speaking of his brother and cousin, priests who read from their books of prayer. He, instead, read in his book of songs that he bought at the Sligo Fair.

> When we come at the end of time
> To Peter sitting in state,
> He will smile on the three old spirits
> But call me first through the gate;
> For the good are always the merry,
> Save by an evil chance;
> And the merry love the fiddle,
> And the merry love to dance.

Some of this merriment could be found in communities of sharing and commitment. Prayer groups were sprouting up without priests (something new for Catholics) as the voice of the Spirit was quietly heard saying, "Behold I make all things new." It was a moment when theology and praxis intertwined.

Home from the Council

When the American bishops arrived home at the close of the council, they brought with them a commitment to a serious and thorough implementation of the council teachings. Cardinal John Dearden of Detroit, who headed the American delegation to Rome, came back with two major goals. The first was to reorganize the bishops' national headquarters so that work at the national level would reflect the areas of reform and renewal that the council had decided were essential. His second goal was to establish a national council largely comprised of laity (two-thirds) but also with members drawn from the clergy (priests and bishops) and from religious orders.

The first national council was appointed, not elected, and the membership reflected the theological depth and breadth of the American church (Avery Dulles, for example, was a member). Because strongly held opinions were part of the members' DNA, it also produced "fireworks." One bishop on the original council told me that it was not until three elements were integrated into the meetings that life calmed down: (1) a professional facilitator was hired; (2) common prayer times, planned by members, were incorporated into the agenda (authentic prayer is the great leveler of egos and other things); and (3) time was made for socializing and for fun (never underestimate the power of a good Merlot). As defenses were lowered, the existing bonds of baptism were experienced more fully, and the outlines of the council's common cause became more visible.

Dearden's plan that this hand-picked council would evolve into a national pastoral council was halted, however. The Netherlands had already established such a council, and its proactive positions on a number of contentious issues had brought an intervention from the Vatican. There would be no national pastoral councils anywhere. So the new council in the United States was confirmed as advisory—and so it remains to this day.

When I worked at the Bishops' Conference, I staffed that council for several years. It met twice a year prior to the meetings of the Bishops' Administrative Committee, the governing arm of the U.S. Conference of Catholic Bishops. I can testify that the pastoral council was always influential in the preparation of documents. If the council felt a statement or action plan was not ready, it was returned to the originating committee and staff.

The council also had a proactive side. Many people either didn't know or have forgotten that the original Call to Action was conceived and promoted by the National Advisory Council. Call to Action was a major breakthrough of historic proportions in terms of involving the people of God, especially the laity, in identifying a pastoral agenda for the church in the particular culture that was America at the beginning of the last quarter of the twentieth century. The nationwide consultation (hundreds of

thousands participated) culminated in 1976 in a Detroit conference with Cardinal Dearden presiding, which is remembered by
most people of a certain age.

Dearden's reorganization of the national headquarters included
establishing a new office, the Secretariat for the Laity. It was to
staff what became a new standing committee of the Bishops' Conference, and that is where I served for twenty years, beginning in
1977 when memories of the national Call to Action meeting were
still present at national headquarters.

Laity Stirring the Church: The Issues

In the course of my work in the secretariat, it became clear that
issues involving the laity could be framed as "living questions."
My responsibilities were to arrange for dialogue concerning the
laity's responsibilities in governance and also to identify the various ways the people of God heard the Second Vatican Council's
universal call to holiness. "All ... of whatever rank or status are
called to the fullness of the Christian life and to the perfection of
charity" (*Lumen Gentium*, 40).

Laity heard these words against a background of a new world
reality: increasing mobility, technology, communication, changing
social mores. As citizens of two worlds, the people went beyond
the traditional sources of truth, namely scripture and tradition,
and dug into the truth of their experience to discover how best
to live in faithful response to the gospel. The ferment of which
many of us were part played out in communal contexts of all sizes
and also included institutions, even the national church structure.
Everywhere throughout the nation, the people, often laity and
clergy together, were shaping prophetic questions.

In a book published twenty years ago[1] I identified six such
questions that, I think, still stand today. Some of the probing edge
may be dulled, but I would argue they have within them the seeds
of redemption for our church and our world. Yves Congar put
it this way: if the church is to have any meaning for contemporary persons, it must be two things. First, it must be a church of
transcendence, that is, of teaching the contemplative dimension
of religion. Second, it must be a church of human liberation—for
God and for humankind.[2]

Six Ways Laity Are Stirring the Church

1. The first is *the hunger and thirst people have for an authentic spirituality.* The council's "universal call to holiness" said to the laity that they can seek direct experiential knowledge of God (as differentiated from knowledge *about* God) where they are. One need not enter a monastery or a seminary for this experience, although that's always an option, but the council said in the ordinary circumstances of everyday life lies the Mystery that is at the heart of life, that which is often hidden in plain sight. In Deuteronomy we read:

> Surely this commandment that I am commanding you today is not too hard for you, nor is it too far away. It is not in heaven, that you should say, "Who will go up to heaven for us, and get it for us so that we may hear it and observe it?" Neither is it beyond the sea that you should say, "Who will cross to the other side of the sea for us, and get it for us so that we may hear it and observe it?" No, the word is very near to you; it is in your mouth and in your heart for you to observe (Dt 30:11-14).

By following many pathways in a spirit of true freedom—from spiritual renewal movements like Cursillo to the practice of Zen, to participation in the ministry of spiritual direction either as directee or director, to an exploration of the arts and of science—laymen and laywomen have become more conscious of living in the Presence. And consequently, they have become more responsive to the segments of human need that are part of our everyday environments. What could be more surprising than the laity feeling they can trust the authenticity of their own experience?

2. The second way that laity have been stirring the church is through *a renewed understanding of marriage and family life as saving grace.* Prior to the 1987 synod on "The Lay Vocation in the World and in the Church," the Secretariat for the Laity conducted a nationwide survey in which we asked people in the parishes to identify the places where, in their own experience, they most readily encounter God. The primary place of encounter was the

family, and these families were of varied configurations, with full measures of sorrow as well as joy.

When the Second Vatican Council emphasized marriage as a covenant rather than a contract, people's expectations took on a personalist tone. The shift yielded new dialogues between theology and the other disciplines, notably psychology. One of the most important theological breakthroughs, in my opinion, has been the description of the family as "the domestic church," meaning that the family is, in fact, a real church and not simply a metaphor for the church. As for surprises, today laity often have the leadership role in preparing people for marriage.

3. The third way the laity have been stirring the church is through *the changing role of women in both church and society*. In referring to "new social relationships between women and men," *Gaudium et Spes* presented the challenge this way: "It is incumbent upon all to acknowledge and favor the proper and necessary participation of women in cultural life" (60). But women have been stirring the church in a most profound way in the last generation through their participation and leadership in the church's mission. While I will come back to this specific point later, I do want to point to a related question, that of women's participation in social, cultural, civic, and political life; it should be noted that whatever problems women have in this regard are not limited to Catholics or to issues of ministry alone.

Some years ago, an ecumenical group formed during the Second Vatican Council to share similarities and differences in spiritual understanding and practice dealt with the question of how to achieve true equality and interdependence between men and women. I was present at the meeting, which included cloistered nuns, a Trappist monk, Protestant clergy, Protestant and Catholic laywomen, Catholic priests, scholars, and so on. Men and women in segregated discussion groups began to explore the question: how has your relationship with women (or men) deepened your relationship with God? I facilitated the men's group. Here are some of the responses: (1) women have introduced me to God affectively; (2) from my marriage I've learned about spontaneity and directness. That's like God, I think. God is not concerned with theories or words so much, but with our joy and our compassion; and (3) I've learned that God knows my cul-de-sacs and will, when necessary, address my male drivenness, and (4) women are mysterious, and this evokes the otherness of God.

The group agreed that sexuality and power are closely related, for good and for ill.

One very gentle, intelligent, and truthful man said that the evolution now under way is a serious threat to what women have been valued and needed for. He asked, "Who will show us how to be receptive to God?"

In plenary session women noted how difficult it was for them as women to express assertively and confidently what they felt they knew. Most expressed the feeling of aliveness in the presence of a real relationship with a man. This probing led to other questions such as: what are the expectations of women as leaders? Such a question is critical not only for the church but for nation-states.

Freeman Dyson, who usually writes about the universe, expressed concern about women adopting a language style he calls "warrior." (He wasn't saying that women leaders were warriors.) The warriors, he said, are typically male, and they speak the language of efficiency and rationality, production and status. The warriors stand in contrast to victims, who are, Dyson says, mostly women and children. The Benedictine writer Joan Chittister certainly agrees with that, pointing out that women and children bear the burden of war.[3]

Having worked in a largely male environment for twenty years, I know how easy it is to slip into warriorism, ignoring the reality of my own vulnerability. The truth is, of course, that men too are vulnerable. We all are. Knowing it makes the difference.

4. The fourth way laity stir the church is *by calling attention to the co-creation with God that we undertake in our work life.* Work is one of the three principal sites of lay life, the others being family and civic life. It is strange that not much is heard about human work either in preaching or teaching.

This strange silence bothered me during my tenure at the Bishops' Conference; it also bothered a number of bishops who served on the Committee on the Laity. We tried to remedy the situation by sponsoring a conference to attempt to discover why there seemed to be a disconnect between religious faith and the world of work. Sixty laywomen and laymen were invited to a three-day meeting with seven bishops on the committee held at the University of

Notre Dame. A few theologians were also present. The invited laity were leaders in a variety of secular fields: business, politics, medicine, the military, the arts, nonprofit organizations, labor, research, science, education, sports, and journalism. The bishops who attended made it clear that their role was to listen and they urged a candid dialogue.

There were two guiding questions:

• What impact, if any, does Catholic faith have on your professional life?

• What kind of ministry is needed now and in the future to help busy lay people committed to secular vocations be consciously Christian in the workplace?

Basically the lay participants replied that their Catholic Christian faith did impact their work life, but this was because of the past: the closeness of the Catholic immigrant groups and the formation they received in Catholic schools. At present, they said, the church's ministry was missing them. What they were looking for was for the church to facilitate small communities of faith where they could pray and talk about the meaning of their lives as Christian workers, and where they could be supported in their family situations.

The Jesuit sociologist John Coleman, who was present as a *rapporteur*, agreed with the value of small communities but opposed what he called "the quick fix" communities with no prophetic edge. When men and women come together in community, he said, they should be asking new questions such as: what is it in work, family, in economics, in shops, in laboratories that gives hope? What connects work with other parts of life? And what integrates life? Where is the sense of call, of vocation? Where and how can we understand that we are co-creating with God?

5. The fifth question is closely related to the previous one, and that is the formation of Christian communities, which can take various forms. One way to think about the parish is as a community of friends befriending the world. (For this terminology I am indebted to Evelyn and James Whitehead.) The interdependent parts together make up the gathered church: homes of parishioners (the domestic church); the religious education programs, both child and adult; the pastoral team of the ordained and laity who are leaders in the parish; and perhaps the school. These comprise the communities of friends befriending the world. Friendship is a

key New Testament word: as Jesus says at the end of his life on earth, "I call you friends."

One way to describe community is to say what it is not. It is not a new elitist enclave that reinforces the cultural and social biases of the members. Quite the opposite. Authentic community helps us to see and to be free of the cultural addictions that can run our lives. It does so through a number of dynamics that I think of as different aspects of the reality of Christian friendship. I want to mention four.

- The first is the cultivation of relationships. In an essay, "Liberating the Divine Energy," Rosemary Haughton speaks of Jesus' legacy as the establishment of a new social order in which the encounter is the key. Jesus knew people not only as acted upon by divine power but as sources of it.[4]
- The second is respect for truth, which includes a willingness to face the truth about oneself. Respect for truth means using language that is not spin, not discriminatory, not cliché-ridden, and not distorted.
- The third is inner work, developing our capacities to open the doorways of the spiritual world and then to walk through those doorways toward the center where God dwells. Authentic spiritual work is not self-indulgent, sentimental, or self-inflating.
- The fourth dynamic is discerning one's personal vocation, including a call to ministry.

6. The sixth way the laity have stirred the church is through *their entrance into ministry and their willingness to share responsibility for the mission of the church.* In 1980 the American bishops approved the pastoral statement "Called and Gifted," which broke from the typical bishops' statement or letter. First, it was deliberately short and written in language accessible to the ordinary layperson. Its basic theme was that the laity are called by God to be adult in their relationships, to be holy as they live the lay life, to engage in ministry in the world and in the church, and to build community. The notion of call and these particular calls are reflective of deeply held beliefs of the chairman of the bishops' committee at that time, Bishop Albert Ottenweller, who at the time of this writing is now ninety-three years old, is still hopeful and still at the cutting edge of ministry.

"Called and Gifted" situates the call to ministry in the sacraments of baptism and confirmation, following the theology of

Vatican II. Lay participation in ministry is presented in two ways: as ministry in the world (called Christian service) and ministry in the church, in which laity are called ecclesial ministers. This is the first time the word ecclesial is used in this way.

As the document was being crafted, there was a conscious decision to place the world before the church in the call to ministry in order to signal the importance of the laity's vocation in secular life. When the bishops met in plenary assembly there was considerable debate about applying the term "ministry" to civic and public life. The debate was not so much about whether laity laboring in secular fields could be considered "the church in the world," but more a debate about precise language. There were a number of attempts to introduce amendments to strike the word ministry wherever it appeared, but they failed. "Called and Gifted" was the first pastoral statement on the laity by a bishops' conference anywhere since the Decree on the Apostolate of the Laity was promulgated in 1965. "Called and Gifted" was passed on the fifteenth anniversary of the Decree on the Apostolate of the Laity.

Fifteen years later, in 1995, the message was updated: "Called and Gifted for the Third Millennium." The revision pledged to support the laity whose call is properly discerned as a vocation to lay ecclesial ministry. This time, there was not the battle over the term ministry that occurred in 1980.

Ten years after the revised "Called and Gifted," the bishops approved "Co-Workers in the Vineyard of the Lord" (2005), a pastoral and theological reflection on the reality of lay ecclesial ministry, the spiritual formation of the ministers, and an affirmation of those who serve in this way. It is a synthesis of the best thinking and developmental practice over the course of twenty-five years, and it was prepared through a process of extensive consultation with ministers and theologians and the involvement of bishops all over the country. Even so, there were bishops who objected to using the term "lay ecclesial minister." Their argument was that Catholics would be confused about the difference between lay ministers and the ordained. It seemed that a generation after "Called and Gifted" the argument had not been fully resolved.

Enter Cardinal Avery Dulles, who asked to be recognized but appeared to be ignored. Finally he waved his cane rather than his place card (the usual method) and was given the microphone.

The cardinal said that he had been a theological consultant to the writing committee and that the drafters of "Co-Workers" had been very careful that the terminology was in accord with the documents of the Holy See and with a whole series of documents previously published by the conference of U.S. bishops. He added "I don't think the term ministry is only used in the Catholic Church for the ordained unless it's qualified in some way, like Petrine ministry or something like that." The document was approved by a vote of 190 to 49.

I doubt that the fathers of the church sitting in ecumenical council all those years ago envisioned the story of lay ministry as it has taken shape over these many years. I am confident, though, that a number of them, including Cardinal Suenens of Belgium, Archbishop D'Souza of India, and Cardinal Ritter of the United States, would be (are) happily surprised.

The State of the Questions Today

As I noted above, I believe that the six ways the laity have stirred the church, as I've described them, still remain relevant for our time. I do so with these caveats.

1. Concerning *spirituality*. To be a living question in our time, spirituality needs to be situated in the context of consumerism. In addition, many are likewise concerned and thinking and writing about a spirituality that recognizes the impact of globalization. This fresh thinking needs to find its way into parishes and bishops' conferences.

2. On *marriage and family*. Clearly this remains of major importance to the laity and is an arena in which they have competence. It is among the new priorities of the U.S. Conference of Catholic Bishops, and the Secretariat for the Laity is currently engaged in writing a pastoral letter on the topic. There is some concern that the language in the letter could be the opposite of "Called and Gifted," in other words, a reprise of arcane and theologically abstract language. Could the emphasis turn to a juridical description of marriage? Yes. Could the narrative take on a romanticized, illusionary tone? Yes. Let's hope not.

3. Concerning *women*. We know that women are leaders in ministry, in higher education, and in diocesan structures. But in their statement "Strengthening the Bonds of Peace" (1994),

the U.S. bishops asked for earnest study of existing obstacles to women exercising juridical authority. I am concerned that this remains unresolved and that the times seem bereft of imagination in pursuing the possible.

4. About *the world of work*. The world has changed in the twenty years since I wrote *Laity Stirring the Church* and so has the work world. Today people worry not so much about finding creativity in their work as simply having a job. Today economic uncertainty burdens family life. While wage earners understandably feel they have to give priority to their work, yet they long for time with their families. The need to balance work life and home life is not new, but what may be new is what Robert Bellah calls sullenness and hyperactivity at work where there should be an environment of care and celebration.[5] I submit this is a field for some imaginative pastoral ministry.

5. Finally, *community*. One of the great postconciliar surprises is how the laity are taking responsibility for responding to the Spirit. The action is on the ground, not in the chairs of power. The new life happening from below is exciting and hopeful. From Voice of the Faithful, to the Leadership Roundtable (a venture in church management skills), to new alliances between vowed religious and laity, new life is flourishing.

Every time I listen to John Haught, professor emeritus at Georgetown University (and now a Woodstock Fellow), speak on evolution, about single cells finding their way out of ponds and lakes to become ... what? I have hope renewed that the most wondrous life comes from the smallest bits and pieces. The Nobel poet Czeslaw Milosz (inspired by Lk 5:4-10) puts it this way:

> On the shore fish toss in the stretched nets of Simon, James and John
> High above, swallows. Wings of butterflies. Cathedrals.[6]

Notes

[1]Dolores R. Leckey, *Laity Stirring the Church: Prophetic Questions* (Philadelphia: Augsburg Fortress, 1987).

[2]Congar's description was at a Vatican-sponsored symposium on the laity in Vienna in 1981, though to my knowledge it remains unpublished.

[3]Dolores R. Leckey, ed., *Just War, Lasting Peace: What Christian Traditions Can Teach Us* (Maryknoll, NY: Orbis Books, 2006).

[4]Rosemary Haughton, "Liberating the Divine Energy," in *Living with Apocalypse: Spiritual Resources for Spiritual Compassion*, ed. Tilden H. Edwards (San Francisco: Harper & Row, 1984).

[5]Bellah used these descriptions at the annual Mark Gibbs Lectureship of The Vesper Society Group, Fuller Theological Seminary, April 27, 1990.

[6]Czeslaw Milosz, "Abundant Catch," in *The Gospels in Our Image: An Anthology of Twentieth-Century Poetry Based on Biblical Texts*, ed. David Curzon (New York: Harcourt Brace, 1995).

"Be Holy for I Am Holy"

Clothing Ourselves in Our Biblical Identity— 1 Peter 1:13-2:10

Carol J. Dempsey

In Leviticus 11:45, the ancient Israelite community received a divine call and challenge: "You shall therefore be holy for I am holy." A similar call and challenge was extended to the people of Jesus' day, "Be perfect, therefore, as your heavenly father is perfect" (Mt 5:48). In early Christianity, perhaps no other letter is more concerned with the call to holiness than 1 Peter, a pastoral letter addressed to a broad and general audience of Gentile Christians in Asia Minor, that offered them a word of clarity about Christian self-identity. The letter also provided a message of hope and encouragement to Christians who faced real problems and crises in the course of their daily lives. In our post-modern world, the call to holiness is no less important than it was centuries ago. The Second Vatican Council re-affirmed this call to holiness, particularly in chapter 5 of *Lumen Gentium*:

> The followers of Christ, called by God not in virtue of their works but by his design and grace, and justified in the Lord Jesus, have been made sons [and daughters] of God in the baptism of faith and partakers of the divine nature, and so are truly sanctified. They are told by the apostle to live "as is fitting among saints" (Eph 5:3), and to put on "as God's chosen ones, holy and beloved, compassion, kindness, lowliness, meekness, and patience" (Col 3:12), to have the fruits of the Spirit as their sanctification (cf. Gal 5:22; Rom 6:22).[1]

This article explores the theme of holiness in relation to 1 Peter 1:13-2:10, and argues that "holiness" is at the heart of the Catholic identity of the laity who, as part of the human community created in God's image, according to God's likeness, have a unique role to play in the evangelization of the world.

1 Peter 1:13-2:10: An Exegetical Analysis

Chapter 1:13-2:10 of 1 Peter is part of the first major section of the letter. This portion of the letter follows a doxology that praises God (1:3a), and includes a word of hope for Christians that assures them of their divine favor (vv. 3b-12). Verses 13-21 of chapter 1 is an exhortation that not only expands on themes introduced in 1:3-12 but also begins to establish a code of conduct befitting Christian life.

Verses 13-16

In vv. 13-16, the first unit of this section of the letter, Christians are given five directives. They are to (1) prepare their minds for action; (2) discipline themselves; (3) set all their hope on the grace that Jesus Christ will bring them when he is revealed; (4) not be conformed to the desires that they formerly had in ignorance; and (5) be holy in all their conduct.

The notion of preparing the mind for action is derived from the idea of "girding one's loins' in preparation for significant activity, as in the case of the exodus from Egypt when the Israelites ate the Passover meal with their loins girded (Ex 12:11).[2] Disciplining one's self pertained to refraining from an over-abundance of food and drink so as to preserve mental and spiritual alertness, free from alcoholic or spiritual "drunkenness" (1 Thes 5:6, 8; 2 Tm 4:3-5; cf. Lk 12:35-49; Eph 5:17-18). The goal was to live a balanced, self-controlled life, free for God and free for God's people. Christian hope was to be rooted in God, the one who graces and who will confer grace through Jesus Christ.[3] The desires once had in "ignorance" relate to those ways and passions characteristic of the Christians' lives before their rebirth through baptism. All of these directives lead up to the final one in vv. 15-16, which forms an antithesis to v. 14:

Instead as he who called you is holy, be holy yourselves in all your conduct; for it is written, "You shall be holy, for I am holy."

This final directive is the crux of all the other directives. The understanding of God as "holy" is unique to the New Testament. In the Old Testament, however, God is frequently referred to as *ho hagios*, "the Holy One," a title that expresses a sense of awesomeness, power, glory, majesty, and distinctiveness associated with the Divine.[4]

In v. 15 the author also makes clear to the Christians that they have been "called" (*kaleō*). Throughout the Old Testament, God is portrayed as summoning a person for a particular task, as in the case of Moses (Ex 3), Samuel (1 Sm 3:1-21), and Jeremiah (Jer 1:4-10). As a people, Israel is also called by God, signifying the community's divine election and privileged status (see, for example, Is 41:8-9; 42:6; 43:1; 45:3; 46:11; 48:12, 15). In his study of 1 Peter, John H. Elliott notes that "the notion of the believers having been called by God runs through 1 Peter both as an affirmation of their special elect status before God (2:9; 5:10) and as a reason for their behavior (1:15; 2:21; 3:9)."[5] Through the Sinai covenant, the Israelites became "a holy people" (Ex 19:6),[6] and now the Christian community addressed in 1 Peter is exhorted to recognize and live out its ancestral heritage. They are to be "holy" themselves.

Added to this phrase is a further qualifier: "in all your conduct." The Old Testament prophets stressed the ethical implications of both God's holiness and the people's holiness as seen in Isaiah 1:4; 5:6 and Ezekiel 36:20-32. The relationship between holiness and ethical conduct is also reflected in the Holiness Code of Leviticus (Lv 17-26), which has as its recurring refrain, "you shall be holy as I the Lord your God am holy" (Lv 19:2; 20:7, 26). Donald P. Senior notes that "the author does not describe 'holiness' as requiring Christians withdraw from the world but rather as the transformation of their 'entire way of life' (v. 15)."[7] Thus, Christians are to attest to their holiness not only as a divine state of being but also as a way of acting and living. In doing so, they become the embodied presence and transparent glory of the Sacred One who is "holy" and who acts within creation accordingly. The author closes the final directive and v. 16 with an appeal to scripture,

"You shall be holy, for I am holy," a quote from Leviticus 19:2. This appeal to scripture lends authority to the specific point being made and adds to the exhortation as a whole.[8]

Verses 17-21

Verses 17-21 comprise the second unit of 1 Peter 1:13-2:10 and continue the theme of holiness introduced in vv. 13-16. Once again, Christians are invited to embrace a transformed life of holiness now signified through new imagery. In v. 17 they are instructed on what they must do if they invoke God: they are to live in reverent fear during the time of their exile. The term "exile" recalls the social situation of the Israelites first as displaced aliens from Canaan who moved into Egypt (Gn 46:1-Ex 12:28) and then as displaced aliens in Egypt and Babylon following the fall of the Southern Kingdom of Judah in 587 B.C.E. Here the term captures the experience of the Christians who, as believers, are "aliens" or "outsiders" in an Asia Minor society. "Reverent fear" indicates how they should live, namely, in a state of awe and reverence toward God.

Verse 17 is also confessional and presents two images of God: one as father and the other as judge. God as "father" not only reflects "the prevailing patriarchal world-view of their male-dominated, patriarchal culture"[9] but also implies "God's progenerating or bringing his human 'children' into existence (Isa 45:9-10; 64:8; 2 Sam 7:14; Pss 2:7; 89:26), his authority over them (Deut 14:1), his paternal affection, protection, and care for them (Ps 103:13; Isa 63:16; Jer 3:19; Hos 11:1), and his function as the 'father of the fatherless' (Ps 68:5)."[10] The term was used by Jesus to help establish his identity as the messianic son of David. The term was also used to welcome people into a covenant relationship (see Mt 6:9; Lk 11:1). This "father" is also a "judge" who judges impartially according to one's deeds. Coupled with the image of "father," the one who "judges" does so as a function of love, distinguishing between right and wrong without criticism or condemnation. Implicit in v. 17 is a further lesson to Christians on God's holiness that provides them with more insight as to how they should live their lives and conduct their affairs.

In vv. 18-21 the focus shifts from God to Jesus. In this passage the author recalls the apostolic teaching the audience has already

received and accepted. That teaching serves as the motivation
behind holy and reverent conduct (vv. 14-17). The Christians are
reminded that they have been "ransomed" from the futile ways
inherited from their ancestors (v. 18). Of note is the fact that this
"ransom" came as a result of God's initiative realized through
the suffering and death of Jesus, a shed blood more precious than
silver or gold (v. 19). The risen, glorified Christ is a testament to
God's love and power, and has now become the testimony as to
why the Christians should have their faith and hope set in God.
Hence, the writer of 1 Peter 1:13-2:10 has situated the Christian
community within Israel's history and "anchors holiness in union
with Christ as well as God...."[11] Furthermore, "their holiness is
grounded in the holiness of God who called them [v. 15] and that
of Christ, the holy lamb by whose blood they were redeemed. The
holiness has both a moral and a social aspect."[12]

Finally, looking at vv. 13-16 and vv. 17-21 as a whole, we see
that, although they are separate units, they have a unifying theme
of hope and holiness as indicated by their chiastic structure:

> A   Hope (v. 13)
>   B   Holiness (vv. 14-16)
> A   B¹   Holiness (vv. 17-21b)
> A¹   Hope (v. 21c)

Verses 22-25

Verses 22-25, the third unit of 1 Peter 1:13-2:10, continue the
theme of holiness. Here the author focuses on the believers as the
purified, holy, and born anew children of God (1:3, 14-19), and
calls them to a life of genuine mutual love from the heart (v. 22).
The call to love echoes Romans 12:9-21 where Paul outlines the
marks of a true Christian. What was eclipsed in v. 15 now comes
to full light in v. 22. The conduct proper to holiness is love. The
reference "from the heart" is central to the theology and spirituality of Israel. The Israelites were called to love God with all their
heart (Deut 6:5)—a God who had set the divine heart in love on
them (Dt 10:15; cf. Dt 7:7).

Moreover, the Israelites were called to circumcise the foreskin
of their hearts (Dt 10:16; cf. Jer 4:4), a deed that would be ac-
complished by God (Dt 30:6). Such is the sacrifice that Israel's God

desired—a sacrifice of love and not a sacrifice of burnt offerings, year-old calves, thousands of rams, or the firstborn of one's flesh as Micah proclaimed (Mi 6:6-8). This genuine, mutual love from the heart echoes New Testament teaching (Mt 22:34-40) and found its fulfillment in and through the life of Jesus, especially through his suffering and death on the cross, an image that draws listeners back to 1 Peter 1:18-19. Sincere and mutual love from the heart is a sign of "authentic conversion."[13]

In v. 23, the author reminds the believers of how they were born anew, namely, through the living and enduring word of God. This "word of God" is not only the gospel but also Jesus. This implied reference draws listeners back again to vv. 18-19 and to the centrality of Christ's life offered as gift and source of faith and hope in God (v. 21). In v. 24, the author links his instruction to Isaiah 40:6-8. He offers a rereading of an ancient prophetic text, thus giving an ancient text a new nuance and a new and deeper understanding as he emphasizes the abiding power of God's word in the midst of a transitory, created world. This imagery complements the contrast between silver and gold and the precious blood of Christ heard earlier in vv. 18-19. Verse 25 closes with a statement that adds additional clarity to the enduring word of the Lord: "That word is the good news that was announced to you." Once again the allusion here is not only to the gospel but also to Jesus who was revealed at the end of the ages for the sake of the believers addressed in this letter (v. 20).

1 Peter 2:1-3

Having been called to a life of love, Christians are now instructed in how to live out this life of love, this life of holiness that needs to be exemplified through righteous conduct. They are to rid themselves of all malice, all guile, insincerity, envy, and slander. Such vices go against the grain of communal solidarity and inhibit the practice of mutual love. Like newborn babes, the Christians are to long for the pure, spiritual milk so that they may grow into salvation (v. 1-3). The idea of growing into salvation serves as a reminder that salvation is an ongoing process, with its final realization still anticipated and hoped for (1:5, 9, 10; 14:18). The segment closes with a line (v. 3) adapted from Psalm 34:9 that functions as a qualifier for vv. 1-2 and a segue into v. 4.

1 Peter 2:4-10

In v. 4 the focus shifts from the community of believers to Jesus who is described metaphorically as a "living stone" rejected by mortals yet chosen and precious in God's sight. To this living stone the believers are to come. This new metaphor is derived from Psalm 118:22. The notion of this living stone being rejected is an image common to the synoptic gospels.[14] Throughout the Old Testament God is often referred to as a "rock."[15] The reference to Jesus as a "living stone" complements the metaphorical language and imagery used for God in the Old Testament, and underscores the relationship that exists between them. Furthermore, in v. 8 Jesus is called both a "stone" and a "rock." The two words are used synonymously, thus giving rise to an implicit suggestion about how Jesus came to be understood in relation to God.

Similar images of "stones" come to the fore in v. 5 where the focus shifts back to the community of believers who are metaphorically referred to as "living stones." Here the author of 1 Peter makes clear that not only is Jesus in God's image and according to God's likeness, but so also are the Christians—these "living stones" that need to allow themselves to be built into a spiritual house, to be a holy priesthood, to offer spiritual sacrifices acceptable to God though Jesus Christ. Together, vv. 4 and 5 establish a bond between God, Jesus, and the Christian community. Just as Jesus was a temple, a spiritual house, for all people, so too the Christian community is to be a temple for all people. Hence, to become a living stone is to be changed into Christ's own image (2 Cor 3:18), and to embody and live out a life of holiness in union with the Holy One, God. Verses 6-8 are almost entirely Old Testament citations used here to describe Jesus as both a precious stone and a stumbling block.[16]

The last part of 1 Peter 2:4-10, specifically vv. 9-10, also focuses on the community of believers. Having been called "living stone," they are now identified as a "chosen race," "a royal priesthood," a "holy nation," and God's "own people." The language used is the language of "election," rooting the Christian community in its ancient Jewish ancestral heritage.[17] Elliott notes that

On the whole, OT and NT material thus indicates that the concept of election of God's people is an intrinsic element of the Exodus and Sinai covenant traditions, according to which a vulnerable and oppressed people is liberated by God, is taken under God's special protection, and is obligated to a particular and distinctive social and moral order.[18]

This "election" was not intended for personal satisfaction, gain, or sanctification. "Election" was for the sake of mission: "that you may proclaim the mighty acts of him who called you out of darkness into his marvelous light" (v. 9).[19] This "chosen race," this "royal priesthood," this "holy nation"—God's own people—was to participate in the mission of evangelization.

The author closes this last section of the exhortation with an instruction that reminds the community of its past and present identity (v. 10). The phrases "once you were/but now you are" are the language of conversion. The entire verse is a citation derived from the thought of Hosea 1:6, 9, 10; and 2:23, 25. Here the New Testament writer rereads an Old Testament passage in a new social situation and in a new theological environment. Originally, the message of Hosea was directed to the Israelites who had fallen out of right relationship with their God. Now used in post-resurrection times, the passage takes on a new nuance, signifying for the Christian community a deeper union and communion with their God through Christ Jesus who remains their cornerstone (2:6).

In sum, 1 Peter 1:13-2:10 has provided the Christian community of its day and today with an identity and a vision of life representative of holiness that is not only a gift bestowed but also a call given down through the ages. This ancient text can be a foundation for understanding Catholic identity and the laity today.

Catholic Identity and the Laity in Light of 1 Peter 1:13-2:10: Implications and Reflections

1 Peter 1:13-2:10 offers several insights and points for further reflection with respect to the identity, vocation, and mission of the laity today. First, as Catholic Christians rooted in Judaism, the laity is called first and foremost to holiness: to be holy, for God is holy (1 Pt 1:16). This call to holiness invites the laity to embody the living presence of the Divine, which is a creative, healing, loving, forgiving, compassionate presence, whose compassion is for every living thing (Sir 18:13).

Second, 1 Peter 1:13-2:10 calls the laity to be "holy" in all their conduct (1 Pt 1:15). While ridding one's self of all the vices that undermine community, such as malice, guile, insincerity, envy, and slander, is important, I suggest that personal transformation must go hand in hand with the work of the transformation of our world, for that is the holy work of God who not only hears the cry of the oppressed but also works through the human community to liberate the oppressed (Ex 2:23-3:12). The holy work of God also involves sustaining all of creation, providing for human and non-human life alike (Ps 104). Thus, engagement in justice issues, particularly with respect to the environment, is indispensable for the laity today, especially in light of Catholic sacramentality that sees all creation as graced, blessed, and holy.

This holy work also involves engagement with the religious and political powers of the day as exemplified by God's Spirit working through the prophets whose concern was not only for the liberation of the oppressed but also for the salvation of the oppressor. Although deeds were judged and condemned, always the prophetic word remained the graced word, holding out opportunity for change while beckoning to "turn back." Thus, the holy conduct of the laity must be prophetic, and prophetic enough to see, as Isaiah did, the coming of the new heavens and the new earth dawning in our midst (Is 65:17-25).

Third, 1 Peter 1:13-2:10 firmly grounds the identity of the Catholic Christian laity who have been redeemed by the precious blood of Christ (1 Pt 1:17) and are therefore sanctified and graced, united to God through Christ while sharing in the very life of Christ, a Christ who is not only a living stone but also the cornerstone of their own lives. As living stones like Christ, the laity are called to let themselves be built into a "spiritual house" (1 Pt 2:5)—in essence, to become the temple of the living God just as Christ was (cf. Jn 2:19, 21; Acts 2:1-4). As temple, as spiritual house (1 Pt 2:5), they, like Christ, are called to be a house of prayer for all nations, all peoples (Mk 11:17; cf. Is 56:7). As a temple or a spiritual house, the call is to a profound hospitality of heart that exercises genuine mutual love not only for one's own (1 Pt 1:22) but also for those who are not members of one's own specific community, just as Jesus embraced the Canaanite woman (Mt 15:21-28) and loved the sinner into deeper life (Lk 7:36-50; Jn 7:53-8:11). This call is one that must also embrace interfaith and interreligious dialogue.

As a temple of this nature, the laity will have a profound role to play in the unfolding vision of the mountain of the Lord's house to which all nations shall stream with peace as the abiding gift in the land (Is 2:1-4; cf. Mi 4:1-5). Such a temple will be the living expression of the presence of God dwelling in the midst of all creation (Rv 21:1-4; 22:1-26): the holy city, the new Jerusalem envisioned by prophets and proclaimed by saints. As living stones, the cost of personal and global transformation will be great, as it was for the prophets and for Christ. The cost will be not less than everything. It is to this reality that the laity are called as Catholics, as Christians, joined to the holy priesthood, called not only to offer spiritual sacrifices as 1 Peter encourages but also to offer the sacrifice of their lives. Such is the burden, the joy, the labor, and the fruit of holiness.

Finally, clothed in the identity of being a chosen people, a royal priesthood, a holy nation, God's own people (1 Pt 2:9), 1 Peter 1:13-2:10 calls the laity to the mission of evangelization: to proclaim the mighty works of him who called you out of darkness into his marvelous light (1 Pt 2:9). These mighty acts were the many divine deeds done on behalf of all people, all creation, that attested to God's inclusive love for all that has been created. This mission of evangelization calls the laity to deep involvement in the world not as proselytizers but as evangelists, the ones bringing the gospel, the good news of salvation, the living experience of God's love for and to all.

When holiness of this depth is embraced and lived out, then and only then will the universal call to holiness that resounded at Vatican II be answered, and will Catholicism understand its true identity of what it means to be "catholic,"[20] and the words "in God's image, according to God's likeness" (Gn 1:27) find a resting place in our spiritually hungry, thirsty world, searching for justice, searching for truth, searching for God. It is to the non-ordained—like Jesus—to whom such a mission, a vision, a task has been divinely entrusted.

Notes

[1]"Dogmatic Constitution on the Church" (*Lumen Gentium*), in *Vatican II: The Conciliar and Post Conciliar Documents*; new rev. ed., ed. Austin Flannery, O.P. (Northport, NY: Costello Publishing Company, 1992), no. 40, 397.

[2] "Girding the loins" was a common practice in Levantine culture. Persons who wore long robes would gather them up and secure them in preparation for certain activities requiring quick or strenuous action (see, for example, Job 38: 3; 40:7; Prv 31:17).

[3] In 1 Peter, the author mentions two revelations of Jesus Christ: (1) his initial manifestation in human history (1 Pt 1:20) and (2) his final appearance at the end time (1 Pt 1:5, 7; 4:13; 5:4). For further discussion, see John H. Elliott, *1 Peter: A New Translation with Introduction and Commentary*, Anchor Bible 37B (New York: Doubleday, 2000), 356-57.

[4] See, for example, Isaiah 1:4; 5:19, 24; 10:20; 40:25; 41:14, 16, 20; 43:3, 14-15, and so on.

[5] Elliott, *1 Peter*, 360.

[6] See Deuteronomy 7:6-13; 14:1-15:23; 26:18-19; 28:9.

[7] Donald P. Senior, C.P., *1 Peter, Jude, and 2 Peter*, Sacra Pagina 15 (Collegeville, MN: Liturgical Press, 2003), 42; see also John 3:17; 17:15-19; Colossians 3:9-10.

[8] The use of scripture to make an appeal "authoritative" is a literary device commonly used by the author of 1 Peter. See, for example, 1 Peter 2:3; 3:10; 4:18; 5:5.

[9] Elliott, *1 Peter*, 364.

[10] Ibid.

[11] Ibid., 380.

[12] Ibid.

[13] Senior, *1 Peter, Jude, and 2 Peter*, 51.

[14] See, for example, Mark 12:1-12; Matthew 21:33-46; Luke 20:9-18.

[15] See, for example, Deuteronomy 32:4; 2 Samuel 23:3; Isaiah 26:4; 30:29; Psalms 1:3; 19:15; 62:3, 7.

[16] See Isaiah 28:16; Psalm 118:22; Isaiah 8:14-15.

[17] For "chosen race," see Isaiah 43:20; for "royal priesthood," see Exodus 19:6; for "holy nation," see Exodus 19:6; for "God's own people," see Isaiah 43:21 and Malachi 3:17.

[18] Elliott, *1 Peter*, 445.

[19] The phrase "that you may proclaim the mighty acts" is an adaptation of the second part of Isaiah 43:21 LXX.

[20] For further discussion on Catholic identity in relation to 1 Peter 2, see "Decree on the Apostolate of the Laity" (*Apostolicam Actuositatem*), esp. 3, 4, and 18 in *Vatican II: The Conciliar and Post Conciliar Documents*, ed. Flannery. This document is also concerned with holiness and evangelization (see 2, 4, 6, 20, and 26; see also *Gaudium et Spes*, 47 and 49).

How We Hold One Another

Spiritual Practices, Accountability, and the Recovery of Lay Identity

Thomas F. Burke

While spiritual practices have long played a role in Christian formation, they have enjoyed a resurgence in recent years, thanks in large part to a renewed interest in the role human experience plays in Christian faith.[1] Grounded in the reforms of Vatican II and supported by the church's openness to the world, spiritual practices today offer lay Catholics, in particular, a deeper understanding of their lives in relationship to the movement of grace in concrete ways. As postconciliar reforms provided greater participation in liturgical practices, for example, by removing or altering restrictions on lay ministry in the celebration of mass, the reforms also yielded greater lay access to spiritual and pastoral leadership in the church through ongoing adult education and participation in spiritual formation. One area that has contributed to the development of lay Catholics today is the practice of the Spiritual Exercises of St. Ignatius of Loyola.[2] Through the efforts of organizations like the Jesuit Collaborative,[3] the Spiritual Exercises have become a way of life for many lay persons, providing a practical and experiential means for discerning God's presence and action in the world, the internalization of what Thomas Merton calls "the mysticism of daily life."[4]

Yet despite the recovery of lay participation in the life and ministry of the church, lay leadership has diminished in recent years. In the liturgy, for example, greater attention is paid today to the unique role of the priest in the celebration of the mass, adding a degree of clarity to previously nuanced instructions and effectively barring lay ministers from assisting the priest at the altar.[5] Similarly, in the aftermath of the sex abuse crisis of early 2002, the chasm between clergy and laity has grown wider. Despite the bishops' calls for greater transparency in the process of removing sex offenders from the clergy and protecting children from further victimization, many lay persons regard their resolution as half-hearted and not capable of fully addressing a systemic clericalism that they believe lies at the root of the abuse.[6] As a result, the relationship between clergy and laity has assumed a kind of contractual character, where accountability becomes the legal threshold for an acceptable relationship rather than the basis for re-building trust and fidelity within the church. The Spiritual Exercises, however, provide a theological framework to address the work of reconciliation needed in the church without relying on rigid distinctions between ordained and lay persons. The Exercises do so by summoning the individual to spiritual growth through an ongoing process in at least three different ways: (1) a period of discernment of one's calling and an unqualified confrontation of sin; (2) an ongoing and imaginative encounter with Christ through a scriptural retelling of his life, death, and resurrection; and (3) the movement toward election in terms of vocation or life choice.

This essay looks to the Spiritual Exercises of Ignatius as a means for analyzing the formation and recovery of a viable lay identity. While there is indeed much discussion of lay ministry in the church today—for good *or* for ill—the Exercises offer an alternative method for thinking about lay identity through practical contemplation of the Christian faith in concrete ways. In exploring the intersection between the Exercises and lay identity, I examine their basic theological structure, highlighting both their epistemological and christological presuppositions. Next, I investigate the specific practices that give flesh to the Exercises and put them in context by reflecting on the experiences of two lay members of my parish community who recently completed the 19th Annotation Retreat, often referred to as "A Retreat in Everyday Life." Finally, I reflect briefly on the notion of accountability and its significance in light of the theological and practical implications of the Spiritual Exercises.

The Process of Spiritual Discernment

The theological import of the Spiritual Exercises is best grasped by beginning with the practices themselves. Broadly speaking, the practices reflect what David L. Fleming calls the "interplay" between memory and imagination in the contemplation of God's grace and human agency.[7] At the heart of this interplay is the biblical narrative—the synoptic account of Jesus' life, death, and resurrection that serves as a contemplative framework for discovering and integrating Christ's approach to God. To grow in unity with Christ is to grow in likeness to Christ, reflecting a kenotic theme in the Exercises as expressed in the second chapter of Paul's letter to the Philippians:

> Let the same mind be in you that was in Christ Jesus, who, though he was in the form of God did not regard equality with God as something to be exploited, but emptied himself and took the form of a slave, being born in human likeness. And being found in human form, he humbled himself, and became obedient to the point of death—death on a cross. (Phil 2:5-8 NRSV)

In order to move closer to God, we must make Christ's attitude our own and, in similar form, empty ourselves in humble service. While the Exercises take their cue from scripture, the content is nevertheless the participant's own life experiences. This kind of theological approach is not unique. It finds its moorings in the early rites of Christian initiation as celebrated by the Mystagogues and in the sayings of the Desert Fathers and Mothers. Although Ignatius's work reflects his own late medieval context, his emphasis on memory and understanding echoes the work of Augustine and Anselm and, no doubt, finds a home among contemporary figures like Karl Rahner. This essay argues that the theology of the Spiritual Exercises comprises two basic paradigms: first, an epistemological model grounded in the experience of conversion and the language of pilgrimage, best expressed through an active engagement with the world; second, a christological model that expands human knowledge through a radical conception of the communication of grace. These two frameworks contribute to the emergence of a critical spirituality of transformation and service facilitated by explicit practices: namely, the challenge of confronting sin, the cultivation of humility, and the discernment of spirits.

The epistemological dimension of the Exercises is clearly laid out in the four-phased approach of Ignatius. The retreatant (or exercitant), through the aid of a director, begins a disciplined examination of his or her life over a four-week period, though the time frame may be adjusted. The self-knowledge gained is bound up in the quest for God and the invitation to discover God's goodness in all things.[8] The desire for God, however, occurs within a horizon of knowing that is fundamentally dialectical. We want to know God and see God in all things, but we cannot. We limit our understanding of the God we seek by the choices we make, the sins we commit, and the self-deception that lies so deep that we may not sense it at all.[9] As J. Matthew Ashley notes, there are "competing theologies" built into the Exercises that give rise to a broad spiritual landscape.[10] For example, the immediacy of the graced relationship between the retreatant and God is held in tension with the mediated work of confronting sin and struggling through unfamiliar realms of loss and failure. The movement toward freedom and personal fulfillment is necessarily balanced by the call of Christ to know and love him. Even the goal of opening oneself in service to the world is tempered by the ongoing need for discernment, to find God in all things, and to avoid the trap of idolatry that remains part of earthly temptation.

The dialectical structure, however, should not give the impression of a sharp distinction between theological categories of sin and grace, freedom and obedience, service and discernment. The work of the Exercises is relational; its aim is the growth and development of the retreatant toward a new relationship with God. For Ignatius, this relationship takes place within a forward trajectory or movement, in Christian terms, a journey or pilgrimage. Spiritual growth, he argues, happens over time.[11] We can see this reflected in his personal experience of injury and recovery, and desolation and conversion, as well as a lifetime of dedication to the discernment of God's will in his life. The idea of movement is a central theological theme in the Exercises because the participant is called to embody different postures—both physically and emotionally— as a means of forgoing sin and moving closer to God.

Like patristic and monastic notions of pilgrimage, the approach of Ignatius owes much to its historical context. By the twelfth century, the influence of the Crusades had supplanted the monastic ideal of pilgrimage as a purely eschatological goal with a more measured approach to pilgrimage as an ongoing "struggle in the world that would reach its completion in heaven."[12] According to Ignatius, the spiritual journey thus requires us to confront the forces that imperil our forward movement or diminish our ability to love God. His use of militaristic and chivalric themes serves to emphasize the quality of the battle in which the participant now engages. To move toward God's reign requires us to entrust ourselves to God, to enter into the fight between the "human and anti-human" forces, and to earnestly seek the knowledge to change our lives so that we may receive "the grace to imitate Christ."[13]

The forward movement of the Exercises occurs against the backdrop of salvation history. The christological framework is built into the entire experience of the four weeks; in the first exercise of the first week, Ignatius reminds the participant that the struggle against sin is only possible because of the created gifts lovingly bestowed by Christ.[14] Because Ignatius structures the Exercises as imaginative encounters with Christ based on scriptural accounts of his life, death, and resurrection, the participant comes to know Christ firsthand, as it were, as friend and confidant in the struggle for wholeness. Christ breaks into our sinful reality and by virtue of his incarnation becomes one with us. As we labor to acknowledge the reality of sinful choices and purge ourselves of the oppressive weight of temptation, we move closer to Christ. Thus, grief and sorrow do not mean we are entrapped by our sins, forced to perpetually gaze over past mistakes, but rather that we come to an awareness of Christ's presence in the midst of our sorrow and allow him to free us from the hidden grief we often harbor. Once we begin to grasp the nearness of God, then the question that lies at the heart of the Exercises—what has God called me to do?—comes into sharp focus. Overcoming sin and becoming one in union with Christ provides a theological foundation for a Christian understanding of God.

Christ's nearness and the participant's assimilation in the Body of Christ signal not only a kind of *imitatio* but also a *communio*. We do not engage the Exercises merely to become an *alter Christus* but rather as a way of welcoming Christ to journey with us.

When we fall into sin or struggle to pray, we are not alone because Christ is present throughout every step. The Exercises become the touchstone for living out the saving work of Christ, and our lives form the context by which this salvation takes shape. The soteriological dimension of the Exercises provides a larger basis for service to the world and a greater awareness of God's presence in human history. Day-to-day struggles become the theological locus for discerning, contemplating, and receiving God's grace.

We can see this dynamic reflected in the gift of love that accompanies the Exercises of the fourth week. Entering into the joy and consolation of Christ's victory over death, we contemplate the immensity of God's saving love. Through prayer, we come to savor the resurrection of Christ and rest in his consoling presence which vanquishes our fears. Christ's unity with us reflects a kind of nuptial quality, by which Ignatius understands the relationship of Christ to the church.[15] As Michael Buckley notes, the driving force behind this nuptial unity is pneumatological.[16] It is the Spirit who guides and upholds the church as the enduring sign of Christ's love. The Spirit of God transforms us through the changes we make in our lives, moving us closer to God and one another. Even as we encounter the incarnate and suffering Christ in the midst of our struggles and sin, so too in the joy and consolation of Christ's resurrection we discover the Spirit of love, who animates our life choices and leads us out in fuller service to the world.

In light of this theological framework, we now turn to examine specific practices in the Exercises that relate to the themes mentioned earlier—those of confronting sin, cultivating humility, and discernment. As a way of illustrating the impact of the Exercises on the formation of lay identity, I will refer to the reflections of two lay Christians who recently completed the Spiritual Exercises.

Spiritual Practices and Lay Formation

The term "confrontation" is never explicitly mentioned in the Spiritual Exercises, nor is the term "conversion." Yet both of these words reflect the quality of the general "disorientation" that may arise from spiritual introspection by bringing to the surface hidden assumptions and choices. While the first week is dedicated to leading the retreatant to a contemplation of God's presence in creation, it also directs the individual to a recollection of sinful experiences. True to their imaginative and colloquial form, the Exercises encourage the retreatant to pray that God might reveal the troubling and alienating aspects of his or her life and assist the individual in examining the choices he or she has made.[17] The activity of examining the conscience becomes a daily part of the retreatant's struggle to acknowledge the pain caused by broken relationships and a willful disregard for others. The practice of the examination is disorienting in that it forces the participant to identify not only sinful behavior, but also the obstacles we erect to distort and trivialize our responsibility for such behavior.[18] As Karl Rahner notes, the Ignatian meditation on sin helps us to recognize that "(o)ur acts penetrate our personal human existence" in an essential way "even when they are no longer noticed on the surface of our consciousness."[19]

The confrontation with sin is not a remote activity. As noted earlier, the practice of the examen takes place in the context of prayer. When we acknowledge our complicity with sin, Christ comes to us and stands with us. Thus, in the face of overwhelming guilt, the retreatant is encouraged to look to God even as she feels herself unworthy of God. This move reflects the dialectical tension of the Exercises: not only do we confront hurtful memories of past sin, but we also confront the possibility of God's forgiveness, the hopeful imagining of a recovered self and the potential of living out God's desire for us in the world.[20] The use of imagination in prayer is an essential component of the Spiritual Exercises because it allows us to place ourselves in communication with God. Through the use of scripture, the director leads the retreatant into different imaginings, placing the retreatant within the biblical story and encouraging her to describe what she sees.

The experience of the imaginative colloquies resonated with the retreatants I interviewed. In almost every phase of the Exercises, each individual remarked on the helpfulness of imagining himself with Christ through the re-telling of the scriptural story not only as a means to achieve greater intimacy with Christ, but also as a way of making Christ's struggles his own. Keep in mind that the content of the Exercises is not so much the biblical narrative or spiritual practice as it is the retreatant's participation and experience of these two. The goal is to bear fruit by discerning one's calling in this life and to move forward in service to the world. At pivotal moments of discernment and choice, Ignatius offers a set of meditations as helpful guides in the cultivation of humility and wisdom.[21]

One of these meditations, which Ignatius calls the "Two Standards," encourages the retreatant to evaluate two opposing realities (namely Christ's and Lucifer's) by imagining their differences in stark, realistic terms. For Tony, a pediatrician of twenty years, this meditation allowed him to conceive of the first standard as an encounter with Christ at different stages of his life, from infancy through adulthood and death. Meditating on the second standard, the concept of evil, however, took on a more visceral expression on a recent visit to a sister parish in Jamaica. Although his medical skills were in great demand and the parishioners were both generous and hospitable, the immense poverty and misery of the place as well as the "world-wide ignorance" of these people's suffering left Tony with a sense of the pervasive and systemic nature of evil. The contrast between the humble joy of his imagined encounters with Christ and the all too real experience of oppression in the lives of the poor led him, in his own words, to a desolation of tears. As with the initial phase of the Spiritual Exercises—the graced struggle to confront sinful behavior—the retreatant at this point is directed to keep in mind the overall goal: to "find" God in all things. But for Tony, finding God in the midst of overwhelming suffering seemed beyond his reach.

The solution came during the next phase of his journey: the period of discernment of spirits. While Tony could distinguish within the "Two Standards" the need for advocacy on the one hand and resistance on the other, especially in terms of the desolation he experienced, the distinction did little to assuage his grief. Although the discernment of spirits posits a similar distinction between good and evil, it also challenges the retreatant to distinguish between divine and human impulses in the midst of contemplation.[22] For Tony, this meant that he had to re-assess the discouragement he felt over the suffering he witnessed in order to better understand God's intentions. Was his grief a confirmation of righteous anger or an attestation of God's steadfast presence in the world? Could the desolation he felt be an expression of true spiritual poverty, or humility and thus a reflection of Christ's call in his life?

Tony shared two experiences that offer some illumination. First, his director had asked him (and others in his group) to locate a childhood photograph. His search turned up only one from the family photo album, and the image was faint and grainy. By reflecting on that photo, however, and imagining himself sharing it with the infant Christ and his mother, he began to see a picture of his own innocence and sinlessness. Although he managed to locate only the one photograph, he was consoled by what he came to understand as an act of genuine love by the one who chose to take the picture. At that moment, he began to see the image of himself through the loving gaze of another, which became a revelatory act of immense hope. Second, through the aid of spiritual direction, Tony began to contemplate his own sense of isolation and alienation, not only experienced on his travels, but also occasioned by a chronic illness and the recent death of his father. He imagined himself standing before a large pit, staring down into a void that represented not only his illness but now his grief as well. The ability to distinguish and distance those things that had become central to his existence led him to an experience of freedom from fear he had not anticipated. In his mind's eye he recognized that he was whole, that he stood on the other side of his suffering, and that, most importantly, he was not alone. Looking up, he sensed God's presence there as well as the communion of saints standing with him.

Tony's experience of discernment deepened his relationship with God by illuminating not only his understanding of what God was asking of him but also God's proximity in the midst of his suffering. God did not desire that he be overcome by his grief—giving in to the influence of what Tony now recognized as a dark spirit. Rather, through further reflection, he was now able to "see the truth of [Christ's] way [before him] ... and to feel the impulse of the Spirit [encouraging him] to live it."[23] He could face the suffering he witnessed, in the world and in himself, without being vanquished in the process.

Although not as elaborate as Tony's experiences, Jane, a psychologist specializing in trauma practice, went through a similar process of discernment. For her, the challenge was to create a balance between action and contemplation. A resident of the Boston area, Jane volunteered to treat flight attendants who had resumed their work only weeks after 9/11, many of them flying for the same airline that had come under attack. Months later, she found herself also involved in the work of Voice of the Faithful (VOTF) as a way of responding to the unfolding sex abuse crisis in the Boston archdiocese. In reflecting on these experiences with her spiritual director, Jane viewed her involvement as a positive use of her gifts. As a trained psychologist she was able to bring comfort and peace of mind to the flight attendants as well as keen insights and expert advice to those caring for the survivors of the sex abuse crisis. In addition, Jane hoped her involvement with VOTF would precipitate further changes in the structure of the church, and lead to greater accountability among the clergy.

Despite the generous use of her gifts, Jane commented that she soon found the work "frustrating" and "exhausting." Caring for the traumatized in both cases created what she called a kind of "vicarious traumatization." The inconsolable grief of the flight attendants and the anger and despondence of the victims of clergy sex abuse fueled her own cynicism and distrust. Looking back, it became difficult for Jane to find God in the midst of this vicarious suffering. Through the aid of her spiritual director, however, Jane used the Exercises as way of restoring the balance between action and contemplation. By integrating her love for music and the reading of spiritual texts, she was able to let go of the frustration and exhaustion she felt, especially in her own church, which seemed intent on covering up evil rather than exposing it. In retrospect, she could sense God's presence during these experiences because without God she would not have been able to initiate her work or persevere in a meaningful way.

For both Tony and Jane, the Spiritual Exercises provided a critical vantage point of discernment. The practice of the "Two Standards" challenged their pre-conceived notions of good and evil, subverting the moral normativity of "right" and "wrong" behavior without denying the emotional grief caused by the powerlessness they experienced. With God's help, they could distinguish between the spirits of goodness and evil, perceiving Christ's presence even in the midst of desolation. With this insight, they could move forward with a renewed commitment to their life's work. While the Exercises emphasize a moment of "election" or choice, Jane and Tony each experienced this component as a reaffirmation of their chosen professions. Through the Exercises, their spiritual directors assisted them in choosing paths that might engage the totality of their lives, affecting the decisions they make every day. After practicing the Exercises over an eight-month period, both Jane and Tony felt ongoing prayer would help them develop a kind of natural rhythm in the process of discerning God's will. By doing so, retreatants like Jane and Tony find it easier to make a decision in the face of suffering, grief, and injustice because they will have inevitably experienced these feelings before.

Lay Identity and Accountability in the Church

I would like to make a few comments on the relationship of the Exercises to the formation of lay identity, especially in terms of the call for greater accountability in the church, and also parse some of the ecclesial and theological implications for spiritual formation. As the title of this essay suggests, the Spiritual Exercises relate to the theme of accountability through the introspective practices of confronting of sin and cultivating humility. If an individual is accountable to self and to God, in honest and direct ways, growing in the image and likeness of God, the person may distinguish between what is truly beneficial and irreparably harmful in the spiritual life.[24] And yet, accountability in the spiritual practices, especially in the process of discernment and election, is not a guarantee that we will make the right decision. Nor does it follow that having made our peace with God and resolved to do God's will, we will not suffer future distress or chaos in our lives. Instead, the Exercises can offer a helpful strategy for facing demons when they arise. Because the Exercises place an emphasis on relationality and growth, they summon us, as noted earlier, not just to *imitatio* but to *communio*: a pairing of our lives together with God so that, as Monika Hellwig notes, we may discover "the courage to takes risks ... make mistakes ... and imagine the world quite differently."[25]

The idea of accountability is prevalent in Catholic discussions these days, especially in terms of the church's self-understanding. After the sex abuse crisis broke in Boston in January 2002, accountability was embraced by both the scandalized laity and the remorseful bishops who were anxious to put the crisis behind them. The Voice of the Faithful, a lay organization born in the early days of the crisis, was perhaps the most prominent voice in calling for accountability and honesty from the bishops. As many in the organization have said, the crisis at that time was not merely the sexual molestation of children by trusted clergy but the elaborate cover-up that occurred after allegations had been raised. The deep scandal facing the church was malfeasance, and the solution, VOTF members argued, was accountability.[26] At their Dallas meeting in the summer of 2002, the U.S. bishops seemed to concur. In their "Charter for the Protection of Children and Young People" they pledged themselves to abolish the atmosphere of secrecy, take responsibility for the problem, and "restore the bonds of trust" with the very people who were demanding nothing less.[27] But the bishops' response and the laity's expectations did not match up; VOTF continued to charge the bishops with a lack of transparency and real accountability, based not only on their exclusion from the Dallas meeting but also the lack of public communication with the organization beforehand and afterward.[28] It is striking, therefore, that although accountability seemed to be the means by which the crisis would be resolved, it failed in part, perhaps because it remained a mere catch-phrase and not a process of honest inquiry as envisioned by Ignatius in the Spiritual Exercises.

Accountability is no doubt an important component to resolving the crisis, just as it plays an important role in the successful development of a spiritual life. I would argue, however, that it is only a first step. Accountability must give way to shared responsibility, which in turn may engender trust and, indeed, friendship and reconciliation. From this vantage the church may begin to cultivate a ministry of service to the world, born not out of regret or merely structural change, but out of communion with Christ, who encounters the world in order to redeem it.

The Spiritual Exercises provide a fitting way to grasp the depth of Christ's love for the world and one way of moving closer to him. As the contemplation of God's love in the fourth week reminds us, we belong to God and everything we have is God's. With Ignatius, we can say, "take, Lord, receive ... everything is yours."[29] In turn, we may learn how to hold one another in bonds of love and respect, and to discern together—ordained and lay—how to bring that love to bear in the world.

Notes

[1]See Walter J. Burghardt, "The Richness of a Resource," in *A Spirituality for Contemporary Life: The Jesuit Heritage Today*, ed. David L. Fleming (St. Louis: Review for Religious, 1991), 1-6.

[2]*The Spiritual Exercises of St. Ignatius*, trans. Anthony Mottola (New York: Doubleday, 1964).

[3]The Jesuit Collaborative is the result of the combined efforts of the New England, New York, and Maryland provinces of the Society of Jesus to meet the increased interest of lay persons in the practice of Ignatian spirituality and to encourage the development of Ignatian identity. In the New England Province under the leadership of Fr. Ronald Mercier, S.J. and Sister Clare Walsh, MHSH, the Collaborative has provided spiritual direction in local parishes through training and formation in the Exercises according to the 19th Annotation or as it is more commonly referred to as the "retreat in everyday life."

[4]Thomas Merton, "Is Mysticism Normal?" *Commonweal* 51 (1949-50): 98.

[5]See the General Instruction of the Roman Missal (Third Typical Edition) (Washington, D.C.: United States Conference of Catholic Bishops, 2003).

[6]Charles Kenney and James E. Muller, *Keep the Faith, Change the Church: The Battle by Catholics for the Soul of their Church* (New York: St. Martin's Press, 2004), 10.

[7]David L. Fleming, S.J., *Like the Lightning: The Dynamics of the Ignatian Exercises* (St. Louis: Institute of Jesuit Sources, 2004), 29.

[8]David L. Fleming, S.J., "The Ignatian Spiritual Exercises: Understanding a Dynamic," in his *Notes on the Spiritual Exercises of St. Ignatius of Loyola* (St. Louis: Review for Religious, 1983), 3.

[9]See Karl Rahner, *Spiritual Exercises* (New York: Herder & Herder), 34-42, on the essence of sin.

[10]J. Matthew Ashley, "Ignacio Ellacuría and the Spiritual Exercises of Ignatius Loyola," in *Theological Studies* 61 (2000): 18.

[11]Fleming, *Notes on the Spiritual Exercises of St. Ignatius of Loyola*, 5.

[12]Michael J. Buckley, S.J., "Ecclesial Mysticism in the *Spiritual Exercises* of Ignatius," in *Theological Studies* 56 (1996): 447.

[13]Ibid., 450 51.

[14]*The Spiritual Exercises of St. Ignatius*, trans. Mottola, 54-55.

[15]Ibid., 139-42.

[16]Buckley, "Ecclesial Mysticism in the *Spiritual Exercises* of Ignatius," 458.

[17]H. Cornell Bradley, *The 19th Annotation in 24 Weeks, for the 21st Century* (Philadelphia: St. Joseph's University Press, 2002), 76.

[18]Ibid., 80.

[19]Rahner, *Spiritual Exercises*, 37.

[20]William A. Barry, S.J., "The Experience of the First and Second Weeks of the Spiritual Exercises," in *Notes on the Spiritual Exercises of St. Ignatius of Loyola*, ed. David L. Fleming (St. Louis: Review for Religious, 1983), 95-102.

[21]The set includes the reflection on the "Two Standards" or types of leadership, the three types of persons, and the three different kinds of humility. While I refer only to the two standards, all three practices are grounded in the movement toward a more humbled existence. The goal of these medita-

tions is the expression of a kind of *imitatio Christi* through the cultivation of humility. See Fleming, *Notes on the Spiritual Exercises of St. Ignatius of Loyola*, 14.

[22]Herbert F. Smith, S.J., "Discernment of Spirits," in *Notes on the Spiritual Exercises of St. Ignatius of Loyola*, ed. David L. Fleming (St. Louis: Review for Religious, 1983), 226.

[23]Ibid., 238.

[24]Fleming, *Like the Lightning*, 53-54.

[25]Monika K. Hellwig, "Christian Responsibility for Today's World," in *A Spirituality for Contemporary Life: The Jesuit Heritage Today*, ed. David L. Fleming (St. Louis: Review for Religious, 1991), 42.

[26]Kenney and Muller, *Keep the Faith, Change the Church*, 284, 302.

[27]"Charter for the Protection of Children and Young People" (Washington, DC: USCCB, 2002), 1.

[28]Kenney and Muller, *Keep the Faith, Change the Church*, 123-29.

[29]*The Spiritual Exercises of St. Ignatius*, trans. Mottola, 54-55.

"To Be Holy in the World"

The Influence of Yves Congar on the Spirituality and Practice of the Community of Sant'Egidio

Laurie Johnston

Amid the variegated landscape of post-Vatican II lay spirituality, the Community of Sant'Egidio offers a rather unique model of lay vocation.[1] While the community is known internationally for its humanitarian and peacemaking work, its interest for theologians also lies in its ability to transcend many of the divides that have plagued the post-Vatican II church. With its "border-crossing charism," its focus on dialogue, and its moderate attitude toward church authority, Sant'Egidio owes much to the theology of Yves Congar. Congar's ideas about history and engagement with the "other," and the ways these ideas have taken shape in the life of Sant'Egidio suggest some key lessons about what it means for lay people to live the gospel authentically in the world today.

The Community of Sant'Egidio was founded in Rome in 1968 by Andrea Riccardi, who was eighteen years old at the time. The community currently counts approximately fifty thousand members in seventy countries, with the largest communities in Europe and Africa. It has become internationally known for its peace work, receiving a nomination for the Nobel Peace Prize for its mediation of a peace accord in 1992 that ended the civil war in Mozambique. Sant'Egidio has also been involved in other conflicts in Africa, as well as in Kosovo, the Middle East, and Guatemala; it is sometimes referred as the "U.N. of Trastevere," after the neighborhood in Rome where it is headquartered.

Yet its self-understanding has relatively little to do with this diplomatic work. Rather, Sant'Egidio is primarily a community of lay people who try to live the gospel through a life of prayer and service to the poor. Members, who do not live together, have their own jobs and homes, but are committed to the spiritual discipline of friendship. They carry out their work of service on a strictly volunteer basis and they use virtually no paid staff. Yet the community has been able to make a substantial difference in the cities where it is active, by running soup kitchens and small group homes for the elderly and AIDS patients, and by providing many services to immigrants and refugees. On a larger scale, it is involved with advocacy on a number of issues such as the rights of the elderly and immigrants, and it has mounted an international campaign against the death penalty, a cause for which it has collected many millions of signatures. Sant'Egidio also runs an award-winning AIDS treatment programs in ten countries in Africa. Though relatively unknown in America, in Europe a number of Sant'Egidio members are public intellectuals, well known for speaking on behalf of the poor and staunchly committed to dialogue with the broader society as well as to ecumenical and interreligious dialogue.

In the early years of the community, some of the founders developed a friendship with the great theologian Yves Congar; this friendship proved extremely influential for the direction of the community, and also important to Congar in the final years of his life. This relationship is not widely known to either Congar scholars or even to most members of Sant'Egidio, but is nevertheless quite significant. While space does not permit a full discussion of the ways in which Congar's rich theology was a fruitful influence on Sant'Egidio, I will highlight here two themes from Congar's thought that have been particularly important for Sant'Egidio: history, and the relationship with the "other."

Congar and the Legacy of Vatican II

Toward the end of his life, Yves Congar was concerned about how the vision of the Second Vatican Council, in which he played a major role, was being put into practice. He had envisioned what he called a new "form of holiness less opposed to the earthly life ... a less narrowly monastic spirituality, one more adapted to men and women who desire wholeheartedly to practice the Gospel perfectly and live the Beatitudes, but feel called to do so in the world, without being dispensed from actively doing the world's works—only without sin."[2]

Though Congar was unsure what such a form of life would look like in practice, he was particularly interested in the ways it could play out in small Christian communities. Writing on the occasion of the tenth anniversary of the Council, he describes his vision of the future:

> In this world, Christians must bring the response of the Gospel, that is, a response less reliant on the classical treasure of Catholic theology that comes out of the middle ages and the Counter-reformation, and more reliant instead on the Gospel and on the spiritual tradition of all the centuries of Christianity. In this regard I have confidence in communities of prayer and of spiritual life, some of them even inspired by the spirituality of the ancient fathers, closer to the contemporary world than to the theology inherited from the middle ages. Thus, the future of the Church, in my view, rests greatly on the existence of spiritual communities animated by a great devotion to the Gospel and to evangelical practice, to the practice of love and charity with the greatest liberty and "sympathetic" openness to what is happening in the world. This is the future of the Church. A future which every community realizes, on its part, and therefore in a partial way, certainly: we are all parts, no one in the Church is everything. But the fact that these communities exist and that they are made up of people who are not out of the world, but live within the current of life, seems to me a quite important fact for the future of the Church.[3]

In fact, he wrote this for *La Nostra Assemblea*, the magazine of the Community of Sant'Egidio. While he indicates only implicitly here that Sant'Egidio is one of the communities "in the world" that will be important for the future of the church, he refers to Sant'Egidio more directly elsewhere. In his book *The Catholic Church and Modern France*, Congar identifies a number of places where he sees authentic forms of Christian discipleship being lived out in the world. "How does the Church of today appear?" he asks. "If one observes the realities, if one gazes beyond the few square feet of our usual space, one finds oneself in the presence of a prodigious diversity. God alone knows it. We cannot do more than just evoke some images of it—and even that, we do badly."[4] But among the images he evokes is this one: "This Community of Sant'Egidio of Rome, that I love to return to every year, young yet charming, dynamic, concerned with literacy, with drugs, with blackshirts, with impoverished elderly, with holding liturgies in the suburbs of the great city.... This is the Church."[5] It is clear that Congar saw Sant'Egidio as one example of the fruit of the Council.

The Friendship between Congar and Sant'Egidio

How, then, did this meeting between Congar and Sant'Egidio take place? In the early days of the community's existence, Riccardi and his companions described themselves as trying to find a way to live as "monks in the city," but needing help to understand how to shape such a vocation. As Andrea Bartoli, one of the earliest members, has explained,

> It's fair to say that without Congar, without Vatican II, we simply could not have Sant'Egidio. Even just the conception of Sant'Egidio, being holy in the world, in a way, that was awkward, because one of the major tensions that I remember in the first four, five years, was that ... some parents were Catholic, some were devout Catholic, but the idea was that you were supposed to be a good Catholic by having a family and by being a good Catholic whatever you were, a good Catholic doctor, engineer, that was the idea. You have your space in society, you were to be a good Catholic in doing that. Family and work, work and family. For us that was a non-starter. We simply could not start thinking that the world was family and work. For us, the world was rich and poor, was life and death, was health and illness. The world was a struggle of what is new and what has to come, and what is living and life-giving, and what is dreadful, horror and terror. We saw the world as a place in which we were constantly living a drama, a passion for life, that was certainly consumed in the family and work; there are conditions, but, for example, for us, it was hard to believe that you could limit yourself to the family, or that in living in your family,

you would be justified in your search for holiness, or in doing your job right, that was enough—when everybody was dying, so many were not able to read and write, where there were those who were abandoned in the hospital, and so on. For us, the idea was ok, many of us will have families, will have jobs, that's not an issue, but that's the beginning of something, and the something was the Community. And the idea that you could have lay people singing vespers, lay people doing the prayer every morning before going to school, or lay people preaching the gospel, was . . . a huge departure from the very conception of what constitutes a spiritual life, a religious life, and an experience of the gospel.

Congar gave us back a sense of vocation that we didn't have. In a way, what was happening before was that the vocation was constrained in the social role. Your vocation was being in the family, was doing your work well. But Congar helped us to say no, the vocation is one, the vocation is living the gospel, is to be holy, to live your life in front of God, the vocation is to be the Church! This was phenomenal, but for us, was a beginning.[6]

Bartoli's description of the world as a drama in which the church must be engaged clearly recalls the preface of *Gaudium et Spes*—"that world which is the theater of man's history"—and indicates the degree to which Sant'Egidio shared the mood of the moment in which *Gaudium et Spes* was written. And Sant'Egidio's response to this sense of drama is clearly dependent on Congar; the work Congar had done in *Lay People in the Church* and elsewhere to legitimize a truly lay vocation as a valid and not inferior position in the Church was critical for Sant'Egidio's self-understanding.

But Congar's gift to Sant'Egidio was also a personal recognition. In a homily he preached at Sant'Egidio in 1983, Congar said:

I feel very small in your midst: you do not believe it, but it is true, because I do theology, and there is also need for it to become reality. You need everything to make a world, as the proverb says—even theologians. But I am not concretely in contact with the poor, with drug addicts, with ex-prisoners, with the elderly, while you are! And so truly it is you who are realizing this Gospel of Jesus not only on a liturgical level but also on a concrete one.[7]

This personal approval from the great theologian was very important for community members to assure them that there was indeed a place for them within the church. As Riccardi himself has said, "He was one of those friends who ... saw that there was something there, that the Community was the bearer of a charism ... that the Community is born as a legitimate child of the tradition. When a legitimate son [of the church] recognizes you as a legitimate child, that is a lot."[8] In 1973, when the community was first given the convent of Sant'Egidio to use as its headquarters (thereby gaining the name of Sant'Egidio in the process), Congar was the very first invited guest. It is more than a little difficult to imagine that first dinner between the group of Italian teenagers and an elderly theologian not generally known for being particularly gregarious or sociable.

A Sense of History

Congar's theological influence went beyond merely giving Sant'Egidio a sense of its own legitimacy, however. Perhaps the most important idea that Congar gave to Sant'Egidio was simply the importance of understanding history. It was partly this emphasis that led Andrea Riccardi to become a historian himself.[9] By reading Congar's *True and False Reform in the Church* as well as other works, Riccardi and others gained a sense of the history of the church that allowed them to take a more nuanced view of it as an institution. Congar's deep understanding of tradition helped convey the idea that it was possible to be faithful children of the church without being slaves to the forms of the past. They learned from him that "the Church can be constructed in new forms, different forms, without betraying its truth, its tradition."[10] Riccardi says, "We liked very much the idea of the church *in* history—because I read in this the idea that history could go on."[11] Riccardi describes Congar as "a bridge to the great tradition" of the church, who helped open his eyes to the riches of the church's historical experience: "When you say you're going to the sea, you don't mean you're throwing yourself into it. You're going to a little place on the shore. Congar is like a place on the shore where you can encounter the great tradition."[12]

This sense of history, while freeing, was also humbling, because it reminded the members of Sant'Egidio that they were not doing something truly unique. While many of their contemporaries had an almost apocalyptic sense that they were creating religious and political utopias never before seen in the world, Sant'Egidio maintained and continues to maintain that it is merely one avenue for living the gospel in a church that has offered and will offer many possibilities. Riccardi explains:

> I think that the great risk run by community experiences is sectarianism, which leads people to live closed up in themselves and to mistake themselves for the Messiah or to believe that they've been officially draped in the mantle of the Gospel.... To avoid that, you have to get to know a wide gamut of experiences and enrich yourself with them. This is one more reason why the Church is beautiful. Father Yves Congar, who came many times to Sant'Egidio and with whom a mutual bond of spiritual brotherhood sprang up, taught us that.[13]

As Congar said in the article written for Sant'Egidio mentioned earlier, "We are all parts, no one in the Church is everything."[14] For a group of young revolutionaries, this was an important reminder, and it has helped shape Sant'Egidio's relatively moderate attitude toward church authority. While quite independent from the hierarchy in certain ways, Sant'Egidio did not hesitate to register as a church public lay association when the category was created in the 1980s—something that some other lay communities hesitated to do. At the same time, the sense that there is room for many realities in the vast sweep of the history of the church also has freed Sant'Egidio from any great sense that its members need to go out of their way to prove their allegiance to the church. While there is a clear sense of love for and fidelity to the church, Sant'Egidio tends to eschew litmus tests and is more focused on the possibilities for the church, rather than potential threats to it. When pushed to talk about questions of ideology and authority in an interview with John Allen, Riccardi responded typically:

JA: Many people believe that Sant'Egidio is "progressive," meaning that in some sense it represents the left wing of the church. Is that true?

AR: You know, I'm a historian. I know that "left" and "right" can't be used in the church. In the history of the church, I've found a number of figures who make this point. Romolo Murri, for example, a great personality of Italian Catholicism, who was left-wing, progressive, even excommunicated, and who ended up with the fascists. Hence I'm afraid of these terms. I would say two things. If you ask me, "Andrea, what's the line of Sant'Egidio?" I would say that we try to have a few points of reference: the Word of God; the liturgy; the poor; we try to stand with the people, to understand their reality, hence not closing ourselves off; and finally the horizon of the world. If this is what it means to be progressive, then we're very progressive. Because everything can become an ideology, you know? Also "Franciscanism" can become an ideology.

JA: You didn't mention fidelity to the magisterium or closeness to the bishops among your points of reference.

AR: Look, we're Catholics.[15]

When Riccardi goes on in the interview to speak of Sant'Egidio's close relationship with Pope John Paul II, one is struck by how much he sees fidelity and freedom as going hand in hand. As he puts it, "I think that the council and the church in the postconciliar period teach us to live in complexity and unity."[16] It is a historical consciousness that allows Riccardi to convey a sense of reverence for the unity of the church while at the same time cultivating a truly catholic sense of its complexity.

There are many other ways to observe the fruit of this historical focus in the actual life of Sant'Egidio. A few examples: In 2000, the community organized a pilgrimage through Trastevere (in Rome) that made explicit its sense of being connected to a long tradition. The pilgrimage sites alternated between ones connected to the church's past service to the poor—such as a hostel where St. Francis had stayed in Rome and which offered hospitality to the poor—and ones where Sant'Egidio currently provides service to the poor, such as a soup kitchen and a center of hospitality for immigrants. This juxtaposition of old and new moments in the church's ongoing mission of charity shows the degree to which Sant'Egidio, like Congar, sees the practice of Christian charity as a central element of the tradition that is to be remembered and continued.[17]

Memory is important to the community: Sant'Egidio holds a memorial service every year to remember a homeless woman who died in the train station in Rome some years ago when emergency personnel refused to load her into an ambulance on account of her smell. This commemoration of one woman becomes a commemoration of all homeless people who die on the streets, and hundreds of homeless people attend the ceremony each year. In another exercise of historical-geographical memory, Sant'Egidio holds yearly candlelight walks along the path that was taken by the Jews being deported from Rome by the Nazis. One final example: Sant'Egidio has been extremely active in interreligious and ecumenical dialogue and has particularly close relations with many Orthodox churches. Riccardi explains that Congar said to him, "Remember, the church was united in the great history."[18] Thus the memory of historical unity becomes a driving force for ecumenism today.

Andrea Riccardi also emphasizes that a sense of history provides motivation and guidance for being engaged in the world today. He says,

> [Congar told us that history] creates a profound sensitivity to reality: "Without history you find yourself like illiterates who can't read the present." That's how I gradually discovered the importance of history for understanding the world.... I think of my experience in the 1970s, which were a time of powerful ideology, with a Marxist cultural hegemony. But even in the first days of Sant'Egidio, though we were rather radical, we never shared an ideological vision. This shows how much we distrusted ideology, the distrust expressed by the boy who said, "First of all you have to change human beings." ... History ... has taught me to distrust ideology, received ideas, oversimplifications, the *clichés* of those who for years have spoken in the name of the "working class." History has always given me a sense of complexity. Cardinal

Martini has written about the community, "It immediately impressed me by its joining together of a profound sense of prayer and Scripture with an intelligent attention to the poorest of the poor and to difficult social situations. At a time when there was a trend towards either the politicization of religion (to the point of adopting revolutionary theories) or towards a concentration on spirituality, the path they followed struck me as responding to what many individuals—and I myself—were looking for: a mode of evangelical Christianity capable of engaging the sufferings of people."[19]

Riccardi explains that it was Congar who helped him distinguish ideology from theology in an important way by seeing this distinction in history: "Congar understood, in the middle ages, the difference between the faith and the medieval Christian ideology."[20] This is what allowed Congar to develop a new church-world theology rooted in the tradition and yet free from the constraints of medieval ideology. The result, in the case of Sant'Egidio, is a theological stance that has produced a fascinating combination of realism and pragmatic political savvy, demonstrated both in local political contexts as well as in international politics—coupled with a firm commitment to remain essentially apolitical. The focus, then, is more on personal conversion and responsibility. Bartoli speaks of

> the responsibility we all have for the history we live, that we cannot be complacent, explaining what doesn't work as the fault of the state, or it's the economic system, or someone else. There is a responsibility that has to be placed in the human heart of the person who is listening to the gospel.... The history you are living in is much more your own doing than you think.[21]

Studying history is understood as an invitation to moral transformation, and it helps avoid both theological and practical errors. Christians, as Congar explained, must think about history analytically and critically, but must also think about history as God's history, as a dramatic story of salvation in which they have a role that they must play well—and effectively.

For Sant'Egidio, then, an understanding of history and an understanding of Christian theology give hope about the possibilities for changing the world, while at the same time relativizing that hope by showing that ideologies are limited and earthly utopias are finally impossible. As Riccardi summarizes, "The great teaching of Congar, reflecting on it today, was that utopias are belied by history, but that one must always dream, and dream *in* reality."[22]

That capacity to dream in reality is at the root of Sant'Egidio's successes in peacemaking. As the community has found, violent conflict—though it may have significant structural elements—is often caused or prolonged by the inability to creatively envision alternatives, and that is precisely where there is room for intervention. Bartoli puts it in this way:

> When you engage, you engage with people who live in the reality in which they live, they don't live in the reality that we fantasize about. Our role is actually to engage them in a way that they will be able to recognize something beyond the constraint of what they see as the only option they have, which is to be in a violent conflict, a destructive conflict.... This work is fundamentally discernment, discernment of something that is possible and hidden, that is there and is not perceived.[23]

An understanding of history helps develop accuracy in this type of discernment and results in Sant'Egidio's capacity to remain both visionary and pragmatic.

The Other

There is another key theme that Sant'Egidio draws from Congar that has been important both for its spirituality and for its work for peace. For Congar, the key moral test for Christians who would be engaged in the world is their attitude toward the "other." Congar explains that true dialogue, which is the foundation for the church's relationship to the world, depends upon the capacity to accept the other as other, and the willingness to be open to what the other can teach us:

> Christian love of our neighbour rests on a certain sense of the other, consisting of an absence of contempt and mistrust

and the presence of an *a priori* openness and sympathy, a
desire to understand and share. Racial prejudice ... implies
not love but contempt and mistrust of the other. The colonial,
in his unfavourable aspect, has been characterized by a lack
of the sense of the other.[24]

Congar was particularly critical of what he called *esprit de
corps*, which he saw as being the root of many of the world's
problems: colonialism, racism, inter-Christian and interreligious
discord, and war. He said,

> [T]he first duty of the Christian ... is ... to keep up a vigi-
> lant resistance to propaganda and images which foster and
> express *esprit de corps*: then to build up in himself, by true
> information and, if possible, by personal contacts (for which
> there is no adequate substitute), a psychological structure
> of potential brotherly communion.[25]

Congar thought that to counter *esprit de corps*, Christians
needed to cultivate "a more truly 'catholic' soul: less provincial,
less stay-at-home, less inclined to see error in what is merely
unaccustomed...."[26] This is precisely what Sant'Egidio tries to
do—so much so that its charism has been described as a "border-
crossing charism." A British journalist, Austen Ivereigh, explains
it in this way:

> When John Paul II addressed the Community some years
> ago, he singled out two of its vital characteristics: on the
> one hand, its *filoxenia*—its love of the outsider—and on the
> other its openness to the universal. The Community tries
> to live "without walls," conscious of the tendency in both
> society and in the Church to build a fortress around itself
> and to create scapegoats. To the temptation of the Church as
> refuge and the nation as fortress, the Community responds
> with a counter-logic of concern for the one who is outside
> and far away.[27]

This emphasis on dialogue and solidarity with the "other" is
evident in the way Andrea Riccardi recently described the life of
the members of Sant'Egidio to an American audience:

In 1968 as in the following years, on the streets of Rome, on the roads of the world, and in the poorer areas of cities, the Community of Sant'Egidio has lived a commitment to dialogue, believing that this is the true expression of convinced Christians who are rooted in the Gospel. Indeed, a Christian community is a dialogue: between men and women, between different generations, between different cultures. Faith itself, as Pope Paul VI said in his encyclical *Ecclesiam Suam*, is "dialogue between God and men." ...

First as young people and now as not-so-young people, we have lived our dialogue in solidarity with the other. During our years of existence, we have lived in close proximity to the poorest, both in Rome and in the slums of many other cities of the world. These are the truly other, so often excluded from solidarity and from dialogue. We students discovered another world, the world of misery, a misery that was close at hand but often ignored.

This is how the 15,000 members of the Community live. We share the joys and the hopes, the anguish and sorrows, of all, but especially of the poor. For us, solidarity does not mean trying to substitute for public institutions. We have considered the poor as our own friends and relatives.[28]

Dialogue and friendship with the other, then, is a constant theme in the life of the community.

What is most interesting about Sant'Egidio, however, is the way that it has followed the logic of dialogue and of its border-crossing charism into a range of activities far beyond direct service to a few poor people in Rome. The community sees a close link between its service to the poor nearby, and a contribution to making peace in the world. In the minds of the members, reaching out in dialogue to the "other" who is nearby is the way one begins to reach out across the many barriers in the broader society and even the world. One of the members of the community, Mario Giro, states this in a clear way as he writes about the community's work in mediating the peace accord in Mozambique in 1992:

An old woman barricades herself in a dilapidated building in the slums of an Italian city. She refuses to open her door. Her neighbours are convinced she's becoming a derelict. A member of the Sant'Egidio community knocks at her door and starts to speak to her. She replies in monosyllables. He leaves but comes back later to continue a dialogue that may go on for months, even a year, until she agrees to open the door and let him in and finally start getting some help. Using these skills in patient communication based on friendship, the community later made contact with a guerrilla chieftain hidden away for years in the heart of Africa, brought him out of his isolation and persuaded him to negotiate instead of fight....

Eventually, the community reluctantly saw it had no choice but to act as a mediator. Lacking experience, it had to learn what to do as it went along. It invented a "language of reconciliation" whose syntax it picked up as a humanitarian organization working for the poor. Sant'Egidio had discovered how to talk to all kinds of people from its work in a wide variety of constantly changing situations in which its members related to the poor, shared their lives, spoke their language, went to the same places they did and regarded them not as welfare cases but as full members of society.[29]

It is interesting to point out that in the human rights community, Sant'Egidio has been severely criticized for being willing to talk even with the perpetrators of truly gross misdeeds—the guerrillas in Mozambique, or the LRA in Uganda, the *janjaweed* in Sudan. (In fact, the U.S. State Department regards Sant'Egidio as more or less a specialist to be called upon to help talk to the worst of the worst in Africa.) This criticism is somewhat justified, but on the other hand, the community says if you want to make peace, you have to talk with the people who are making war, no matter how much you would prefer to isolate them. In fact, this is simply the logical extension of a policy of solidarity that began with reaching out to the most marginalized people in Rome. The commitment to dialogue with anyone and the faith that any person is capable of changing—these are things that have come partly from Congar.

There is much more that could be said about Congar's vision of the church as immersed in the history of the world, in dialogue with the world, and his rich vision of catholicity and about Sant'Egidio's interpretation of them. But all of these themes come together in a quote that captures a sense of both Congar's thought and the personality of Sant'Egidio. Nearly twenty-five years after they were preached, Andrea Bartoli clearly recalls Congar's words:

> I remember when he spoke in Sant'Egidio, "You need everything to make a world, to make a world you need everything"; it was beautiful, it had this sense of, it's very Catholic in a very good, welcoming sense. It was very simple but very engaging. For us it was a beautiful thing. It was this invitation of saying "bring life on," don't seclude yourself in a Catholic ghetto, welcome what is in the world because you can make it holy, because it should be holy, and because you are meant to be holy in the world....[30]

Notes

[1]For the purposes of full disclosure, I wish to mention here that I am a member of the Community of Sant'Egidio in Boston.

[2]Yves Congar, *Christians Active in the World* (New York: Herder & Herder, 1968), 99-100. Published originally as the second half of *Sacerdoce et Laïcat*.

[3]Yves Congar, "L'apertura 'simpatica' della Chiesa al mondo," *La Nostra Assemblea* II, no. 1 (February 1976), published by the Community of Sant'Egidio, Rome. All translations here are my own.

[4]Yves Congar, *Église Catholique et France Moderne* (Paris: Hachette, 1978), 75.

[5]Ibid., 77.

[6]Interview with Andrea Bartoli, September 25, 2006, New York.

[7]Archives of the Community of Sant'Egidio, Rome, from June 4, 1983. Congar's homilies at Sant'Egidio were preached in French with sequential translation into Italian, and the archives contain only the Italian.

[8]Interview with Andrea Riccardi, November 24, 2006, Convent of Sant'Egidio, Rome.

[9]Riccardi is a professor of history at the Third University of Rome and at the time of his appointment was the youngest full professor in Italy.

[10]Interview with Andrea Riccardi.

[11]Ibid.

[12]Ibid.

[13]Andrea Riccardi (interviewed by J. Dominic Durand), in Andrea Riccardi and Peter Heinegg, *Sant'Egidio, Rome and the World* (London and Maynooth: St. Paul's, 1999), 30.

[14]Congar, "L'apertura 'simpatica' della Chiesa al mondo."

[15]John L. Allen, Jr. "Interview with Sant'Egidio Founder Andrea Riccardi," *National Catholic Reporter,* July 23, 2004; available at http://ncronline.org/mainpage/specialdocuments/riccardi.htm; accessed December 1, 2008.

[16]Ibid.

[17]A guide to the pilgrimage has been published: see the Community of Sant'Egidio, *Pilgrims in the Heart of Rome: A Journey through Trastevere* (Milan: Guerini, 2000).

[18]Interview with Andrea Riccardi.

[19]Riccardi, *Sant'Egidio, Rome and the World*, 41-43.

[20]Interview with Andrea Riccardi.

[21]Phone interview with Andrea Bartoli, May 20, 2008.

[22]Interview with Andrea Riccardi.

[23]Phone interview with Andrea Bartoli, May 20, 2008.

[24]Congar, *Christians Active in the World*, 201.

[25]Ibid., 202.

[26]Ibid., 170.

[27]Austen Ivereigh, "Changing the World Via the Crucified: The Community of Sant'Egidio," December 22, 2005; available at http://www.godspy.com/reviews/Changing-the-World-Via-the-Crucified-The-Community-of-Sant-Egidio-by-Austen-Ivereigh.cfm; accessed July 10, 2007.

[28]Andrea Riccardi, "Promoting Democracy, Peace, and Solidarity," *Journal of Democracy* 9, no. 4 (1998): 157-67 at 159-60.

[29]Mario Giro, "Sant'Egidio's Diplomacy of Friendship," *UNESCO Courier* (January 2000), 33.

[30]Interview with Andrea Bartoli, September 25, 2006, New York.

PART II

THE LAITY IN THE MODERN WORLD

Sex and Love as a Pathway to God

Toward a Vision of the Catholic Vocation of Marriage Today

Ann M. Michaud

At this time we seem to be at a juncture between two phases—a postmodern perspective that questions the value of anything, and a "return to the tradition" (a sort of *risorgimento*) that seeks to reinculcate the values of the past. However, too often "the tradition" is no more than a set of customs with unknown histories and purposes.

In regard to marriage, a frequently asked question today of "postmoderns" is, "Why bother to marry at all?" Why be a married couple—what does a commitment to marriage have to offer a couple if you can just live together and have kids (and split up if you need to)? If half of marriages end in divorce, what's the point? On the other hand, those who maintain a *risorgimento* perspective embrace the notion of the long-standing tradition of marriage, but do they know why?

This essay explores sex and love as a primary part of the Catholic vocation of marriage—as a pathway to God, rather than as a source of temptation or the "approved" means of allaying concupiscence. It also intends to focus primarily on the relationship between the spouses.

The first part focuses on the sacramentalization of marriage and the vision of sex and marriage in scripture. The next part examines sex and love as the work of marriage. The final section proffers a case study that demonstrates the impact of marital sex and love on the totality of life.

Tradition and Scripture

The first purpose here is to trace briefly the sacral history of marriage to see how the erotic and the sacral were linked from earliest times. This demonstrates both why and how certain elements were incorporated into the tradition of the sacrament. It is also of interest to note the original sources of many of today's "essential" wedding customs.

Even before the Roman Catholic Church's process of sacramentalizing marriage, marriage had been a sacral event. In ancient Roman and Greek societies, marriage was based primarily upon a "religion of the hearth."[1] Each family maintained its own household gods and "its own liturgy with its own rites, prayers, hymns, and sacrifices,"[2] and each was considered to be a separate religious community. The family hearth, a symbol of this set of ancestors and household gods, was symbolically kept perpetually burning, and the *paterfamilias* was the priest with the duty of caring for it. This responsibility passed from father to son. Procreation assured that this particular "religion" continued to exist. Because a barren marriage threatened the continuance of this religion, it would be dissolved.

For a woman, marriage meant changing from one religion to another. First the bride was "excardinated" from her paternal religion, a religion into which she had been initiated when her father accepted her after her birth. Then she was handed over to the bridegroom by an offering to the household gods of the father. This process involved not only a sacral, but also a legal action.

Next the bride was dressed in a white ceremonial gown, a veil, and a garland. Seated in a carriage, she was led to the house of the bridegroom in a public procession while hymns were sung. Upon arriving, she could not enter of her own accord, because the rites of this new religion were still unknown to her. Instead, a simulated abduction was performed in which the bridegroom carried her over the threshold, which she could not touch, and the marriage ceremony took place; the ceremony also "incardinated" her into her new religion. She was led to the household altar (the hearth), sprinkled with water, and permitted near the fire. Prayers and offerings were made. The final part of the ceremony for which the entire sacred marriage service was named—the *confarreatio*—

consisted of the bride and bridegroom sharing the wedding cake, which constituted the "very holy pledge of marriage."[3] This pledge was both a religious and a legal act.

During the fourth century, a truly liturgical celebration of marriage began in Rome, but it applied only in the case of a first marriage. It was obligatory for clergy who married, but optional for the laity.

After the sixth century, the Greeks developed a "certain distaste" for marriage, yet it was still considered a religious and a civil duty, and a sacrifice or an entry into a marital register was evidence of the validity of the marriage. Michel Foucault offers us insight into this Greek "distaste" when he asks:

> How, in what form, and why were sexual relations between husband and wife "problematical" in Greek thought? ... [He discovers the answer] at the end of the legal argument ... attributed to Demosthenes, [where] the author delivers a sort of aphorism that has remained famous: "Mistresses we keep for the sake of pleasure, concubines for the daily care of our persons, but wives to bear us legitimate children and to be faithful guardians of our households."[4]

So while marriage has become the necessary legal and moral obligation, it was in other relationships that pleasure lay. This separation of the sense of sexual pleasure and intimacy from the marriage bed rendered the marital relationship merely a pragmatic necessity and, hence, "distasteful." The church denied both Greek sexual promiscuity and the Manichean rejection of the body in its eventual sacramentalization of marriage.

The process of sacramentalization developed in response to the writings of Augustine, who named marriage a *sacramentum*; in other words, it had the indissoluble bond of a "sacral" nature and was a sacred sign.[5] At this point, "both the pagans and the Fathers of the church" viewed marriage primarily as the means of producing legitimate children.[6] (Remember what happened with the Greeks!) Augustine, too, believed that propagation was the first and most legitimate purpose of marriage.[7] But he did cite three goods of marriage: fidelity (*fides*), offspring (*proles*), and sacrament (*sacramentum*). He saw fidelity as confining sexual activity to one's spouse. Offspring meant not only procreating, but also accepting children in love, nurturing them with affection, and raising them in the faith. Sacrament, to Augustine, meant that the marriage bond would not be severed nor the spouse abandoned, even for another.[8]

It is important not to impose the contemporary understandings of "sacrament" on the term at this point. Theodore Mackin explains, "In using the word *sacramentum*, Augustine did not mean to call marriage a sacrament of the New Law, a religious sign or manifestation in human conduct of God's grace-giving entry into the lives of the persons involved in this conduct ... he is here describing marriage as it is found among all human beings, pagans included."[9] Augustine wavered throughout his writings as to whether or not to also consider marriage a form of friendship, and more than once he assented to its being a source of mutual help and support.[10] Augustine's thought had a long-lasting and highly influential effect; throughout the development of the sacramentalization of marriage, Augustine's understanding of primary threefold goods was foundational. Later on, his secondary considerations would offer support for the contemporary broadening of the vision of marriage.

Throughout the patristic and medieval periods, according to Edward Schillebeeckx, validity of a Christian marriage depended only on the mutual consent of a baptized man and woman "in the Lord." The marriage contract itself was in the hands of a mutually consenting man and woman, even if no witnesses were present, and it was sealed upon the first act of sexual intercourse. It was not until the tenth century, when the juridical power of the kings and the feudal system waned and legislative functions were handed over to the church, that a marriage ceremony was assimilated by the church. The nuptial mass included a separate blessing by means of a veiling together of both the bride and the groom, and frequently a blessing of the bridal chamber followed.[11]

As the sacramentalization process continued, debates occurred as to what constituted marriage, the mutual consent of the couple or the act of sexual intercourse between them. Theologians favored consensus and canonists preferred *copula*. Three basic schools of thought eventually emerged. The first claimed that "the desire for sexual intercourse belonged to the mutual consent to marry."[12] The second school claimed that marriage was basically a spiritual communion and that sexual intercourse was not an essential element.[13] The third claimed that marriage made a woman into a mother and therefore marriage was an institution for the purpose of bringing up children.[14]

There was also a debate between the theologians of the University of Paris and the canonists of the University of Bologna as to whether it was the consent of the couple to marry—irrespective of sexual intercourse—that constituted a valid marriage, or whether the subsequent act of sexual intercourse was necessary.[15] Gratian, a canonist and master at Bologna, made the next advancement, attempting to resolve the debate through his complex response in his work *Concordantia Discordantium Canonum*, better known as the *Decretum*.[16] He utilized a distinction of the Parisian theologians between a *matrimonium initiatum* (an inchoate marriage) and a *matrimonium ratum*. Gratian declared that *matrimonium initiatum* is created by *desponsatio*; it is made *ratum* by the first act of intercourse.[17] To explain *ratum*, Gratian referenced Augustine's three goods of marriage.[18] Gratian held that consent and subsequent intercourse could act as co-causes to create a marriage.[19] However Gratian left himself open to debate by his unclear use of the term *desponsatio*, which commonly referred to betrothal, and he had already declared in his own work that *desponsatio* was insufficient to create the marriage.

In speaking for the Parisian theologians in his famous *Sentences*, Peter Lombard took a different tack and proclaimed the necessary element to be the parties' mutual consent *de praesenti* that created the marriage before and apart from intercourse.[20]

After much debate, it was Cardinal Rolando Bandinelli, soon to be Pope Alexander III, who was credited with the resolution. Consensus remained the critical element, while *copula* determined the legal status. Marriage *de praesenti* with consent but without subsequent consummation (the biblical *unitas carnis*) was judged to be incomplete and thus could be dissolved.[21] The common vision then accepted and incorporated the ideas of all three schools from the prior debate and saw marriage "as a primarily sexual community, as a spiritual communion which was open to sexual intercourse, and a social institution for the bringing up of children."[22] In judicial matters, consent *de praesenti* constituted a valid but incomplete marriage (but not consent *de futuro* or betrothal), while *copula* or consummation meant that the marriage could no longer be dissolved.

From then on, the main focus of the ecclesial history of marriage quite often became the guaranteeing of paternity and fatherly support, prevention of spousal abuse (usually of the wife), the ecclesial and social encouragement to enter marriage as the "approved" means of allaying concupiscence, and the assurance that the procreative and unitive aspects of marriage were never separated. While Augustine's interpretation of original sin and concupiscence allowed for only very limited circumstances in which sexual intercourse, even within marriage, was not sinful,[23] Thomas Aquinas argued that the inclination to marriage and sexual intercourse "must of its nature be good."[24] Only in recent years was love added to the standard trilogy as a viable reason for marrying. Most recently, sexual love or *eros* was portrayed by ecclesial authority as a virtue or value to be promoted. We will take a closer look at this recent trend when examining the work of marriage.

It can be noted that the same three threads that came together in the Catholic image of marriage also existed in other religions and cultures. Vajrayana Buddhism, the Tibetan form of Buddhism also known as the Diamond Way, utilizes a variety of forms of energy in an attempt to reach its ultimate goal of Nirvana in a single lifetime. Among these energy forms, sexual intercourse and the numerous practices associated with it are given priority. Vajrayana sees the desire and consent of the couple as a clear means in seeking to attain Nirvana, a spiritual goal as well as a means of pleasure.

Michel Foucault points out that, in stark contrast to the Greek division of sexual pleasure and marital duty, ancient Chinese culture provided the means for a young woman to develop a spectrum of techniques designed specifically to give sexual pleasure to the couple (or at least to the husband), as well as the knowledge to optimize the chances of producing children. Such skills were not only considered pragmatic, but also necessary, since at that time Chinese society was polygamous and a wife's level of skill was her only assurance of maintaining her status.[25]

Jewish tradition recognizes sexual relations between wife and husband as a moment to be hallowed, and sexual relations on the Sabbath are considered especially blessed. Children are deemed a special gift and blessing from Yahweh. So sexual intercourse in Jewish understanding is the union of the couple, a spiritual encounter, and the possibility of the gift of progeny. The issues introduced in the sacramentalization process in Catholicism also exist in these and other religious traditions and cultures.

Having examined the Catholic tradition, as well as making a brief foray into other traditions, I turn now to another foundational source on sex and marriage for Catholicism—sacred scripture. Although images related to sexuality and marriage appear throughout the Catholic scriptures in both the Old and New Testaments, this essay will consider only three.[26] The first is Genesis 2:18-24, the Yahwist creation account, in which woman is considered a gift to man from God. Schillebeeckx reads this text, against some of the "subtle linguistic hairsplitting ... not all of it philologically sound,"[27] not in terms of man being given the power to choose woman for himself, but rather as man recognizing woman as his one true equal, which the animals were not: "She is a human being as he is, a partner at the same level of life."[28] That is also the intent behind the image of woman being formed from the rib of man: she is his blood-relation, of the same clan or the same "flesh and blood." Man and woman do not only complement each other sexually; they need one another to survive, and in joining together in the act of sexual union, they form one person, one flesh. And the term "helper" did not mean an assistant in his daily tasks; in Israelite understanding, it meant a refuge and support in whom one finds security, as God is the help of Israel (Ps 23:20). The later submission of a wife to her husband "was seen, even in Genesis, as a sinful situation."[29] This passage and Schillebeeckx's interpretation of it (with which I concur) demonstrate the deep intertwining of the various issues at play—sexual partnership, helper and comforter in the daily struggles and joys of life, and of course the possibility of producing progeny.

A second passage of interest is 1 Corinthians 7:16. Set in the context of a discussion of the possible dissolution of marriages between believing and unbelieving partners, Paul offers this reason for the believing partner to remain in the marriage if she/he so desires: "Wife, how do you know that you will not save your husband; or you, husband, that you will not save your wife?" The passage alludes to a deeper purpose to marriage: it is truly a means to salvation, a pathway to God. The spouses are not only to be of help to one another in the daily tasks of life; they are intended to help one another grow toward God. There is a deep spiritual partnership to a marriage, but one that must be cultivated.

A third passage is from the Gospel of Matthew 19:3-12.[30] It is often cited as a "problematic" passage concerning marriage because, while it offers Jesus' clear support of the notion of monogamous marriage, it also introduces the sometimes hotly debated prohibition against divorce in most cases, and, in the second part, it seems to favor celibacy over marriage. It is this later section that concerns us here, for it actually confirms both celibacy and marriage with its sexuality as viable vocations or paths to God. In v. 10 a disciple suggests that it is better not to marry, but in verse 11, Jesus responds with an important proviso—"only [for] those to whom it is given to do so." Verse 12 clarifies that this is to be done "for the sake of God's reign" and "Let him accept this teaching who can." Celibacy or abstaining from marriage and sexual activity is to be taken on voluntarily only for the sake of devoting one's self to doing God's work and only if one has been given (by God) the ability to accept this teaching—only if one is "called" to do so. This is basically the language of vocation. The implication is that marriage with its sexual relationship and celibacy are both pathways to God, and it is better to take on the one that one is given to do.

Sex and Love (and Procreation)—The Work of Marriage

The issues of *consensus* (love) and *copula* (sex) were foundational for the definition of marriage. So how are these two, apart from the issue of procreation, foundational for today? From a theological perspective, what is the work of marriage?

First, sex has a purpose beyond procreation—it brings a person to self-knowledge.

In his book *Love, Human and Divine*,[31] Edward Vacek illuminates the values that all relationships, including solid marital relationships, contain and aspire to. Vacek states, "Full acceptance of God's love requires not just acknowledging God's goodness, but also being genuinely affected by God's gift. An emotional acceptance of being loved is essential to a full Christian life.... The experience of being loved should be gladly welcomed and savored; it should not immediately be converted into a duty or power to love others."[32] Part of the work, and joy, of marriage is coming to this emotional acceptance of being loved—a necessary part of a full Christian life and a full relationship with God.

So, too, sex is not extrinsic to love and spirituality: sex and *eros* are not merely inherently self-absorbed; sex is a means of deepening love and of deepening and maturing spirituality.

Pope Benedict XVI (long known to theologians as Joseph Ratzinger), in his first encyclical *Deus caritas est* (part I, 5), points out that

> man is a being made up of body and soul. Man is truly himself when his body and soul are intimately united; the challenge of *eros* can be said to be truly overcome when this unification is achieved. Should he aspire to be pure spirit and to reject the flesh as pertaining to his animal nature alone, then spirit and body would both lose their dignity. On the other hand, should he deny the spirit and consider matter, the body, as the only reality, he would likewise lose his greatness.... Yet it is neither the spirit alone nor the body alone that loves; it is man, the person, a unified creature composed of body and soul, who loves. Only when both dimensions are truly united, does man attain his full stature. Only thus is love— *eros*—able to mature and attain its authentic grandeur.

Thus those who seek to avoid sexuality only for the sake of self-purification and those who seek only sex for the sake of self-enjoyment are equally missing the mark.

In his exploration of the three forms of love—*agape, eros*, and *philia*— Vacek points out that "Eros ... is no external, 'using' relation, but rather a union of our self with the beloved."[33] While *eros* may inherently involve a certain amount of acquisitiveness, it naturally progresses over time to a concern for the beloved that rightly evolves into a desire to seek what is best for the beloved. Huston Smith articulates it thus: "At the moment of mutual climax, where what each most wants is what the other most wants to give, it is impossible to say whether the experience is more physical or spiritual, or whether the lovers sense themselves to be two or one."[34] In the marital act of love-making, the temporal and the spiritual achieve unity, the lovers achieve unity, and sometimes a sense of union with the Divine as well. This, too, is the work of marriage—learning to love with both the body and the spirit.

What of that "secondary" issue of marriage as a form of friendship-philia? So, too, is the philia form of love also found in the marital relationship. Mutuality among persons is possible only with freely offered self-revelation.... When we communicate ourselves, we become *vulnerable*. Philia essentially includes a vulnerability that can be absent from agape. James Nelson well observes: "Agape comes from one who is self-sufficient and strong...not only is it more blessed to give than to receive, it is also easier. A man can stay in control of things...when he is self-sufficient and not needy, when others depend on his largesse, not he on theirs. What we risk in mutuality is the identity we have thus far formed. We open ourselves to what is beyond our control."[35]

And this is another work of marriage—to go beyond the self-seeking self-gratification, which may have been part of the initial sexual attraction, and to open oneself in vulnerability, receiving as well as giving, needing as well as providing, being known as well as knowing.

Yet another—and sometimes the most difficult—work of marriage is living the moments that call for agapic love: a love that seeks to give to the other what she/he needs without thought of the cost. Any married couple will attest to the fact that marriage is filled with opportunities to express multiple forms of agapic love. During sex, that agapic urge can produce delight; at other times, agapic love can be painful, calling for forgiveness of a deep wounding. In a healthy marriage, each spouse is willing to proffer agapic love to the other, and together toward others— toward family, friends, and above all, toward their children. It is the moments of *eros* and *philia* that the couple have experienced with and from one another that prepare and sustain them in the times of challenging agapic loving. This nature of sex and love in marriage lead a couple beyond themselves, even apart from the issue of procreation—and, in fact, a healthy relationship is the best milieu for having children and the best example to provide children for their own future marriages.

However, marriage is not always easy. To ignore this truth or to speak of marriage as a romantic fairy tale is neither helpful nor responsible. The best way to alter today's trend in which half of marriages end in divorce is to adequately prepare those entering marriage to expect that marriage will be work—sometimes hard work—and to help couples to commit to this work before they say "I do."

A Case Study: Dr. Rose

As a final method of examining the effects of sex and love in marriage—or in this case, the effects of its absence—I proffer a case study.

Rose is a well-respected internist, called in to consult on the most difficult cases. In her mid-twenties, Rose met and married a man. He was her soul-mate, she said. Her life suddenly experienced new dimensions. She found ways to express and share herself, sexually and otherwise, that had previously been forbidden. Even her spiritual life experienced new dimensions. She now found moments where she palpably felt God's presence with amazing intensity when with her husband, and he felt the same. These, she said, rivaled her own contemplative experiences, and there was something special about the fact that these were also now shared experiences.

Twelve years into their marriage, Rose and her husband divorced. Rose expected a time of adjustment, but found herself increasingly recognizing more and more parts of herself that she had lost with the relationship. She missed the sexual relationship. She had many offers, but they were for "just sex," as she put it, and she wanted much more, the intimacy, the trust, the soul-mate. Social engagements seemed less appealing. She attended some events alone. At other times, she would go places with her female friends. But more and more she missed the "otherness" of a male companion—the erotic element—and the parts of herself that she had been able to express in that relationship.

More than that, she discovered her loss had a major impact on two other areas of her life that had been so solid. While Rose could still give full intellectual assent to the tenets of her faith (as requested by her confessor), she no longer had any sense of God's love or presence in her life. She had no more "encounter" moments, nor even any general positive sense, just intellectual assent. While her spiritual director assured her that that was sufficient, Rose was not satisfied. And after twelve years, having now been divorced as long as she had been married, she felt things should have "improved." (And, yes, she had spoken with the appropriate professional colleagues about depression.)

Rose's situation had also, in recent years, begun to impact the practice of her profession, the one always reliable area of her life. While her skills had certainly not deteriorated and her colleagues consulted with her more often than ever, she was finding it increasingly difficult to arouse empathy for her patients, a previously automatic skill for Rose. She confessed that she had to exert much emotional energy to focus on each patient in order to offer appropriate personal as well as medical care. This disturbed her because she had always considered her work to be her ministry. Now it was becoming a job, a job she excelled at professionally, but still a job. Without the means to express the deepest parts of herself that her marriage had afforded, Rose was finding it difficult to offer the heartfelt emotional and personal support that her own life lacked. Overall, Rose described her situation as "increasingly constrictive." While she was smart enough to keep searching for life-giving situations, the results seemed increasingly superficial to Rose.

Rose's case demonstrates amply the widespread and devastating effects that the loss of a marital relationship can impose on one whose vocation is marriage. While Rose was always a self-assured, responsible, giving, and contributing person, she discovered untapped treasures when she entered the relationship with her soul-mate. She uncovered parts of herself she had not known, and was able to release parts that it would have been professionally or personally inappropriate to express in other relationships.

Rose had previously had a very strong spiritual life. By her own account, her marriage added to and deepened it in surprising ways. The loss of her partner, however, seemed to drain Rose of the emotional connection she had to the Divine. While her intellectual faith remained, it was woefully insufficient to Rose, who had experienced so much more. The holistic spiritual experience she had had was strikingly diminished by the loss of her marriage.

And the impact was not only affecting Rose. Although others may not have been aware of it, Rose was struggling to offer "gifts" she once found easy to give. The absence of her enriching marital relationship left Rose impoverished in terms of what she could offer to others. Many of her patients and friends were losing a special caring and sensitivity that Rose had shared, that had been magnified during her years of marriage. Few people had known Rose throughout that time (so few might notice the difference), but I had known her since just after the breakup, and I could see the waning energy and emotional unavailability of which she spoke. By the world's standards she was still "a well-respected, contributing member of society, admired by her peers and colleagues, as well as her patients" (as read the award she recently received). But Rose was experiencing something very different—spiritually, personally, and sexually—as the deep resources of her marital experiences ceased to exist. Her marriage had enriched her self-awareness and self-expression. It had expanded her social dimensions and had deepened her spiritual experiences. Without all of that, Rose's life felt empty to her, despite the fact that others saw her as an outstanding member of the community. Her marriage was about much more than just sex or just spiritual companionship, or just the opportunity to raise children (they had had none). The sum of the whole had been far greater than its parts, and the price of the loss far greater than the loss of just one relationship. And, yet, Rose acknowledged that the treasures she had lost were gifts she would not have possessed to such a great extent had she never been married.

Conclusion

From the earliest times, marriage was tied to religious meaning. We have seen how its characterization and traditions developed into what is now recognized in the Catholic Church as the sacrament and the vocation of marriage. We recall that Augustine acknowledged that the purpose of marriage extended beyond procreation: he cited *proles* (progeny), *fides* (fidelity), and *sacramentum* (the sacred bond of permanence) as the primary goods of marriage. In recent years the Catholic Church has expanded its understanding of marriage beyond these threefold goods. Today the church sees love in its threefold form—the unitive power of *eros*, the friendship and mutual support of *philia*, and the self-giving of *agape*—as an essential element of the marital bond.

And the case of Dr. Rose demonstrates how marriage can deepen one's awareness of the Divine, of one's self, and of one's relationship to spouse, family, and even the wider community. Rose's case also indicates clearly that the disintegration of a marriage can have devastating consequences, spiritually and emotionally, effects that extend beyond the confines of the relationship itself.

Such all-too-frequent breakups are significant, especially when we consider that most lay adults in the Catholic Church are, were, or will be married. Marriage is a pivotal element in the life of the laity of the church, and therefore in the life of the church. Marriage is more than the approved and private locus of procreation. The state of Catholic marriages affects not only the personal lives of the participants; it has an enormous impact on the life of the church community and on all of the communities in which married laity participate.

The institutional and juridical concerns of the church regarding marriage—such as what is necessary to make a marriage valid and what constitutes grounds to allow its dissolution—are a proper and necessary function of the hierarchy. But much more is at stake. The entire church community—all of the laity as well as the institutional hierarchy—share in and are therefore responsible to the married laity to provide whatever help and support they can to keep marriages healthy, while simultaneously respecting the vital privacy of the marital bond.

So the question to ask is: In what creative ways can we contribute to the well-being of Catholic marriages today? How can we address today's concerns that impact marriage within our own communities as well as globally: concerns of fostering commitment one to another, of nurturing and protecting our children, of economic considerations—from states of dire poverty and the ravages of war, to the impact of the economy on the "middle class" and the struggles of both single and two-parent families to provide for themselves and for their children financially and emotionally—concerns about the ecological future of our planet, the consequences of increased longevity of life, and so forth?

What is the responsibility of the institutional church to provide assistance before problems develop or become overwhelming and when such situations do occur? What is the responsibility of the church community as a whole, of the people of God?

Are the current programs (pre-Cana, marriage renewal, and so forth) sufficient? What more could be offered? How could church communities create a network of support for married couples? Who could best organize and participate in such an endeavor?

Marriage is a vocation that contributes to the participants, their offspring, their faith community, and the world. It, in turn, deserves spiritual sustenance, emotional encouragement, social support, and compassionate care in the face of devastating break-ups. Marriage is an indispensable part of the life of the Catholic Church today. In light of the high number of divorces, it is incumbent on all members of the church to live their vocational call to the best of their ability, on the hierarchy and pastoral leadership of the church to do all in its power to encourage and assist married couples in living out their vocation, and on all Catholics to support one another in whatever ways are possible.

To the postmoderns—yes, marriage is a risk, but so is living together. So is never discovering the best in yourself and your partner by playing it safe. The greatest gifts of Dr. Rose's marriage came with the risk of committing to and becoming someone's soul-mate, not just a mate. These are the very gifts Rose so ardently desires to recover. Is the lesser risk of just living together worth the casting away of these deeper, more intimate, and more fulfilling possibilities?

To the *risorgimento*—yes, the tradition has much to offer. There is a reason it has long recognized the vocation of marriage and continues to expand its vision of the goals and gifts of marriage. But marriage requires work and effort and often outside support. The success of marriage is not guaranteed. The tradition as a set of precepts is necessary but insufficient to sustain a marital relationship. Each member of the couple must carefully consider the reasons for entering into the marriage bond with this particular person before they make a lifelong commitment to one another. Marriage faces many challenges today. Its success depends upon us working together, as couples and as a faith community, in support of one another.

Notes

[1]Edward Schillebeeckx, O.P., *Marriage: Human Reality and Saving Mystery*, trans. N. D. Smith (New York: Sheed & Ward, 1965), 167.

[2]Ibid., 234.

[3]Ibid., 235.

[4]Michel Foucault, *The Use of Pleasure: Volume Two of The History of Sexuality*, trans. Robert Hurley (New York: Vintage Books, 1986), 143. Foucault cites Demosthenes, *Against Neaera*, French ed. trans. L. Gernet (Collection des universites de France); English trans. A. T. Murray (Loeb Classical Library).

[5]Ibid., 281.

[6]Ibid., 282.

[7]Theodore Mackin, S.J., *What Is Marriage?* (New York: Paulist Press, 1982), 142. Mackin notes that this view is expressed by Augustine in both *De Bono Coniugali* (On the Good of Marriage), written in 401, and eighteen years later in 419 in *De Adulterinis Coniugiis* (On Adulterous Spouses).

[8]Ibid., 129. Mackin is quoting (in translation) Augustine's *Commentary on the Literal Meaning of Genesis* (Book 9, chap. 7, n. 12).

[9]Mackin, *What Is Marriage?*, 139.

[10]Ibid., 139-42. Mackin cites *De Bono Coniugali*, chaps. 3, 5, 6, 9, 11, 17, 19, and 24; *De Moribus Ecclesiae Catholicae*, Book 1, chap. 30; and *De Sermone Domini in Monte*, Book 1, chap. 15, n. 42.

[11]Schillebeeckx, *Marriage*, 278-79.

[12]Ibid., 291. This was the school of Astenasus, which claimed that the desire for sexual intercourse belonged to the mutual consent to marry.

[13]This was the school of Hugh of St. Victor, which set forth the marriage of Mary and Joseph as its example.

[14]The third was the school of St. Isidore of Seville. At this point, Gratian took over the view of the canonists (*copula*) and Peter Lombard that of the theologians (consensus).

[15]Mackin, *What Is Marriage?*, 159. What was at stake in the argument was the concern of the school of Hugh of St. Victor—if intercourse was necessary, then Mary and Joseph were not truly married according to the teaching that Mary remained a virgin her entire life. Also, by this definition, a brother and sister could marry, so long as they did not consummate the marriage.

[16]Mackin, *What Is Marriage?*, 158.

[17]Theodore Mackin, S.J., *The Marital Sacrament* (New York: Paulist Press, 1989), 289.

[18]Ibid., 289. According to this argument, Mary and Joseph were indeed married, even without sexual intercourse according to *matrimonium initiatum*. For *matrimonium ratum*, Gratian offered an explanation of a "different and richer completion" of their marriage utilizing Augustine's three goods of marriage.

[19]Ibid., 289.

[20]Ibid., 290.

[21]Ibid., 291-92.

[22]Schillebeeckx, *Marriage*, 302.

[23]Mackin, *What Is Marriage?*, 130-31. According to Augustine, sexual intercourse was sinless only within marriage and with the express intent to conceive without attempt at carnal pleasure or to prevent the other partner from committing the more serious sin of adultery. Sex propelled by concupiscence and passion, within marriage, was venially sinful. Sexual intercourse with the intent of avoiding conception, within marriage, was mortally sinful. Sexual intercourse outside of marriage was mortally sinful.

[24]Ibid., 179.

[25]Foucault, *The Use of Pleasure*, 143. Foucault is referencing R. Van Gulik, *La Vie sexuelle dans la Chine ancienne*, 144-54.

[26]Some texts, such as Hosea, utilize marriage to demonstrate symbolically

the relationship between God and God's people. Their central message does not regard marriage itself. These complex comparisons require the unpacking of many texts in order to arrive at the premise, which at its most basic (e.g., for Hosea) is that God loves God's people in spite of their sinfulness. See the commentary by Dennis J. McCarthy, S.J. and Roland E. Murphy, O.Carm., "Hosea," in *The New Jerome Biblical Commentary*, ed. Raymond E. Brown, S.S., Joseph A. Fitzmyer, S.J., and Roland E. Murphy, O.Carm. (Englewood Cliffs, NJ: Prentice Hall, 1990), 217-28, esp. 219-20. Another important biblical text, the Song of Songs, is a complex poetic work that refers literally to human sexual love (not necessarily to marriage) and figuratively, depending upon interpretation, to the love of God or Christ for God's people or to the belief that human love contains a reflection of divine love. It warrants further detailed treatment in a separate essay. See, in the same source, Roland E. Murphy, O. Carm., "Canticle of Canticles," 465, esp. the introduction on 462-63. Other texts that utilize marriage as an analogy, for example Ephesians 5:21f, pose an additional dilemma. Biblical scholars such as Elisabeth Schüssler Fiorenza argue that the "household codes" could demonstrate the imposition of the Greco-Roman cultural standards on the more egalitarian early Christian communities, or could show how early Christian *ekklesia* were rifled with the hierarchical power structure of Roman colonial imperialism or the politics of Empire. Pauline interpretation, which allows for both readings, is not self-evident, but is influenced by the interpreter's view of reality. See Elisabeth Schüssler Fiorenza, *The Power of the Word: Scripture and the Rhetoric of Empire* (Minneapolis: Fortress Press, 2007), esp. 69-109, and also the works of Richard A. Horsley and others. If one wishes to follow a more traditional reading, again more unpacking would be necessary. The text in its essence states that it is the duty of husbands to love their wives in all circumstances as Christ loves (and as they love themselves), that wives should accept this Christ-like love and care, and that everyone should "defer to one another out of reverence for Christ," as demonstrated in the exegetical work of Paul J. Kobelski, "The Letter to the Ephesians," also found in *The New Jerome Biblical Commentary*, 883-90.

[27]Schillebeeckx, *Marriage*, 17.

[28]Ibid., 18.

[29]Ibid., 19.

[30]Matthew 19:3-12: Some Pharisees came up to him and said, to test him, "May a man divorce his wife for any reason whatever?" He replied, "Have you not read that at the beginning the Creator made them male and female and declared, 'For this reason a man shall leave his father and mother and cling to his wife, and the two shall become as one?' Thus they are no longer two but one flesh. Therefore, let no man separate what God has joined." They said to him, "Then why did Moses command divorce and the promulgation of a divorce decree?" "Because of your stubbornness Moses let you divorce your wives," he replied; "but at the beginning it was not that way. I now say to you, whoever divorces his wife (lewd conduct is a separate case) and marries another commits adultery, and the man who marries a divorced woman commits adultery." His disciples said to him, "If that is the case between man and wife, it is better not to marry." He said, "Not everyone can accept this

teaching, only those to whom it is given to do so. Some men are incapable of sexual activity from birth; some have been deliberately made so; and some there are who have freely renounced sex for the sake of God's reign. Let him accept this teaching who can" (*The New American Bible* [New York: Thomas Nelson Publishers, 1983]).

[31]Edward Collins Vacek, S.J., *Love, Human and Divine: The Heart of Christian Ethics* (Washington, D.C.: Georgetown University Press, 1994).

[32]Ibid., 128.

[33]Ibid., 252.

[34]Huston Smith, *The Illustrated World's Religions: A Guide to Our Wisdom Traditions* (San Francisco: Harper Collins, 1994), 92.

[35]Vacek, *Love, Human and Divine*, 290-91. The quote from James Nelson is taken from *The Intimate Connection* (Philadelphia: Westminster, 1988), 55.

Justice, Peace, and Catholic Identity in Archbishop Hunthausen's Letter on Matrimony

James T. Cross

A commitment to the pursuit of social justice, which includes the pursuit of peace, became a prominent characteristic of Catholic identity in the twentieth century.[1] It was this century that saw the development of modern Catholic social teaching, a continuing corpus of official documents wherein the Catholic Church elucidates its social conscience and challenges its members to fulfill it. As *Gaudium et Spes*, the central modern social document, makes clear, the lay members of Christ's faithful people are especially particularly responsible for such fulfillment: "Since they have an active role to play in the whole life of the Church, laymen are not only bound to penetrate the world with a Christian spirit. They are also called to be witnesses to Christ in all things in the midst of human society" (43).

This same document also points out that one of the ways that the laity can pursue (and realize) social justice is via the sacramental vocation that is uniquely theirs, the sacrament of matrimony. The chapter on marriage (47-52) in *Gaudium et Spes* repeatedly insists upon the existence of a moral interdependence between families and the societies of which they are parts. Especially noteworthy is the following: "The family is a kind of school of deeper humanity.... Thus the family is the foundation of society. In it the various generations come together and help one another to grow wiser and to harmonize personal rights with the other requirements of social life" (52).

Archbishop Raymond G. Hunthausen's *Pastoral Letter on the*

Sacrament of Matrimony[2]—like *Gaudium et Spes*—bases social justice and peace upon characteristics essential to the lay vocation of sacramental marriage. Given this fact, the letter's contribution to understanding the relationship between Catholic identity and the laity promises to be significant.

Context and Content of the Letter

The 1982 Convention of the International Worldwide Marriage Encounter was held in Seattle. The episcopal moderator of the convention was Raymond G. Hunthausen, the Roman Catholic archbishop of Seattle. Theological and pastoral themes central to the convention were gathered and elaborated upon in a *Pastoral Letter on the Sacrament of Matrimony*. This letter resulted from the collaboration of Archbishop Hunthausen, Thomas L. Vandenberg, and Charles A. Gallagher, S.J.,[3] and focuses on what Gallagher calls "a need for a marital spirituality based on sexual intimacy as a sacramental symbol."[4]

The seventy-four-paragraph letter begins by acknowledging and valuing Judaism's understanding of marriage as a sacred covenant (3).[5] It also does so with regard to Protestant views of marriage as a sanctifying bond (3). Then, from the fourth paragraph through to the final paragraph, the letter is devoted to the Catholic understanding of marriage as a sacrament. Specifically, the letter asserts that this sacrament is the evolving relationship of a baptized husband and wife (5), one that is to signify the church's call to intimacy and belonging (8-9). The latter two qualities are said to be "integral to the life of the church" (9), and they can (and ought to) be exemplified in the relationships of Catholic couples (8).

The last seventy-one paragraphs of the letter can be summarized in the five following points. First, pursuing social justice is urgent, but it is subordinate to and dependent upon the church's primary vocation to realize communion-love or intimacy. Second, such intimacy consists in mutual self-giving. Third, since the greatest possible degree of human intimacy can be experienced only in sacramental marriages, the latter are necessary in order for the church to fulfill its primary vocation. Fourth, such marriages are essentially sexual, sacramental, agapic, exclusive, permanent, and parental. Fifth, such marriages can heal the brokenness of the church and the world.

Priority of Love over Justice

The first New Testament quotation cited in the letter is Jesus' *agape* commandment in John 13:35: "By this all will know that you are my disciples, if you have love for one another" (11). This should serve to remind us that we are called to "communion, not just ... cooperation; and to a oneness of life, not just ... shared endeavor" (13). This "communion" is said to be much more than a community, since the latter includes social structures of which "heaven will be devoid" (30). It is, rather, an intimacy that, if not imbued in the church's social programs, will leave the church looking like "just another service organization" (56). To be a Christian disciple is to be called to relationship more than to productivity (14). Although "rights and responsibilities ... must be honored and observed ... the gospel mandate of love must always have first place" (29). In fact, experience shows us that love (in the form of forgiveness, for example) is our only recourse when the rectification of specific injustices remains elusive (59-63).

Intimacy

The word "intimacy" is recurrent, appearing in twenty of the seventy-four paragraphs, and it is often coupled with the word "belonging." Several meanings for the term "intimacy" are offered throughout the letter. One of the first of these is "complete self-giving of each to the other," a giving that was first perfectly modeled by Jesus (13). "Openness and vulnerability" are associated with intimacy, if not identified with it (16). Sexual intimacy "summons the couple to rise above egoism" (22), and is related to a couple's "bonding of life, of heart, and of spirit" (26). Intimacy is also being absorbed with one's spouse and by "giving up our independence" (32). Intimacy must be fostered by a person-centered love (34). The most intimate question husband and wife can ask each other is: "Will you empower me to become a parent?" (47). If they become so blessed, their shared parenting deepens their intimacy (50). Sulking, bitterness, distrust, pride, indifference, and stubbornness are condemned as barriers to intimacy (59-60).

The Church's Mission Depends upon Its Married Couples

The pastoral letter claims that in scripture marital love is the primary image of God's love for us (15). This unique imaging ability of married couples is seen as "indispensable for the church's well-being" (16), since witnessing to God's love is the "central mandate" given to the church (12). The sexual union of a Catholic couple, as sacramental, "challenges the couple to translate what is signified into living reality" (22), and simultaneously "equips the church for its mission to the world, calling forth greatness from us all" (23). Since they alone experience perfect intimacy, the married achieve "a dimension of witnessing which unmarried persons cannot offer, no matter how great their gifts or how profound their holiness" (26). Such intimacy "incarnates ... the church's ideal of communion in God," creating in the church an environment of hope (32), and heralding the gospel "more profoundly than the words of the teaching office of the church" (40). Even the church's ministry as God's servant to the world depends upon sacramental marriage: "Without the daily servanthood of its married couples, the church's ministries to people in need would be an empty institutional gesture" (44).

This servanthood consists fundamentally and especially in the creation and nurturing of new life within a community of mutual interpersonal love (45-49). Not only does the church depend upon sacramental marriages, the latter deserve constant and considerable support from the church (24, 73).

Essential Characteristics of Marriage

The letter sees sacramental marriages as essentially sexual, agapic, sacramental, exclusive, indissoluble, and parental. The mutual sexual desire experienced in a sacramental marriage is fundamental, for it "energizes [the couple] to pursue a love which knows no bounds" (23). This desire and its fulfillment in sexual intimacy are sacramental, since they cause and are caused by the couple's exclusive and permanent[6] agapic union (21), and since this union is a sign of God's creative love (35). Since their love knows no bounds, it does not ignore or suppress its procreative potential (48). Procreativity and parenting are seen as simultaneously essential in and yet subordinate to the marital relationship (46). It is even suggested that appropriate parenting of children may be more important than procreating them (49). Procreativity is called a "charism" that a truly loving partner must be willing to give to (and receive from) her or his beloved (47). Parenthood is to be a shared responsibility based upon the couple's shared intimacy (49). Children believe that life is sacred when they directly witness and experience their parents' unconditional love (52). Such education is impeded if the family meal is poorly celebrated or neglected (52-53). Parenthood also reminds the whole church to attract and welcome converts (54).

Healing Church and World

The church is called to heal the world's brokenness. It will do so as well as it heals its own brokenness (57). Married Catholic couples can lead a healing process because they possess a healing charism and experience in using it (59). They know so well that conflict resolution and forgiveness are necessities, not noble alternatives (60). A prominent sign of the Catholic Church's brokenness is its exclusion of married couples from its structures of leadership (67). To maintain such a course is to unjustly discriminate (68) and to defy a tenet of the Second Vatican Council (71).[7]

Critical Assessment

The letter does have some lacunae, the first of which is the absence of a bibliography. The letter does not include actual footnotes, endnotes, or bibliography, although some of the theological sources informing it are easily recognizable. The latter are (some modern translation of) the Bible, *Gaudium et Spes*, *Lumen Gentium*, and Avery Dulles's *Models of the Church*.[8] Assessing the letter is thus possible, but it is impeded by a degree of uncertainty about its authors' dialogue partners.

Also absent is evidence of historical-critical exegesis of the biblical passages that are cited throughout the letter. Various theological points are argued proximate to fourteen seemingly supportive quotations from scripture. Even though these quotations appear to fit the point argued, and even though readers of official Catholic documents often experience these documents' exegetical deficiencies, the absence of biblical scholarship should give readers pause.

If there is a theological claim in the letter that biblical scholars would surely question, it is calling the "love one another" commandment in John 13:34 "the central mandate of the Gospel" (12). This commandment can, indeed, be said to be central, but it is central along with a theologically prior command that is omitted in John: the "greatest" commandment is to love God (Mt 22:37-38). Actually, the New Testament books contain four distinct love commandments. The love commandment in John involves *koinonia*, a fellowship love shared among community members. Matthew and the other evangelists include the other three commands: the aforementioned command to love God (also in Mk 12:30), the command to "love your neighbor" (Mt 22:39; also Mk 12:31), a love that includes love of enemies (Mt 5:44; also Lk 6:27), and the command to love oneself (Mt 22:39; also Mk 12:31).

Love of God includes worship, thanksgiving, and being alone with God.[9] Love of neighbor involves *diakonia*, charitable service extended to any and all.[10] The *Pastoral Letter on the Sacrament of Matrimony*, by preferring John above every other biblical book,[11] and by reading John uncritically, thus both obscures the priority of love of God and subscribes to what could be called a "passive *diakonia*":

> The witness of sacramental couples reminds the church of its primary mission: to proclaim Jesus to the world *through its members' relationship of love for one another*. When this truly happens, the church becomes ... *attractive*... (56; italics mine).

The letter's preference for Johannine morality might also explain why it omits reference to Thomas Aquinas's classic understanding of love. Aided by, yet transcending, the thought of Aristotle, Aquinas points out that love of God—charity—is the highest virtue because God is its primary object and because it guides all other virtues, including the virtue of justice.[12] In fact, human persons cannot act lovingly or justly without God's love first justifying and empowering them.[13] It is only God's love that gives humans "the capacity to love God above all else and the ability to love others as themselves."[14] Furthermore, charity demands that we love (not merely work dutifully for) the common good, since God, the supreme good, is the foundation of this good.[15] The virtue of justice, in turn, "challenges charity to beam its love ... on all social relationships and not simply to restrict love to interpersonal relationships."[16]

Three consecutive sentences situated near the end of the letter elicit my final criticism, which is mixed. The sentences that span paragraphs 67 and 68 challenge Catholic bishops and priests to include married couples in the church's structures of leadership. At the time the letter was written, and still today, the Second Vatican Council's vision for the lay apostolate is unfulfilled, and some of this failure can be blamed on the "sin of clericalism."[17] Nevertheless, official Catholic documents such as *Apostolicam Actuositatem* (especially paragraphs 10, 20, and 25) remind us that Catholic laity can (and sometimes must) circumvent this sin; they need not wait for the hierarchy to invite them to lead. Also, the letter at this point seems to forget its earlier subordination of the institutional model to the communion model of church. If it is true that "heaven will be devoid of social structures; love alone will suffice" (30), then why insist that "our structures of leadership ... change to include married couples" (72)? Should not the latter's ability to signify communion inspire us to replace— not merely change—church structures? Dolores R. Leckey seems to agree:

> [I]n the past quarter of a century, laity (a large proportion of them women) have professionally prepared for lay ministry within the church, at all levels.... The presence of the laity introduces a new context as they pursue studies while still inserted in their homes (the domestic church) and serving as responsible citizens of their larger communities. One could say they consciously live in two worlds, neither of which is like the seminary culture....[18]

Strengths

While the letter's preference for the Gospel of John can be criticized, it can also be praised. In focusing upon the Johannine themes of mutual love and unity, the letter reflects John Paul II's inspiring emphasis upon mutual self-donation while simultaneously avoiding the pope's questionable emphasis upon gender complementarity. The latter emphasis is rooted in John Paul II's dominant biblical source of Genesis 2.[19] Luke Timothy Johnson points out that, "If Genesis 1—which has God creating humans in God's image as male and female—had been employed more vigorously (in the pope's "body" audiences), certain emphases would be better balanced."[20] In contrast, the letter on matrimony finds such balance through its dependence upon the Gospel of John.

This balance enables the letter's esteem for and grand vision of a "nuptial mindset." The end of the letter, in its call for inclusion of sacramental couples in leadership roles, regrets the prevalence of "exclusionary procedures" and a "single person's mentality" in the church (69). But the regret is accompanied by hope, since the "couple perspective" can effect needed reforms (72). Here is where another major difference between John Paul II's theology of marriage and that of the letter can be discerned. John Paul II limits the duty to develop a "nuptial mindset" to each heterosexual couple's marriage, while the letter sees this mindset as a charism that challenges and leads the entire church through couples that exercise it:

> The deeper remedy would be a conversion of heart so that all those who are in decision-making positions would have a nuptial mindset ... would have the achievement of intimacy as their basic goal, and would have some skills in that achievement.[21]

This nuptial mindset must inform the church's efforts at service: "We who provide services must do so as a means of fostering the intimacy that is our salvation. More importantly, we must live in intimacy as we provide those services."[22]

Another charism of sacramental marriage—one seen as essential—is parenthood (47). This traditional emphasis, like the emphasis on mutual self-donation, seems to be close to that of John Paul II. However, again the letter goes in a different direction. While John Paul II holds that a marriage's procreative dimension is on a par with its unitive dimension, the letter holds that the couple's relationship is primary (47). Also somewhat different is the letter's exaltation of education over procreation (49), and its insistence that the tasks of education are to be shared equally (50). The letter's awareness of its "new" distinctions is said to be based upon recent conciliar teaching (46). Such newness is a strength since children—the future of society—need to see interpersonal relationships, especially their parents' marriage, as having intrinsic (not utilitarian) value. It also supports couples who might prefer the adoption of children over the procreation of them.

In Roman Catholicism, prayer and fasting are simultaneous and climactic in the sacrament of eucharist. At eucharist, Catholic laity, religious, and clergy prayerfully lift up their bodies, hearts, and minds with Jesus, whose fast is symbolized in his "not drink[ing] again the fruit of the vine until the day when I drink it new in the kingdom of God" (Mk 14:25). In their communion with Jesus, Catholics learn that that kingdom of justice and peace will only come after prayer and fasting, after faith and works, after celebrating and living the eucharist. In the letter on matrimony, the eucharist is called "the church's family meal" during which Catholics fast from "individualism and private concern" (53). Furthermore, this meal of the universal church is seen as being enhanced by the meals of the domestic church:

> The family meal is an especially important aspect of par-
> enting.... [E]ach day the main meal can be a kind of home
> liturgy.... The meal should begin with a meaningful prayer.
> Conversation during the meal should be directed to a sharing
> of each person's life, hopes, joys and fears.... Some sacrifice
> will be entailed because the secular world sets up competing
> demands.... (52)

Lay Catholic theologian Julie Hanlon Rubio confirms that there are aspects of the family meal upon which social justice and peace depend: prayer remembers our fundamental dependence upon God; conversation increases interpersonal intimacy, teaches moral values, and inspires civic responsibility; hospitality practices inclusivity and sharing. She concludes, "If families do not gather as communities of love in their homes, they cannot then be communities of love for the world...."[23]

Conclusion

Catholic colleges and universities today continue to value justice and peace education as a major component of their Catholic identity. As Archbishop Raymond G. Hunthausen's alma mater, Carroll College, plans to inaugurate its justice and peace center during its imminent centennial, it and other colleges would do well to found such centers upon the theology contributed in his pastoral letter on matrimony. This letter, like *Gaudium et Spes*, bases social justice and peace upon characteristics essential to the lay vocation of sacramental marriage. Prominent among these characteristics is a nuptial mindset whereby Christian spouses are called to model for the church and the world the self-donating love that is a prerequisite for justice. Furthermore, the letter is both similar to, and corrective of, the nuptial theology of John Paul II. Those who may be tempted to reduce lay Catholic identity to sexual morality, and those who may be tempted to reduce it to social activism, should note that the letter celebrates the marriage of the one to the other.

Notes

[1] This commitment has roots in the first modern Catholic social document, Pope Leo XIII's 1891 encyclical *Rerum Novarum* (see, for example, no. 13). See the English translation in David J. O'Brien and Thomas A. Shannon, eds., *Catholic Social Thought: The Documentary Heritage* (Maryknoll, NY: Orbis Books, 1992), 14-39. On the inseparability of justice and peace, see the Second Vatican Council's pastoral constitution *Gaudium et Spes* 78 in O'Brien and Shannon, *Catholic Social Thought*, 220.

[2] This letter (hereinafter called "the letter") is available in *Origins* 12, no. 15 (23 September 1982), 229-38. It is sequentially the first of only thirty-one episcopal documents on marriage currently highlighted at the official website of the United States Catholic bishops (accessed 7 June 2008 at http://www.usccb.org/laity/marriage/statements.shtml).

[3] Thomas L. Vandenberg, a priest of the Seattle Archdiocese, shared this information with me in personal correspondence. Rev. Gallagher is the founder of Worldwide Marriage Encounter.

[4] Charles A. Gallagher et al., *Embodied in Love: Sacramental Spirituality and Sexual Intimacy* (New York: Crossroad, 1983), 3.

[5] The paragraphs referred to or quoted will be cited numerically according to their sequence in the letter, and parenthetically within the text and endnotes of this essay. The paragraphs of the letter are not numbered in the

Origins printing. See Charles A. Gallagher and Thomas L. Vandenberg, *The Celibacy Myth* (New York: Crossroad, 1987), 155 n.5, for evidence of the letter's paragraphs being numbered.

[6]Paragraphs 37 and 38 of the letter seem to see this union as eternal, not as ending when one spouse dies. Such a view challenges the permissibility of remarriage in the church. See, for example, Canon 1141 in the *Code of Canon Law* (Washington, D.C.: Canon Law Society of America, 1983), 413.

[7]"Church leadership ... is the corporate responsibility of all the baptized" is a tenet present—although worded differently—in *Lumen Gentium* 33. During my interview of him on 23 May 2008, Archbishop Hunthausen underlined this tenet when he stated that "My strongest feeling about what the Church needs to do has always been: shared responsibility."

[8]Avery Dulles, *Models of the Church* (Garden City, NY: Doubleday, 1978).

[9]See Edward Collins Vacek, *Love, Human and Divine: The Heart of Christian Ethics* (Washington, D.C.: Georgetown University Press, 1994). Vacek cogently argues that love of God is distinct from love of neighbor, and that it is the foundation of the moral life. Those guilty of neglecting this foundation may be, may become, and/or may raise what Christian Smith calls "Moralistic Therapeutic Deists." See his chapter "Is Moralistic Therapeutic Deism the New Religion of American Youth? Implications for the Challenge of Religious Socialization and Reproduction," in *Passing on the Faith*, ed. James L. Heft (New York: Fordham University Press, 2006), 55-74.

[10]See Timothy E. O'Connell, *Principles for a Catholic Morality*, rev. ed. (New York: Harper Collins, 1990), 43-44, on the *koinonia* v. *diakonia* distinction.

[11]The letter's preference is understandable, given that the theme of the 1982 Worldwide Marriage Encounter convention was based upon Jesus' prayer for unity in John 17.

[12]What the New Testament books call *agape*, Aquinas calls *caritas*. See Thomas L. Schubeck, *Love That Does Justice* (Maryknoll, NY: Orbis Books, 2007), 116. The letter, like the fourth gospel, focuses Christians on exercising agapic love for fellow humans; this focus excludes God, strangers, and self, at least explicitly.

[13]Thomas Aquinas, *Summa Theologiae* II-II.23.

[14]Schubeck, *Love That Does Justice*, 123.

[15]Aquinas, *Summa Theologiae* I-II.19.10. Schubeck points out how this theocentric view of the common good opposes viewing a nation's or dictator's good as the highest good (*Love That Does Justice*, 138).

[16]Aquinas sees justice as the greatest of the cardinal virtues because of two reasons: it extends beyond one's self, and it calls the subject to obey reason when obligations ought to be satisfied.

[17]This is a phrase uttered by Bishop Carter vis-à-vis the Council's original schema on the lay apostolate. See Xavier Rynne, *The Third Session: The Debates and Decrees of Vatican Council II, September 14 to November 21, 1964* (New York: Farrar, Straus & Giroux, 1965), 73.

[18]Dolores R. Leckey, *The Laity and Christian Education: Apostolicam*

Actuositatem, Gravissimum Educationis (Mahwah, NJ: Paulist Press, 2006), 89.

[19]See, for example, the papal audiences contained in John Paul II, *Man and Woman He Created Them*, trans. Michael Waldstein (Boston: Pauline Book & Media, 2006). A persuasive critique of gender complementarity is included in Lisa Sowle Cahill, "Marriage: Institution, Relationship, Sacrament," in *One Hundred Years of Catholic Social Thought*, ed. John A. Coleman (Maryknoll, NY: Orbis Books, 1991), 103-19.

[20]Luke Timothy Johnson, "A Disembodied 'Theology of the Body': John Paul II on Love, Sex, and Pleasure," *Commonweal* 128, no. 2 (26 January 2001): 11-17.

[21]Gallagher et al., *Embodied in Love*, 126.

[22]Ibid., 127-28.

[23]Julie Hanlon Rubio, *A Christian Theology of Marriage and Family* (Mahwah, NJ: Paulist Press, 2003), 196-99. This concern shared by Rubio and the letter is fittingly complemented by Hunthausen's memories of his parents. He informed me that his mother, Edna, often took her children to daily eucharist, and that his father, Arthur, often extended credit to customers who could not pay their grocery bill. In feeding their needy neighbors, and in fasting from debt collection, the Hunthausen family fulfilled the agapic meals that formed them.

Is There a Light under That Bushel?

Hidden Christian Identity
in *Wise Blood* and *The Moviegoer*

Jonathan Malesic

On two separate occasions when my in-laws were taking bids on some work they wanted done on their house, the contractor made sure to point out that he was a member of the First Baptist Church in some nearby town. In that context, such a confession could only have been intended as a selling point, evidence, perhaps, that the contractors were hard workers, honest men, not of the sort who break contracts or run off with the money. These contractors clearly echoed a typical statement of religious identity that Max Weber heard during his visit to the United States at the turn of the twentieth century: when a physician in Cincinnati asked his patient how he was feeling, the patient said, "I am from the Second Baptist Church in X Street." Weber reasoned that the statement was a way of telling the doctor, "Don't worry about your *fee*!" Weber concludes that in America, "The question concerning church affiliation, officially frowned upon, but privately still highly significant, is on par with the Homeric question regarding place of birth and parentage."[1]

Religious identity has long been a form of currency in many sectors of American life. Because it is unconstitutional to require public officials to pass a religious test or to inquire about religion on census forms, a particularistic religious identity and American

---

This essay is adapted from my *Secret Faith in the Public Square* forthcoming from Brazos Press, a division of Baker Publishing Group (2009).

political life have "officially" nothing to do with each other. In spite of this, it is often said that an atheist couldn't get elected dog-catcher in this country.

If that is true, then it may also be true that an atheist will not get very far in some American businesses. Some corporations now routinely build chapels and meditation rooms in their offices and hire chaplains to minister to employees during work hours.[2] Is it hard to imagine a supervisor in such an office taking note of who visits the chapel regularly, and making promotion decisions accordingly? Is it hard to imagine an employee visiting the chapel in the hopes of being noticed by a Christian supervisor? This trend mirrors one in which many evangelical Christian corporate managers are making their religious identities more visible and drawing upon networks of well-placed coreligionists to attain and fill positions.[3]

Such practices rest on the presumption that religion, and Christianity in particular, has much to contribute to secular political and economic life (which in this essay I collect under the term "public life"). As the Catholic bishops of the world stated at the Second Vatican Council, "It is the special vocation of the laity to seek the kingdom of God by engaging in temporal affairs and directing them according to God's will. They live in the world, in each and every one of the world's occupations and callings and in the ordinary circumstances of social and family life which, as it were, form the context of their existence."[4] On its face, this principle seems entirely sound and benign. But the "context of [the laity's] existence" in many corners of the contemporary United States also includes the tendency to treat Christian identity as a form of political or social capital. Although lay persons must be the means for the Christian transformation of the world, their worldliness entails being tempted to use their Christian identity to get ahead in the world. Certainly, many who explicitly present themselves as Christians in public life are sincerely trying to do God's work. Others are just as surely trying to bring attention and esteem to themselves, and their apparent piety may mask self-serving and unchristian motives.

Applied uncritically, then, the principle that Christians should bring the world more in line with God's will through their secular occupations can in fact contribute to the distortion of Christian identity. When the rules of a highly competitive American public life and the rules of being a Christian bleed into each other, Christianity stands to lose its distinctive self-conception and ultimately the force of its message. The sharp truths of the gospel are dulled when the church becomes a constituency, network, or market, and when Christian identity becomes a brand. We are faced, then, with the question of how the laity can be visibly holy in contemporary America without their Christian identity being used as currency in secular life.

Turning up the volume on lay persons' Christian witness in the public square will not be the answer, even if this is what virtually every theologian who has written on the subject recently advocates, in one form or another. Charles Mathewes, for instance, claims in a recent book that "Vigorous Christian belief entails a serious commitment to expressing the faith. Conversely, a lack of expressing the faith leads to pallid believing. Christians cannot hide their lamp under a bushel; real Christians will not do so, and are not doing so."[5] The trouble with this theological position is that it plays directly into the hands of opportunists who want to parlay their Christian identity into social, economic, or political advantage. It is not only "real Christians" who are committed to expressing their faith in public; plenty of "fake" ones are also out to exploit the synthesis between Christian identity and public life. This has been the case for as long as Christian identity has been acceptable in public life, as the sermons of several fourth-century Christian bishops attest.[6]

In order to preserve the integrity of Christian identity in our age, when every identity is for sale all the time, theologians need to consider a vastly different paradigm for Christian identity in American public life. I suggest that lay Christians in America need to consider *concealing* their religious identity in their public lives as workers, consumers, candidates, and voters.[7] Only by taking their religious identity out of public view entirely will Christians be able to break free of the assumption that making their identity public is only a benign activity that contributes to their vocation to bring the kingdom of God to the world.

Although there are very good reasons for this secrecy being a sound general strategy for Christians in the public life of any historical context, I see it mainly as a therapy needed by the church in America right now. We remain in what Charles Taylor calls a "neo-Durkheimian" relation between religion and public life, in which Christian denominations collectively function as unofficial civil religions.[8] A "post-Durkheimian" future, in which religion is fully disembedded from public life, has not materialized, despite the increasingly vocal impatience of many non-religious Americans toward religious speech and symbolism in the public square. Perhaps a post-Durkheimian situation would result from this therapy. Like any therapy, especially one that has not been tested on similar patients, there is no telling how long it will be necessary. Perhaps for a generation or two. Perhaps for as long as there is a United States of America. My hope is that if American Christians took this therapy seriously, they would find one day that their religious language was no longer tainted by the materialistic self-interest that helped to melt down and mint their Christian identity into a coin of the realm.

The coin might go out of circulation if ordinary lay Christians stopped accepting it. As a whole, we Americans expect our public officials to exhibit a religious identity. In pockets of American public life, we expect them to exhibit a religious identity that is quite particularistic. In my city in 2006, for instance, a candidate for a seat in the state legislature felt compelled, after a telephone poll seemed to insinuate that he was a Scientologist, to affirm publicly that he is a committed Catholic. According to a newspaper report, the candidate "belongs to St. Therese's Church in Wilkes-Barre and attends Mass every Sunday with his family." That the reporter also noted that the candidate "receives Communion" weekly suggests that in my district simply claiming belief in God or allegiance to a Christian church is not enough to convince voters of a candidate's religious bona fides.[9] Something more particular is expected, and there needs to be visible evidence of that religious commitment.

In the remainder of this essay I discuss these expectations that we, the public, have of those who need our support in order to get ahead in American public life. It would be very easy for an academic writing to his or her peers to blame politicians and CEOs and Hollywood producers for the damage their opportunism has done to Christian identity. There aren't very many of them, and they generally are not interested in the activities of the College Theology Society. We can blame them for anything we want, and they aren't likely to cry foul.

If Christian identity has been distorted by its circulation in

American public life, then the public must share much of the blame, insofar as Christians who are also voters, consumers, and workers have allowed religious pandering to be an effective marketing strategy. Changing their expectations will mean making a hidden Christian identity normative, so that our first-order judgment about anyone who *did* display a Christian identity would be that he or she was not sincere about his or her faith.

Changing this expectation will be hard. One will inevitably encounter people who exhibit some ambiguous signs of Christian identity. They might let slip a word loaded with Christian significance, or perform the visible acts of holiness and forgiveness enumerated in the gospels, or be seen walking into a church on a Sunday morning. It would surely be tempting to demand that such people explain themselves and say, definitively, whether they are Christians. (And in fact, CNN and YouTube gave in to this temptation during one of the 2008 Republican primary debates, confronting the candidates with a Bible-wielding questioner who wanted to know if they believed "this book that I am holding in my hand."[10])

It would be frustrating not to get an answer to that demand. This frustration, though, is born of a toxic cynicism about the purpose of having and exhibiting a Christian identity. The assumption that Christian identity is *for* any worldly purpose is finally what needs to disappear, in order to save American Christianity from Christendom.

Two novels written in the middle of the last century by Catholic authors, Flannery O'Connor's *Wise Blood* and Walker Percy's *The Moviegoer*, indict their readers for expecting that Christian identity is there to be exploited for benefit in a person's public life. What these novels do is put the reader in the position of observing a character who performs actions that seem to bear religious significance. In *Wise Blood* we find out about Hazel Motes's self-mortification, done perhaps out of penitence for real sins he has committed. In *The Moviegoer* we spy on a black man who goes into and out of a Catholic church on Ash Wednesday. In both cases, the reader has access to the thoughts of a second character who is observing the suspected signs of faith. In both cases, those signs are hidden, although in *Wise Blood*, the signs are eventually revealed. Because of the ambiguity this hiddenness lends to the signs, the observers in both cases are led to speculate about what they really mean. The fact that, in both cases, the observers assume that the men they are watching perform the actions in order to profit materially from them suggests that for these observers, bringing the believer into closer relation to God is at best a secondary purpose for religious activity. To the extent that the novels invite readers to share the perspective of the observers, then we are also implicated in their cynicism.

I will show in what follows that in the end readers cannot know whether Hazel Motes or the man at the church really have faith. The novels seem to be saying that we shouldn't care. Given the authors' reputations for interrogating American culture's purported openness to the possibility of authentic Christianity, we should perhaps not be surprised that their work calls the neo-Durkheimian matrix into question.

It is worth noting that these novels, published in 1952 and 1961, bracket the McCarthy years in American politics, when the suspicion and investigation of secret commitments became highly relevant to our public life. It was also a time when Catholics themselves were poised to become more fully integrated into that public life. McCarthy himself of course embodied both trends. Historicizing these novels might therefore reveal that they express some trepidation about Catholicism's acceptance into the neo-Durkheimian synthesis. It's as if they are asking if lay Catholics really want to embrace public religion, as Protestants did historically, allowing their religious commitments to be folded into the American civil religion.[11]

In *Wise Blood*, Hazel Motes is the street-corner evangelist of the Church Without Christ ("where the blind don't see and the lame don't walk and what's dead stays that way"[12]). Near the end of the book, Haze is driven to murder by the madness and scheming all around him. He chases after his double, the "Prophet" Solace Layfield, and runs him over with his car, killing him. After this, Haze loses his car and blinds himself with quicklime. He begins to eat less and to spend his days walking—not just in the streets, but around his rented room, apparently without purpose. To his landlady, Haze's new habits make him like "one of them monks ... he might as well be in a monkery."[13] Later, after she has learned more about Haze's self-mortification, she says, "It's not natural...."

[I]t's something that people have quit doing—like boiling in oil or being a saint or walling up cats.... There's no reason for it."[14]

The air of mystery around his actions frustrates the landlady, named Mrs. Flood. The narrator tells us that Mrs. Flood "didn't like the thought that something was being put over her head. She liked the clear light of day. She liked to see things."[15] She assumes that, like a monk who is no doubt up to something in his "monkery" (unlike Protestants or ordinary Catholic lay people, who do their work in the open), Hazel is keeping a secret from her, and she can no more tolerate the secret than she can Hazel's strange behavior. In fact, she would prefer death to blindness, which would forever keep her from nosing into others' secrets.

Still, she is drawn to her tenant. At first, her suspicion of Hazel is matched by her opportunism, as she wants the small fortune she assumes he must have, since he never spends his money on anything and in fact throws away any "left over" money.[16]

Mrs. Flood's suspicion is in fact warranted, as Hazel *is* keeping secrets. Mrs. Flood discovers evidence of Hazel's self-mortification one day while she is cleaning his room: the insoles of his shoes are covered with sharp stones. After discovering this, she wonders, "Who's he doing this for? ... What's he getting out of doing it? Every now and then she would have an intimation of something hidden near her but out of her reach."[17] She guesses that Haze might have a religious reason for his behavior, but to her that would be the most sinister explanation of all. As she says to Haze, "You must believe in Jesus or you wouldn't do these foolish things. You must have been lying to me when you named your fine church. I wouldn't be surprised if you weren't some kind of agent of the pope or got some connection with something funny."[18]

Hazel eventually falls ill, and while ministering to him, Mrs. Flood sees that he has been wearing barbed wire around his torso, concealed by his shirt. She presses him for an explanation, and the reasons Hazel only grudgingly gives for the stones and the barbed wire make no sense to her: he says only, "to pay" and "I'm not clean." He seems to invest the terms with moral meaning, though for her, they are literal, as her responses to his reasons show: "What have you got to show that you're paying for?" and "You ought to get you a washwoman."[19]

The semantic distance between Hazel and Mrs. Flood *might* be attributable to a genuine religious conversion that has taken place in him. As Søren Kierkegaard writes in *Works of Love*, a religious and a non-religious person "say the same things: yet there is an infinite difference, since the latter has no intimation of the secret of the metaphorical words." The landlady "is using the same words, but not in their metaphorical sense. There is a world of difference between" her and Hazel, but this difference is only noticeable to "the person who has ears to hear."[20] What might identify Haze as a Christian is a secret to the rest of the world. In that world, one can only pay in order to receive something visible in return, cleanliness applies solely to outer appearances, and religion is meant to serve material and public ends.

O'Connor states in a brief note introducing the second edition of *Wise Blood* that whereas many contemporary readers will see Haze's "integrity" in his attempt to run away from Jesus Christ, O'Connor herself believes that his "integrity lies in his not being able to do so."[21] A reader who took O'Connor's commentary here at face value would have to say that Haze has some form of incipient faith. O'Connor seems to want her readers to see Haze as a genuine penitent who has (perhaps unconsciously) recognized how far short of the glory of God he falls, and who thus is open to receiving grace.

But O'Connor's interpretation notwithstanding, we cannot be sure that Haze has any faith at all, even an incipient faith. It is tempting to think that he became a genuine disciple late in the novel, in part because other preachers in the book are frauds and opportunists. Asa Hawks has the public trappings of what seems like discipleship in the world of the novel: he circulates the reputation of having blinded himself as a testimony to his own faith, he talks about Jesus and invites passersby to repent, and he preaches (and begs for money) openly. Secretly, as Haze eventually learns, Hawks can see out from behind his dark glasses.

Hawks isn't the only pretender, though. A man named Hoover Shoats thinks that Haze has a good racket going and so imitates his style, starting a Holy Church of Christ Without Christ as a rival to Haze's Church Without Christ. At first, Shoats tries to co-opt Haze into his ministry. When Haze refuses, Shoats brings in the "Prophet" Solace Layfield, who is made up to be Haze's double. The church is successful, which means it is profitable. To Haze, Shoats's and Layfield's anti-discipleship is inauthentic:

just before he runs Layfield over, Haze accuses him of secretly believing in Jesus.[22]

With these foils around him, Haze can seem like the only character in the book who has any religious integrity. At first, he makes no secret of his unbelief. Later, his disdain for the poseurs who want to make money from their preaching is real. And by the end, his self-mortification, done in secret, grants him no benefit in material goods or status. He may have, in renouncing selfishness, taken the first necessary step toward loving God and his neighbor.

But it would be presumptuous to say that definitively. Hazel kept a secret from his landlady, but even after that secret is found out, Mrs. Flood still senses that he is hiding something deeper. Haze finally dies, and as Mrs. Flood contemplates Haze's dead body, the narrator tells us that "She felt as if she were blocked at the entrance of something."[23] O'Connor may want the reader to think that that something was genuine Christian faith—and indeed, the notion that Mrs. Flood is like a catechumen drawn toward Hazel by his secrecy but barred from the deeper mystery within him is compelling. But there is no good reason within the novel itself to think that Hazel's faith, if he has any at all, has progressed beyond the faith he had as a child, when he tried to "satisfy" Jesus and pay for his sins by walking a mile with stones in his shoes.[24] The reader has no way of determining the truth about Hazel. By the end of the novel, the narrator has lost all access to Hazel's mind. While we are told the contents of Mrs. Flood's thoughts in the final chapters, we read only about Haze's actions. Hazel's hermeneutical intransigence thus rebukes the *reader's* curiosity about him as well as it does that of the fairly unsympathetic character of Mrs. Flood. In inquiring whether Hazel is really a Christian, the question is turned back on us as investigators: Why do we want to know? Who are we doing it for? What are we getting out of it?

We stand in a similar situation near the end of *The Moviegoer*. The narrator in Percy's novel, the young ironist Binx Bolling, has just made perhaps the first real commitment of his life, agreeing to marry his cousin Kate. Binx and Kate can hardly believe what they are getting themselves into as they sit in her parked car in the

French Quarter in New Orleans, on Ash Wednesday, watching people go into and out of a Roman Catholic church. Watching these people without being watched himself, Binx allows himself a final exercise in irony. Sitting in the car, he can remain stationary and detached, sizing up others who are engaged in everyday activity.

One person in particular catches Binx's attention in the rearview mirror. Binx, the narrator, watches as, in his words, "a Negro gets out [of his car] and goes up to the church. He is more respectable than respectable." The man sees that Binx is watching him and "plucks a handkerchief out of his rear pocket with a flurry of his coat tail and blows his nose in a magic placative gesture (you see, I have been here before: it is a routine matter)."[25] A few minutes pass, and, as Binx tells us,

> The Negro has already come outside. His forehead is an ambiguous sienna color and pied: it is impossible to be sure that he received ashes. When he gets in his Mercury, he does not leave immediately but sits looking down at something on the seat beside him. A sample case? An insurance manual? I watch him closely in the rear-view mirror. It is impossible to say why he is here. Is it part and parcel of the complex business of coming up in the world? Or is it because he believes that God himself is present here at the corner of Elysian Fields and Bons Enfants? Or is he here for both reasons: through some dim dazzling trick of grace, coming for the one and receiving the other as God's own importunate bonus?
> It is impossible to say.[26]

Binx very much wants to make several assumptions about what he cannot see. His restricted, inverted view of the man in his Mercury does not allow him to see what the man is looking at in the passenger seat. It may very well be a sample case or an insurance manual. But it hardly need be. Binx also wants to draw a direct link between whatever artifacts of public life the man is studying and the ashes that, presumably, the man went into the church to receive. Ash Wednesday is after all a perfect opportunity to display Christian identity without seeming to want to display it. If receiving ashes, perhaps to be seen by Catholics with whom this man works, is "part and parcel of the complex business of coming up in the world," then the man is doing a poor job of ensuring that the right people notice him. The ashes, if he has in fact received ashes, disappear into his complexion. The sign of the man's faith, if he has faith, is hidden.

The endings to both of these novels say more about the people observing the ambiguous Christians than they do about Haze and the black man themselves. In fact, Binx knows nothing at all about the man he's watching. As he perhaps realizes in the end, Binx can only project expectations onto him, including the expectation that Christian identity is meant primarily to serve one's public life. Binx is right—"it is impossible to say" if either the black man or Hazel Motes has genuine faith. That the signs of faith are hidden is just as well, since what really makes a Christian a Christian is itself hidden within the person. Our impatience with its invisibility is what prompts our desire to find signs of faith in others and in ourselves: ashes on a forehead, Christian language, economic prosperity, snake handling. But these signs do not necessarily tell us any more than that the person wants to exploit the Durkheimian synthesis between religion and public life. In public life, we have no choice but to evaluate people by the visible actions they perform. The same is not true in Christianity, where the ultimate judge sees in secret.

The obscure, reflected image of the man in the car behind him perhaps causes Binx to reflect on the post-Durkheimian possibility that receiving ashes serves a non-social end. To the extent that Binx even considers that the man he watches might believe "that God himself is present" in the liturgy, Binx is much further on the way to shedding his cynicism than is Hazel Motes's landlady. We might very much like to have access to the secret world of another person's faith, but we never can have it, and we must resist the temptation to act as if we do. And those who have faith must resist the temptation to treat it as something that could be told—and sold.

The expectation that religious identity be visible is abetted by a second expectation that religious identity will be worth something in a person's public life. The gospel reading for a Catholic Ash Wednesday service (Mt 6:1-6, 16-18) thwarts the first expectation: Jesus warns his listeners to keep up good appearances when they fast, washing their faces, keeping their clothes tidy, anointing their heads. But the second expectation, the Durkheimian expectation, is the more pernicious. *This* expectation is the one that truly distorts the point of having Christian faith. Without this expectation, the visibility of Christian identity in American public life would not pose a problem to the integrity of the faith.

The possibility that Haze and the black man in New Orleans are Christians and do not make their religious identity public is simply frustrating to the curious. But the possibility that they are Christians and do not care to use their religious identity as a means of getting ahead in the world is downright shocking. It goes against one of the longest-standing American traditions. Its longevity should not be mistaken for immortality, however. Killing the tradition will require cutting off what nourishes it: the assumption that Christian identity should be publicly displayed.

Eliminating this assumption need not entail forgoing the laity's responsibility to "consecrate the world itself to God."[27] Although *Lumen Gentium* states that "resplendent in faith, hope and charity [lay Christians' lives] manifest Christ to others," their task of sanctifying the world is to be done "from within [the world], like leaven."[28] This means that there is visible work to do, but the ones doing the work do not have to make themselves visible specifically as Christians while they do it. The metaphor of leaven is a good guide here. Leaven, once mixed into the dough, can neither be removed from the dough nor visibly distinguished as leaven. It disappears. Its effects, however, are visible and undeniable.

Notes

[1]Max Weber, " 'Churches' and 'Sects' in North America: An Ecclesiastical and Sociopolitical Sketch," in *The Protestant Ethic and the "Spirit" of Capitalism and Other Writings*, ed. and trans. Peter Baehr and Gordon C. Wells (New York: Penguin, 2002), 205.

[2]"Praying for Gain," *The Economist*, August 25, 2007, 60.

[3]D. Michael Lindsay, *Faith in the Halls of Power: How Evangelicals Joined the American Elite* (New York: Oxford University Press, 2007). See esp. Part IV.

[4]Vatican Council II, *Lumen Gentium* 31 (Dogmatic Constitution on the Church), in *The Basic Sixteen Documents*, ed. Austin Flannery, O.P. (Northport, N.Y.: Costello, 1996), 49.

[5]Charles Mathewes, *A Theology of Public Life* (Cambridge, England: Cambridge University Press, 2007), 25.

[6]See, for example, Cyril of Jerusalem, *Procatechesis* 5, in Edward Yarnold, S.J., *Cyril of Jerusalem* (London & New York: Routledge, 2000), 81.

[7]I make the complete case for this in my *Secret Faith in the Public Square*

(Grand Rapids: Brazos, forthcoming). See also the evangelical theologian Charles Marsh's call in *Wayward Christian Soldiers: Rescuing the Gospel from Political Captivity* (New York: Oxford University Press, 2007) for a "season of silence" as a remedy to the damage American evangelicals have done to their religious identity through their political activity and influence. Catholic theologian Tom Beaudoin makes a brief case for Christian politicians' downplaying their religious identity in "Talk That Diminishes Faith," *The Washington Post*, October 24, 2004, A25.

[8]Charles Taylor, *A Secular Age* (Cambridge: Belknap Press, 2007), 455, 487.

[9]Jennifer Learn-Andes, "Scientology Question Surfaces in 121st Poll: Candidate Brian O'Donnell, Who Studied the Religion, Calls Tactic 'A Whisper Campaign,'" *The Times Leader* (Wilkes-Barre, PA), March 24, 2006.

[10]Video available at www.youtube.com/republicandebate#qa_RF-nMaY-q3QE. Accessed June 30, 2008.

[11]The sociologist Alan Wolfe charts the accommodation of American religious practice to American public life in *The Transformation of American Religion: How We Actually Live Our Faith* (New York: The Free Press, 2003).

[12]Flannery O'Connor, *Wise Blood* (New York: Farrar, Straus & Giroux, 1962), 105.

[13]Ibid., 218.

[14]Ibid., 224.

[15]Ibid., 218.

[16]Ibid., 220.

[17]Ibid., 222.

[18]Ibid., 225.

[19]Ibid., 222, 224.

[20]Søren Kierkegaard, *Works of Love*, ed. and trans. Howard V. Hong and Edna H. Hong (Princeton: Princeton University Press, 1995), 209-10.

[21]O'Connor, *Wise Blood*, 5.

[22]Ibid., 203.

[23]Ibid., 232.

[24]Ibid., 63-64.

[25]Walker Percy, *The Moviegoer* (New York: Vintage, 1961), 233.

[26]Ibid., 234-35.

[27]*Lumen Gentium* 34, in Flannery, *The Basic Sixteen Documents*, 52.

[28]*Lumen Gentium* 31, ibid., 49.

The Social Teaching of Pope Benedict XVI

Clergy, Laity, and the Church's Mission for Justice

John Sniegocki

In his first encyclical, *Deus Caritas Est,* Pope Benedict XVI devoted significant attention to the themes of charity and social justice in the mission of the Roman Catholic Church. Some commentators have interpreted Benedict in this document as deliberately marginalizing the pursuit of justice.[1] This claim, I argue, is largely mistaken. At the same time, there are features of Benedict's ethic that may inadvertently limit the ability of the Catholic Church to realize its full potential in the struggle for justice. An exploration of these limitations will be the main focus of this paper. Benedict makes distinctions, for example, concerning the means by which clergy and laity are called to work for justice, assigning to the "lay faithful" a direct role and to "the Church" (by which he seems to mean primarily clergy) an indirect role. These distinctions are motivated by important concerns, especially the need for the institutional church to avoid entanglement in partisan politics. Yet this division of roles, I contend, is ultimately problematic. It fosters unhelpful clergy/laity and spirituality/social justice dualisms, excludes clergy from valuable experiences in social activism that could deeply enrich their ministry, and deprives the struggle for justice of the important leadership that clergy and the broader institutional church could provide. In addition, Benedict (in contrast to John Paul II) seems hesitant to encourage participation in grassroots social activism even by the laity, seeking instead to bring about justice in a more top-down and less conflictual manner. As a result, Benedict's social teaching, while still affirming the importance of justice, may lack effective means of implementation.

The Church and Social Justice

"The Church," Pope Benedict states in *Deus Caritas Est*, "cannot and must not take upon herself the political battle to bring about the most just society possible." The construction of a more just social order "must be the achievement of politics, not of the Church."[2] What then is the mission of the church? In an address to the bishops of Brazil, Benedict states: "This, and nothing else, is the purpose of the Church: the salvation of individual souls."[3]

It is easy to see how the above statements could give the impression that Benedict marginalizes social justice and affirms a privatized understanding of Christian faith. A deeper examination, however, suggests a more nuanced interpretation. While Benedict states that working directly for social justice is not a task of "the Church," he at the same time argues that work for justice is in fact a major obligation of the "lay faithful." "The direct duty to work for a just ordering of society," says Benedict, "is proper to the lay faithful."[4] Although this contrast between "the Church" and the "lay faithful" can rightly be viewed as problematic (as it seemingly excludes laity from the definition of "Church"), it is important to see that Benedict does in fact emphasize the importance of justice and social transformation in Christian life. The laity are called to directly work for social justice, he says, endeavoring to "bring the light of the Gospel into public life, into culture, economics, and politics."[5] The institutional church, meanwhile, aids in this task indirectly through the spiritual formation of the laity. In doing so it contributes to what Benedict terms "the purification of reason" and to "the reawakening of those moral forces without which just structures are neither established nor prove effective in the long run."[6]

When Benedict argues against a direct role for the institutional church in the struggle for justice, what he seems most concerned about is excessive involvement in partisan politics. "If the Church were to start transforming herself into a directly political subject," says Benedict, "she would do less, not more, for the poor and for justice, because she would lose her independence and her moral authority, identifying herself with a single political path and with debatable partisan positions. The Church is the advocate of justice and of the poor, precisely because she does not identify with politicians nor with partisan interests."[7]

While Benedict thus strongly cautions against direct involvement in politics by the institutional church, the implications of this stance require further exploration. What in practice constitutes inappropriate political involvement? Should priests and other church leaders, for example, simply refrain from speaking out on social issues or particular pieces of legislation? Clearly Benedict does not think so, as he himself regularly makes public statements on topics ranging from abortion and homosexual marriage to war and peace, globalization, and ecology, including at times taking firm stands on particular legislative initiatives. The sections that follow provide a brief overview of Benedict's teaching on several of these topics. With this overview as background, I then resume discussion of Benedict's reflections on clergy, laity, and the role of the church in social change.

Abortion

One of the major social justice issues addressed by Pope Benedict is abortion. "[E]veryone," the pope declares, "must be helped to become aware of the intrinsic evil of the crime of abortion."[8] Benedict emphasizes that abortion should be made illegal. Legislators who are unwilling to support the criminalization of abortion, he argues, are complicit in grave moral evil. In the case of abortion Benedict is clearly willing to express strong support for specific public policy proposals.

War and Violence

Benedict, like Paul VI and John Paul II, has repeatedly made strong, broad comments condemning war and other forms of violence: "Violence, of whatever sort," Benedict says, "cannot be a way of resolving conflicts."[9] The Catholic Church, he asserts, "emphatically rejects war as a means of resolving international disputes, and has often pointed out that it only leads to new and still more complicated conflicts."[10] While affirming the theoretical possibility of a just war, Benedict has expressed strong doubts that any modern war could in fact meet the just war criteria. In an interview prior to becoming pope, Benedict defended Pope John Paul II's criticisms of the war in Iraq. "There were not sufficient reasons," he said, "to unleash a war against Iraq. To say nothing of the fact that, given the new weapons that go beyond the combatant groups, today we should be asking ourselves if it is still licit to admit the very existence of a 'just war.' "[11]

Pope Benedict has also been very critical of excessive levels of military spending, urging the transfer of funds to meet basic needs.[12] He has called for the elimination of entire categories of weapons that indiscriminately harm the innocent, including nuclear weapons, land mines, and cluster bombs, and has unequivocally condemned war-related practices such as torture. We again see here, as in the case of abortion, the willingness of Benedict to take strong stands on specific public policy issues.[13]

Economic Justice and Globalization

Pope Benedict has expressed sharp criticisms of both Marxism and capitalism.[14] Of particular concern to him in the present context are rising levels of inequality throughout the world, as well as the ecologically destructive nature of current capitalist models of economic development. "Starvation and ecological emergencies stand to denounce, with increasing evidence," Benedict asserts, "that the logic of profit, if it prevails, increases the disproportion between rich and poor and leads to a ruinous exploitation of the planet." What is needed instead, says Benedict, are forms of economic life guided by the "logic of solidarity and sharing."[15] While Benedict does not express a formal preference as pope for any particular economic system (and does not see it as a task of the Catholic Church to do so), it is notable that in his private writings he speaks favorably of "democratic socialism."[16] In his papal teaching Benedict speaks more generally of the need for policies that "promote an equitable distribution of the goods of the earth."[17] "We cannot remain passive," he says, "before certain processes of globalization which not infrequently increase the gap between rich and poor worldwide. We must denounce those who squander the earth's riches, provoking inequalities that cry out to heaven."[18] Among the specific economic policies that Benedict calls for is the cancellation of the debt of poor countries.[19]

Ecology

One of the most prominent themes in Benedict's social teaching has been the urgent need to address the world's many ecological crises. "Before it is too late," Benedict declares, "it is necessary to make courageous decisions that reflect knowing how to re-create a strong alliance between man and the earth.... A decisive 'yes' to the protection of creation is necessary and a firm commitment to reverse those tendencies that run the risk of bringing about situations of unstoppable degradation."[20] Benedict stresses the need for "particular attention to climate change."[21] "Our earth is talking to us," he states, "and we must listen to it and decipher its message if we want to survive."[22] Significantly, the Vatican has committed to becoming the first "carbon neutral" state in the world, through a combination of the use of solar energy and carbon offsets derived from planting a forest in Hungary.[23] Many commentators believe that heightened concern for ecology is likely to be one of Benedict's most lasting contributions to Catholic social teaching.

The United Nations and International Law

Benedict envisions a major role for international organizations such as the United Nations in responding to many of the political, social, and ecological issues highlighted above. He has repeatedly emphasized the need for enhanced international regulation and enhanced international cooperation.[24] Benedict strongly rejects unilateral decision-making by the world's major powers. "It is essential," he says, "to choose the path of dialogue rather than the path of unilateral decisions."[25]

Benedict XVI, John Paul II, and the Role of the Church in Social Change

The statements of Pope Benedict cited above clearly place him in continuity with earlier Catholic social teaching. Benedict's opposition to abortion, profound skepticism that any modern war could be legitimate, critical views of both capitalism and Marxism, deep reservations about current forms of globalization, emphasis on the importance of ecology, and stress on the value of international institutions and multilateral cooperation closely reflect the views of Pope John Paul II. With regard to the implementation of Catholic social teaching, however, some significant differences exist. In particular, John Paul expresses greater recognition of the important role to be played by grassroots social movements. Benedict, in contrast, is generally quite skeptical of mass social movements. He views them as being prone to irrational excesses, as will be explained more fully below.

Traditionally the Catholic Church has advocated what I have termed a "chaplaincy" model of social change.[26] In this model the church contributes to social transformation primarily by helping to shape the consciences of the economic and political leaders of society. This has been the dominant model of social change in Catholic teaching since the time of the Constantinian transformation of the fourth century. Beginning especially in the 1960s, however, an alternate model of change began to be articulated in Catholic social teaching. This model focuses on the importance of grassroots movements and acknowledges an important role for constructive nonviolent conflict. Rather than understanding change as coming largely from the top of society, from the moral conversion of the leaders, this model sees the primary catalyst for social change coming from below, from mobilization of the poor, the marginalized, and their allies. This perspective is strongly expressed in the 1971 Synod of Bishops' document *Justice in the World*.[27] It is also reflected in the social teaching of Pope John Paul II, such as in his affirmation of the "need for ever new movements of solidarity of the workers and with the workers" and his emphasis on "the positive role of conflict when it takes the form of a 'struggle for social justice.'"[28]

Pope Benedict clearly favors the chaplaincy model of social change. He emphasizes, for example, the church's role in "shaping in the political and entrepreneurial classes a genuine spirit of truth and honesty geared to seeking the common good."[29] It is this behind-the-scenes task of conscience formation, rather than direct involvement in social struggles, that is the primary social responsibility of the church. This is especially the case, as we have seen, for clergy. The prohibition of a direct role for clergy in social justice struggles rules out the participation of clergy in political office, a point on which John Paul and Benedict agree.[30] But what about other forms of political involvement by clergy and the institutional church? When the Catholic Church, under the leadership of Cardinal Jaime Sin, played a central role in the nonviolent overthrow of the Marcos dictatorship in the Philippines, was this inappropriate involvement in politics or a positive contribution to the political and moral well-being of Filipinos? Pope John Paul II has spoken in very positive terms about this nonviolent revolution.[31] Can one assume that Pope Benedict would view the Catholic Church's role in this process positively as well? Pope John Paul II himself also provided strong support for the Solidarity union movement in Poland that played a major role in bringing an end to the communist system of that country. Was this an acceptable manifestation of the justice concerns of the church? If so, can priests or bishops in other places, such as Latin America or Africa, similarly express direct support for grassroots movements pursuing social change in the face of oppressive political or economic systems?

Interestingly, a few years ago Pope Benedict intervened to tell the Filipino bishops *not* to get involved in a broad public movement calling for the resignation of current Filipino president Gloria Macapagal Arroyo, who was accused of massive corruption.[32] Was the difference in response between Benedict and John Paul (who supported church involvement in the overthrow of Marcos) due to a different set of circumstances or a different underlying attitude toward the role of the church in social change? In reality, both of these factors—a higher level of human rights abuses under Marcos and greater skepticism about direct church involvement in social change efforts on the part of Benedict—seem to have been present.

Benedict affirms the obligation to address the moral dimension of social issues, but strongly cautions against improper involvement in politics. Again, however, what constitutes this improper political involvement? Benedict himself, as we have seen, has made numerous recommendations for public policy. Concerning Third World debt, for example, Benedict sent a letter to German Chancellor Angela Merkel declaring it to be "a grave and unconditional moral responsibility" to provide "rapid, total, and unconditional" debt relief for the poorest nations, a very specific policy request. In this letter he also calls for increased foreign aid, more just trading policies, and investment in efforts to combat AIDS, malaria, and other diseases.[33] If it is proper for the pope to speak out on these policy issues, is it appropriate then for other priests and bishops to do the same? Is it appropriate for a parish to organize a letter-writing campaign on these issues or to put informational materials in the church bulletin? What about forming a parish-based chapter of the Jubilee debt relief movement? If a parish-based Jubilee group is appropriate, what about a parish-based antiwar group? Again, at what point for Benedict would this activity cross over into unacceptable forms of direct church involvement in politics? The answer is not entirely clear.

With regard to the laity, both John Paul and Benedict affirm a responsibility to work directly for justice. Benedict, however, seems hesitant to encourage even lay participation in active grassroots struggles. While Benedict argues that the laity have an obligation to work for more just economic and political structures, this task, as he envisions it, appears to be rooted in a largely non-conflictual, top-down vision of social change. Benedict is much more likely, for example, to call upon business owners to treat their workers justly than to encourage active mobilization by workers to defend their rights. While he regularly calls upon politicians to prioritize the common good, he is less likely to encourage the building of broad-based grassroots coalitions that may engage in acts of protest, demonstration, or civil disobedience as means of seeking to change policies.

Some of the reasons for this reticence to support grassroots social movements are explained in Benedict's pre-papal writings. Most significantly, he tends to view such movements as susceptible to "irrationality," setting up utopian goals that are unachievable and then being prone to disillusionment and/or the acceptance of immoral means (such as violence or class hatred) to pursue these unrealizable goals. "[T]he first service that Christian faith performs for politics," says Benedict, "is that it liberates men and women from the irrationality of political myths that are the real threat of our time." "It is of course always difficult," he adds, "to adopt the sober approach that does what is possible and does not cry enthusiastically after the impossible."[34]

Benedict is deeply influenced by a strong Augustinian notion of human sinfulness. His doctoral thesis was on Augustine's understanding of the church and the proper relationship of the church to the broader world. His postdoctoral dissertation was on Bonaventure's theology of history. He devoted particular attention to Bonaventure's critique of Joachim of Fiore, who sought to replace Augustine's emphasis on the transitory and relative

nature of human history with a vision of human-God cooperation in bringing about the kingdom of God on earth. Too much
emphasis on the potential of humans to bring about social change
within history, warns Benedict, leads to the marginalization of
God and a lessening of authentic eschatological hope. "Christian
faith may not know any utopia within history," Benedict states,
"but it does know a promise of the resurrection of the dead, the
last judgment, and the Kingdom of God."[35] With regard to social
change, Christian faith recognizes that only incremental, moderate
change is possible due to human sinfulness. The church, Benedict
declares, "can be content with this because it knows that man's
greater expectation lies hidden in God's hands.... To renounce the
mythical hopes of a society free of domination is not resignation
but honesty that maintains men and women in hope."[36]

Along with his theological predisposition to be wary of the
influence of human sinfulness on mass social movements and to
be skeptical of plans for far-reaching social change, biographers
of the pope also highlight negative, even traumatic, experiences
that Benedict had with the radical student movements of the
1960s. This included numerous disruptions of his lectures, which
seems to have played an important role in his resignation from
a teaching position at the University of Tübingen.[37] It is striking
that in his reflections on this era Benedict focuses almost entirely
on the excesses of the protestors, with nearly no mention of the
very real evils (the Vietnam War, fundamental injustices in the
global economy, the historical alliance of the Catholic Church
with exploitative elites, and so on) that were at the root of many
of the protests. These negative experiences of student protestors,
as well as the legacies of Nazi and communist mass movement
irrationality, strongly color Benedict's perception of social movements. They also help to explain his antipathy to certain forms of
liberation theology, which he views as similarly prone to irrational
excess and which he understands (wrongly, according to critics) as
improperly reducing Christianity to a quest for worldly liberation
while ignoring the primacy of God and of eternal redemption.[38]

Assessing Benedict's Social Teaching

As one considers Benedict's social teaching, it is important to
stress that Benedict has been actively addressing many important

social and ecological issues, such as war and peace, capitalist models of development, globalization, and ecology. These are not issues that received much attention in Benedict's pre-papal writings, and some wondered if they would be neglected in his tenure as pope. While his first formal social encyclical has not yet been released (as of October 2008), these topics have nonetheless already been addressed in numerous shorter statements in strong and insightful terms.

While Benedict has developed the foundations of strong social teaching with regard to specific issues, what seems to be lacking is a realistic method for bringing about the kinds of changes that Benedict and the broader tradition of Catholic social teaching call for. I would argue strongly that the church must not rely merely on moral appeals to the political and economic leaders of society. Rather, it needs to actively encourage grassroots efforts for change. Almost never has substantive social change been brought about without strong grassroots pressure, as can be seen in cases such as the abolitionist movement, the Civil Rights movement, the labor movement, and the movement for farmworker justice in the United States. In most of these movements Christians played a central role.

It is important that clergy and other representatives of the institutional church not be excluded from participation in these social movements. While I strongly affirm Pope Benedict's concern that the church not identify narrowly with partisan political agendas, it seems to me that there are ways to address this concern other than making strong clergy/laity (or church/laity) distinctions with a strict division of direct and indirect roles in the pursuit of justice. These distinctions, I believe, are problematic on several grounds. First, distinguishing between the "lay faithful" and "the Church" seems to marginalize the laity as something other than "Church." At the very least it seems to indicate that what the laity do in their professional and civic lives is not really integral to what it means to be "Church." At the same time, I would argue that establishing too strong of a barrier to the direct involvement of clergy and the broader institutional church in struggles for justice is similarly problematic. It excludes clergy from valuable experiences of solidarity and social activism that could enrich their own faith and ministry and undercuts the effectiveness of the overall social mission of the church.

In my own ecclesial experience I have found that the parishes that are most spiritually alive and socially engaged tend to be those in which a parish priest is personally involved in grassroots movements of solidarity and social change and allows these experiences to inform his preaching and other forms of ministry. The modeling of social engagement by the clergy (and the experiential knowledge derived from it) makes for much more convincing witness than mere exhortation of the laity to such engagement. "Our preaching will be heard," said the 32nd General Congregation of the Jesuits, "to the extent that witness accompanies it, the witness to the promotion of justice." This direct work for justice, the Jesuits contend, "is an integral part of the priestly service of the faith."[39]

It is also crucial to recognize the very important roles that priests and other Christian clergy, as well as Catholic nuns, have played in past social struggles.[40] If clergy are not to be directly involved in work for justice, does this mean that the ministry of Martin Luther King, Jr., a Christian clergyperson, was inappropriate? What about the important role played by the institutional Catholic Church (including numerous bishops) in the farmworkers' struggle for justice led by Cesar Chavez or the social justice ministries of priests such as Daniel Berrigan and Roy Bourgeois and nuns such as Helen Prejean and Dorothy Stang? Would Pope Benedict object to any of these ministries as being too directly political? While his views need further clarification, I suspect that he would likely have some serious misgivings.

What Pope Benedict seems to fear are two major dangers. One is that deep involvement in social struggles (especially on the part of clergy) will lead to the reduction of Christianity to a social justice movement, thereby losing the fundamental importance of the transcendent and placing hope wholly within history. While this is certainly a danger, it is not inevitable. There exist many examples of clergy and others who maintain a healthy balance, persons who understand, for example, the importance of christocentric contemplative experience as the source of their social justice action and who recognize the need for both deep personal and structural change.

Benedict's second fear is that the ministry of the church (the salvation of souls, holistically understood) will be hindered by its becoming identified with partisan political interests. Again, while certainly a very real danger, this is not inevitable. I would suggest that the most sure way to avoid such partisan identification is to always keep the focus on specific moral issues, not on particular candidates or political parties, and to ensure that a broad range of issues (rather than just one or two issues with clear partisan implications) are consistently addressed. This holistic, multifaceted approach to church involvement in justice issues seems to me to be much more helpful than suggesting that direct work for justice is something that laity are to do largely on their own, in their capacity as citizens, in relative isolation from "the Church," while priests and the institutional church are to refrain from such direct involvement and to focus on the primacy of the spiritual. Such a dualism between the realm of the spiritual and the realm of social justice, I contend, hinders rather than assists the church in being faithful to the fullness of its gospel calling. "Fidelity to our apostolic mission," the 32nd General Congregation of the Jesuits insightfully states, "requires that we propose the whole of Christian salvation and lead others to embrace it. ... Since evangelization is proclamation of that faith which is made operative in love of others, the promotion of justice is indispensable to it."[41]

Notes

[1] For an argument that Benedict marginalizes the pursuit of justice, see Tissa Balasuriya, "Benedict XVI's *Deus Caritas Est* and Social Justice," in *Catholic Social Justice: Theological and Practical Applications*, ed. Philomena Cullen, Bernard Hoose, and Gerard Mannion (New York: Continuum, 2001), 41-62.

[2] Benedict XVI, *Deus Caritas Est*, 28. Unless otherwise stated, all writings and speeches cited are by Benedict XVI.

[3] Address to the Bishops of Brazil (May 11, 2007), no. 2. All the speeches of Pope Benedict XVI can be found in English translation on the Vatican website at http://www.vatican.va/holy_father/benedict_xvi/speeches/index_en.htm.

[4] *Deus Caritas Est*, 29.

[5] Address to the Fifth General Conference of the Bishops of Latin America and the Caribbean (CELAM) in Aparecida, Brazil (May 13, 2007), no. 4.

[6] *Deus Caritas Est*, 29.

[7] Address to Fifth General Conference, no. 4.

[8] Address to Presidents of the Episcopal Commissions for the Family and Life of Latin America (December 3, 2005), no. 5.

[9] Address to "Men and Religions Meeting" in Lyon, France (September 12, 2005).

[10] Address to New Syrian Ambassador to the Holy See (December 14, 2006).

[11]Interview with ZENIT News Agency (May 2, 2003).

[12]"On the basis of the available statistical data," asserts Benedict, "it can be said that less than half of the immense sums spent worldwide on armaments would be more than sufficient to liberate the immense masses of the poor from destitution. This challenges humanity's conscience" (Address to Diplomatic Corps, January 10, 2006). Also see his Message on Disarmament, Development and Peace (May 7, 2008).

[13]Reliance on nuclear weapons for security, Benedict declares, is "not only baneful but also completely fallacious" (Message for 2006 World Day of Peace, no. 13). With regard to torture, Benedict argues that its prohibition "cannot be contravened under any circumstances" (Address to Meeting on Pastoral Prison Care, September 6, 2007). For further discussion of Catholic teaching on war and peace—and the unfortunate failure of the church to adequately support these teachings with institutional action—see John Sniegocki, "Catholic Teaching on War, Peace, and Nonviolence Since Vatican II," in *Vatican II: Forty Years Later*, ed. William Madges, College Theology Society Annual Vol. 51 (Maryknoll, NY: Orbis Books, 2006), 224-44.

[14]See Address to Fifth General Conference of CELAM (2007).

[15]Angelus (September 23, 2007).

[16]"Democratic socialism," Benedict asserts in an essay written in his capacity as a private theologian, "was and is close to Catholic social doctrine, and has in any case made a remarkable contribution to the formation of a social consciousness" ("The Spiritual Roots of Europe: Yesterday, Today, and Tomorrow," in Joseph Ratzinger and Marcello Pera, *Without Roots: The West, Relativism, Christianity, Islam*, trans. Michael Moore [New York: Basic Books, 2006], 72).

[17]Benedict XVI and Chrysostom II, "Common Declaration" (July 5, 2007).

[18]*Sacramentum Caritatis*, 90.

[19]See the discussion below of Benedict's letter to Angela Merkel.

[20]Homily to Youth of Loreto, Italy (September 2, 2007).

[21]Message to Symposium on Religion, Science, and the Environment (September 7, 2007).

[22]Address to Italian Priests (July 24, 2007).

[23]"Vatican Announces Plans to Become First 'Carbon Neutral State' in the World" (July 13, 2007); http://www.catholicnewsagency.com/new. php?n=9868.

[24]For example, Benedict stresses the importance of "establishing rules for better control of economic development, regulating markets" (Address to the Diplomatic Corps in Turkey, November 28, 2006).

[25]Message for 2008 World Day of Peace, no. 8.

[26]See John Sniegocki, "Implementing Catholic Social Teaching," in *Faith in Public Life*, ed. William Collinge, College Theology Society Annual Vol. 53 (Maryknoll, NY: Orbis Books, 2008), 39-61.

[27]For example, the Synod of Bishops highlights the importance of social "movements" and stresses the need for "social and political action" to combat and overcome concentrations of economic and political power. *Justice in the World*, 4, 9.

[28]John Paul II, *Laborem Exercens*, 8; *Centesimus Annus*, 14.

[29]Message for Italian Catholic Social Week (October 12, 2007).

[30]John Paul, for example, harshly criticized the Catholic priests who had key roles in the Sandinista government in Nicaragua. Pope Benedict has voiced strong displeasure at the decision of former bishop Fernando Lugo to run for the presidency of Paraguay, an election that Lugo recently won on a reformist social justice platform heavily influenced by Catholic social teaching. The Vatican, in reprimanding Lugo, stressed that the task of a bishop is to work "for the salvation of souls, and not to govern a political community" (see Cindy Wooden, "Vatican Denies Laicization for Paraguayan Running for President"; http://www.catholicnews.com/data/stories/cns/0700644.htm). Lugo was suspended from priestly ministry once he announced his presidential candidacy. His request to be laicized, however, was initially denied by the Vatican on the grounds that the episcopacy is an eternal, irrevocable commitment. Later, however, Pope Benedict did allow Lugo to be laicized, apparently the first time in history that a bishop has been allowed to voluntarily return to the lay state.

[31]For discussion of John Paul's support for church involvement in the nonviolent overthrow of Marcos, see Mary Ann Walsh, *From Pope John Paul II to Benedict XVI* (Lanham, MD: Rowman & Littlefield, 2005), 35.

[32]See Carlos Conde, "Vatican Silences Philippine Bishops," *International Herald Tribune*, July 12, 2005; http://www.iht.com/articles/2005/07/11/news/phils.php.

[33]See Pope Benedict's letter to Angela Merkel, Chancellor of the Federal Republic of Germany (December 16, 2006).

[34]Joseph Ratzinger, *Church, Ecumenism, and Politics: New Essays in Ecclesiology* New York: Crossroad, 1988), 149.

[35]Ibid., 272.

[36]Ibid., 148.

[37]For discussion of the impact on Benedict of the student protests of the 1960s, see John Allen, Jr., *Pope Benedict XVI: A Biography of Joseph Ratzinger* (New York: Continuum, 2005), 49, 113-17.

[38]See Congregation for the Doctrine of the Faith, "Instruction on Certain Aspects of the 'Theology of Liberation.'" Benedict's understanding of liberation theology is controversial. David Gibson, for example, states: "As he often does with ideas he opposes, Ratzinger painted liberation theology in stark tones that distorted the movement's tenets beyond all recognition. Whatever the undeniable excesses of some proponents of liberation theology, Ratzinger was in reality criticizing a movement that did not exist" (David Gibson, *The Rule of Benedict: Pope Benedict XVI and His Battle with the Modern World* [San Francisco: HarperSanFrancisco, 2006], 193).

[39]32nd General Congregation of the Society of Jesus, Decree 4, nos. 41, 18.

[40]A striking feature of the volume *Living the Catholic Social Tradition: Cases and Commentary*, ed. Kathleen Maas Weigert and Alexia Kelley (Lanham, MD: Rowman & Littlefield, 2005) is the central role played by priests and nuns in many of the cases of successful social change.

[41]32nd General Congregation, Decree 4, no. 28.

The Liturgy as a Basis for Catholic Identity, Just War Theory, and the Presumption against War

Tobias Winright

The twenty-fifth anniversary of the U.S. Catholic bishops' pastoral letter *The Challenge of Peace: God's Promise and Our Response* has come and gone. On May 3, 1983, 238 out of the 247 bishops assembled in Chicago voted to accept this statement, the product of a thirty-month process, in order "to help Catholics form their consciences and to contribute to the public policy debate about the morality of war" during a time when the threat of nuclear war was an important concern of the Roman Catholic Church and indeed the rest of the world.[1] Over the years following the document's publication, a number of persons credited it with helping Catholics and other Americans to become more familiar with just war principles. Mennonite theologian John Howard Yoder believed that *The Challenge of Peace* (TCOP) familiarized people in the church and in wider society with the existence of the just war tradition, as evident in the use of just war language by politicians, military commanders, the media, citizens, and church members in connection with Grenada, Panama, and the Gulf War of 1990-1991.[2] In the view of Drew Christiansen, TCOP had "two important byproducts": it increased public awareness of just war principles and brought about a growing acceptance of nonviolence as a legitimate alternative to just war within the Christian tradition; both "byproducts" share what the bishops refer to as a common presumption against war.[3]

However, although he too regards TCOP as a "watershed event,"[4] the American Catholic public intellectual George Weigel accuses it of being part of a "great forgetting of the classic just war tradition" during the past forty years, in which a distorted version of just war theory has been taught by "the nation's moral philosophers, moral theologians, and religious leaders."[5] In Weigel's view, just war is "a tradition of statecraft" rather than "a casuistry of means-tests that begins with a 'presumption against violence' "[6] and ends at a "default position" reducing just war to a "functional or *de facto* pacifism."[7] These allegations are curious, though, given how most Americans, including Catholics, supported the Bush administration's war against Iraq. As Patrick T. McCormick has noted, the actual "default position" of the "vast majority of American Catholics and Christians" is that they evidently "approach the moral analysis of every call to arms with a strong presumption in favor of war."[8]

If McCormick's assertion about the Catholic laity's proclivity toward war is accurate, has the bishops' pastoral letter been effective in informing Catholic laity about the morality of war? Is familiarizing Catholics with just war language and principles sufficient to form their consciences? Or is something more necessary—something that speaks more to their identity as Catholics? This essay focuses on the first purpose, or audience, that the bishops identified for TCOP. It proposes that the liturgy of the mass offers a more coherent theological basis—one that is more integrally connected with Catholic identity and the forming of the consciences of the laity—for Catholic teaching on the morality of war and the presumption that the bishops claim just war teaching and nonviolence share in favor of peace and against war.[9] For as Kenneth R. Himes has observed, "The vast majority of Catholics do not read magisterial statements.... It is not the intellectual appeal of theological documents which moves people at the level of the daily life of the church. For Roman Catholics it is the Sunday Eucharist that continues to be the important ecclesial experience."[10]

I begin with a brief account of the bishops' attempt to speak to two audiences in TCOP and how their effort to form the consciences of the Catholic laity falls short. I then turn to the work of L. Edward Phillips, who provides a schema of the various ways in which the link between liturgy and ethics may be understood. Next, I turn to Virgil Michel, O.S.B. who, while well known in the early twentieth century for his writings on liturgy and social justice, also began his treatment of just war by reminding his readers of the primacy of peace in the mass. Finally, I consider the liturgy of the mass in order to glean a frame of reference or starting point for Catholic identity, just war theory, and the presumption against war—and I attempt to address some of Weigel's objections to this version of just war. This is important because, as he says, "beginning at the wrong place almost always means arriving at the wrong destination."[11]

A Tale of Two Audiences

Because the bishops wanted to help Catholics form their consciences and to contribute to the public policy debate about the morality of war, TCOP addressed "two distinct but overlapping audiences" that required "two complementary but distinct styles of teaching."[12] The teaching style the bishops employed involved different language, depending on audience.[13] The first audience, which is the "Catholic faithful," holds a specific faith perspective informed by the gospel that yields implications for the moral life. Within the four major sections of the pastoral letter, the first ("Peace in the Modern World: Religious Perspectives and Principles") and the fourth ("The Pastoral Challenge and Response") appear to have this audience more in view. These sections delve into how the Bible, the Catholic tradition, and practices such as prayer and penance inform the church's perspective on war and peace. The language in these sections, therefore, tends to be more theological and specifically Catholic.

The second audience consists of other Christian and religious communities, fellow citizens, and persons of good will. Although they may not necessarily share the faith perspective of Catholics, members of the wider civil community are "equally bound by certain key moral principles" that are discernible through reason. The document's second ("War and Peace in the Modern World: Problems and Principles") and third ("The Promotion of Peace: Proposals and Policies") sections are written with this audience more in view. These sections of TCOP presuppose more of a natural law approach and tend to use "mediating language and detailed analysis of intricate policy issues."[14] Most of the attention that the document received in the wake of its release focused on these two sections, especially in connection with what the bishops had to say about initiating nuclear war, the possibility of limited nuclear war, deterrence policy, and disarmament.

Todd D. Whitmore recently has noted, "The significance of the document in American Catholic history is unquestioned."[15] He bases this observation on the quantity of responses to TCOP from the media (including a cover story in *Time* magazine), members of Congress, and the Reagan administration. Most of these reactions came from the document's second audience. Less evident is its reception by Catholics, and in particular the laity. According to Kristin Heyer, while the United States Council of Catholic Bishops relies on "more widely accessible approaches" when dialoguing with the wider political community, which as the pastoral letter notes includes Catholics, the bishops' "first audience is the church itself."[16]

To be sure, the pastoral letter generated responses within Catholicism. In this connection, Whitmore mentions the Vatican. Additional Catholics who were interested in what the American bishops had to say included episcopal conferences in other countries, such as the Federal Republic of Germany.[17] But what about Catholic laity in the U.S.? Attention has been devoted to how notable the document was in the way that it involved a conversational process that included input by experts (military, political, theological) and by members of the church.[18] Thus the bishops not only spoke to these audiences with the release of TCOP, but they also listened to members of their two audiences during the process that led to it. With regard to its first audience, TCOP was written in response to the concern of the laity, including both those Catholics working in arms factories and those protesting against nuclear-armed submarines. The inclusion of the laity in the process culminating in TCOP led Yoder to observe that the document was a significant ecclesiastical event.[19] The bishops involved, listened to, and responded to the laity.

But after its publication, how effective was TCOP in helping them to form their consciences on just war theory and its presumption against war? McCormick certainly expresses some troubling doubts. Far from lapsing into the functional pacifism that Weigel alleges results from the bishops' teaching in TCOP, most American Catholics apparently supported the 2003 invasion of Iraq—even though the bishops expressed serious reservations about whether this particular war was justified.

Before and during the war in Iraq, the bishops issued several statements to the national press and also posted them on the

USCCB's website.[20] Some of these statements were voted on if their timing coincided with the bishops' annual November meetings. Others were issued under the name of the president of the USCCB on behalf of the bishops in the form of a letter to government officials, including President Bush. Composed by bishops and their staff, these brief statements did not undergo a consultative process. The fears and concerns of the laity with regard to this new crisis are not mentioned by the bishops. In their statement from November 13, 2003, the bishops use the criteria of the just war tradition to lift up "moral concerns and questions" that they hope "will be considered seriously by our leaders and all citizens." Their primary audience appears to be the wider civil community, especially government officials, rather than the Catholic laity. Only half of one paragraph in this twelve-paragraph statement specifically refers to "Catholic lay people—who have the principal responsibility to transform the social order in light of the Gospel—to continue to discern how best to live out their vocation to be 'witnesses and agents of peace and justice' (*Catechism*, 2442)."[21] Formation of Catholic consciences with regard to the Iraq war seems secondary in this statement. Knowledge of just war criteria is necessary, but is it sufficient, when such principles "do not exhaust the gospel vision" for Catholic laity?[22]

Daniel M. Bell, Jr., a United Methodist theologian, maintains that despite the frequency with which the just war tradition is invoked, "few Christians know about the kinds of judgments and disciplines upon which the tradition is built. Few can name the criteria, much less unpack how they might be faithfully applied."[23] Like Weigel, Bell does not think the just war tradition should be reduced to "a tidy checklist," but unlike Weigel, he does not reduce the just war tradition to a theory of statecraft. Rather, it is a form of Christian discipleship and practical rationality—that is, more an ecclesial tradition that should be embodied by Christians. In other words, in order to form Christian consciences about the morality of war, there is "much to do between wars, not only teaching the criteria but also nurturing the virtues commensurate with the tradition—justice, temperance, patience, courage and so forth—through preaching and teaching, liturgy and works of mercy."[24] Such an approach would put the Catholic laity front and center, take their identity as Catholics seriously, and hopefully better form them so as to not have a presumption in favor of every call to arms that comes along.

Mass Appeal: Liturgy and Ethics

Given that a major mark of Catholic lay identity is the mass, what bearing does this have on how the Catholic just war tradition addresses the moral issue of war? Toward the end of TCOP—in the final section directed more specifically to Catholic clergy, educators, and laity—the bishops devote a paragraph to the importance of the liturgy: "The Mass in particular is a unique means of seeking God's help to create the conditions essential for true peace in ourselves and in the world."[25] Here the bishops mention the communion rite, the Lord's Prayer, the sign of peace, and petitions for peace during the general intercessions at mass. However, these references to the liturgy and its significance for Catholic morality and war are brief, more like an afterthought. If the liturgy of the mass plays a central role in the identity of the Catholic laity, and if what they experience during worship should spill over into their earthly affairs—which one would assume includes the moral issue of war—then instead of mentioning this toward the end of TCOP perhaps the bishops should have made the mass their starting point. Before considering how the mass offers a basis for Catholic teaching on the morality of war, including the presumption against war, some attention needs to be given to the connection between liturgy and ethics.

The relationship between liturgy and ethics was a novel topic thirty years ago when several eminent scholars—including Paul Ramsey, Margaret A. Farley, and Philip J. Rossi, S.J.—devoted essays to the subject in the *Journal of Religious Ethics*.[26] Since then, many moral and liturgical theologians have contributed to this discussion, so that today, according to liturgical scholar L. Edward Phillips, most theologians generally accept the claim that a correlation exists between liturgy and ethics.[27] A consensus exists that there is "an intimate connection between how the church prays, what it believes, and how it acts"—*lex orandi, lex credendi, lex agendi*.[28] The question that remains, though, is *how* liturgy and ethics are related.

Phillips provides a schema consisting of four ways in which

theologians understand the link between liturgy and ethics.[29] First, liturgy is viewed as a textual source for ethical reflection. As with scripture or the writings of major theologians in the tradition, liturgical texts—such as prayers, responses, hymns, and litanies—can serve as a basis for formulating an argument about a moral issue. In addition, rites and gestures—such as baptism, the eucharist, and the passing of the peace—can function as a normative source for constructing a moral argument about an issue. An example may be found in Julie Hanlon Rubio's chapter on "The Catholic Marriage Liturgy: A Different Vision of Marriage" in her book, *A Christian Theology of Marriage and Family*. "Reading the Catholic wedding as a text," she writes, "will give us the basics of Catholic theological thinking on marriage."[30] Accordingly, she reflects on what the texts (the rubrics, the prayers, the readings, the vows, hymn lyrics, and so on) as well as the practices (for example, how people dress, the procession, the participation of the assembly) teach theologically and ethically about marriage.

The second way scholars understand the link between liturgy and ethics views liturgy as formative and as a motivational tool for ethical behavior. Christian worship provides a normative vision or a distinctive language that, through repeated practice, trains participants to see and speak about moral issues in a certain way. Worship's habitual practices shape and nurture Christian virtues, dispositions, and affections. Worship informs worshipers, but also forms them, so as to orient and motivate them to act in ways congruent with what they have experienced in the liturgy. Don E. Saliers's essay in the *Journal of Religious Ethics* represents this understanding of the link between liturgy and ethics. He writes, "When worship occurs, people are characterized, given their life and their fundamental location and orientation in the world."[31] For Saliers the liturgy is a school of the affections and has more to do with an ethics of character and virtue.

Third, some scholars focus on liturgy as an object of ethical critique. Worship sometimes involves injustice, or it sometimes perpetuates moral deformation. Paul Wadell, for example, distinguishes between "sham worship," wherein worshipers focus on themselves, feeling good, and being entertained, and "true worship," wherein worshipers glorify God and thereby allow themselves to be challenged and changed more into the image of

Christ.[32] Feminist and liberation theologians have also brought attention to how liturgy (e.g., non-inclusive language, only males serving as worship leaders, etc.) can perpetuate oppression and social injustice. Drawing on the prophets (for example, Amos 5:21-24) who criticized the people's worship while they neglected the weightier matters of social justice, especially for the poor and marginalized, some argue that the authenticity of the liturgy is conditioned by the quality of the ethical life of those who participate in worship; in other words, liturgy is not authentic unless there is justice.[33]

The fourth way views liturgy and ethics as integrally related aspects of Christian life. Their connection is fundamental and essential. Worship of God is itself a moral activity, and the moral life glorifies God. For example, at Duke Divinity School, Episcopal ethicist Harmon Smith and Stanley Hauerwas structured their introductory courses in Christian ethics around "Liturgy as Ethics/ Ethics as Liturgy."[34] In this way, Christian identity hinges on liturgy and ethics fused together as two sides of the same coin. According to Smith, "Liturgy both reflects and teaches us the kind of people we are and are meant to be."[35] Moreover, gathering for worship is a moral act, because it acknowledges that worshiping God is right and a good thing to do.[36] Similarly, William T. Cavanaugh, in his book *Torture and Eucharist*, questions dichotomizing liturgy, ethics, and politics, and he argues that the eucharist is an ethic or a "counter-politics" whereby the church as the body of Christ offers an alternative to the nation-state, violence, and oppression.[37] Dramatic examples of what is meant by this may be found in some scenes in the film *Romero*, where the archbishop and the oppressed Catholics of El Salvador chose to have mass in nonviolent resistance to the military.[38] In each instance, when Archbishop Romero said, "Let us begin the Mass," witness was given in the midst of a tumultuous country to an alternate way.

All four of these ways that liturgy and ethics are understood to be related surface in the following section that expands upon the brief paragraph in TCOP that mentions the importance of the mass in connection with the morality of war and peace. First, however, I retrieve the work of Virgil Michel, who provided a precedent for what I am proposing in considering the morality of war on the basis of the liturgy.

Worship and War

Dom Virgil Michel (1890-1938) is remembered for his prominent role in the liturgical movement during the early twentieth
century in the United States. He founded the Liturgical Press and
the journal *Orate Fratres* (now *Worship*) in 1926 at St. John's
Abbey in Collegeville, Minnesota. Attention to Michel's work
has focused on his identification of the connection between the
liturgy and "the social question,"[39] a topic about which Michel
often wrote in the pages of *Orate Fratres*.[40]

A syllogism that Michel formulated encapsulates his project:
"Pius X tells us that the liturgy is the indispensable source of the
true Christian spirit; Pius XI says that the true Christian spirit is
indispensable for social regeneration. Hence, the conclusion: The
liturgy is the indispensable basis of social regeneration."[41] The
liturgy offered a solution to the problems of America at that time,
including individualism, materialism, and indifference to economic
injustice. The mass provided "the best model and guide" for society.[42] The mystical body of Christ was a metaphor that Michel
used to describe the church as a dynamic, living community and
the Christian life as active, participatory and social.[43] According
to Michel, the Catholic "who lives the liturgy will in due time feel
the mystical body idea developing in his mind and growing upon
him, will come to realize that he is drinking at the very fountain
of the true Christian spirit which is destined to reconstruct the
Social Order."[44] The liturgy thus makes present a different reality that witnesses to how human society ought to be. The liturgy
also forms and shapes worshipers, transforming them to become
instruments of change in society. As Michel put it, "The liturgy is
the ordinary school of the development of the true Christian, and
the very qualities and outlook it develops in him are also those
that make for the best realization of a genuine Christian culture."[45]
In all of this, Michel focused especially on the Catholic laity and
parishes as fulcrums of social justice and change.[46]

The "social question" was not the only moral issue that seized
Michel's attention. Toward the end of his life, at the dawn of World
War II, he dealt with war, just war principles, and conscientious
objection in his book *The Christian in the World*, posthumously
published in 1939.[47] In the foreword, Michel wrote that his aim

was to "stress the vital truths of the Christian tradition in their relation to the worship of the Church and to the daily life of the Christian—and always in reference to the special characteristics of our present civilization and its needs."[48] It is in this context that he provides reflections on the "evil of war."[49]

Michel began by reciting from the introit of the second Christmas mass, "A light shall shine upon us this day: for our Lord is born to us; and he shall be called Wonderful, God, the Prince of peace."[50] Then he quoted a canticle sung during the morning Lauds of the divine office, which concludes with the comment that Christ came "to enlighten them that sit in darkness, and in the shadow of death: to direct our feet into the way of peace" (Lk 1:79). In addition, Michel mentioned the kiss of peace and the greeting "Peace be with you," which were part of the eucharistic liturgy of the early church. As with his treatment of social justice, Michel proposed, "The Eucharist as the sacrament of the mystical body of Christ, or of the perfection of love, is preeminently the sacrament of the peace of Christ."[51] In the wake of the destruction from World War I, where Christians killed Christians in opposing nations, Michel held that war is "always a tearing apart of the mystical body of Christ" and "a most terrible evil."[52] By initiating his discussion with reference to the church's liturgy, Michel made a strong claim for peace as the starting presumption for Christian reflection on the morality of war.

For Michel, however, beginning with the emphasis on the peace in the mass did not necessarily translate into pacifism as the norm for Catholics. To be sure, unlike most others at the time, including the Catholic Church, he called for the acceptance of conscientious objection for Catholic laity. Yet, Michel continued to employ the reasoning and principles of the just war tradition, which were for him informed and directed by the peace of the liturgy. He thus took up and treated seriously each criterion and how it applied to modern warfare. So, for example, with regard to the *jus ad bellum* criterion of just cause for embarking upon war, Michel wrote that "even a legitimate war of self-defense must be considered a great evil (even if not a moral evil, or a sin), for it, too, will be fraught with all the horrible consequences that modern warfare entails."[53] Likewise, with respect to the *jus in bello* criteria for actions during war, Michel stressed that war "must be rightly conducted: restrained within the limits of justice and love."[54]

Because just war is such a serious moral matter for Catholics, Michel warned Catholic citizens to be ever vigilant, carefully investigating the moral rightness of any conflict that their government undertakes. When competent civil authorities demonstrate that a war is justified, it is the citizen's duty to respond to the call of the country. But Michel recommended that Catholics should consult with their spiritual advisors for prudent counsel, and if there remains any doubt about whether a particular war is just, the person should refuse to take up arms. Thus, although he did not mention it by name, Michel advocated selective conscientious objection. In the end, Michel underscored that war "between nations or civil war within a state is indeed a most serious matter for the Christian since it is always a tearing apart of the very body of Christ."[55] For him, just war was not simply a checklist of criteria but a serious mode of moral reasoning that, while it included principles, was anchored in the peace of the mass. As Bell suggested earlier in this essay, it would be a Christian casuistry embedded in and formed by the practices and virtues of the Christian community. The default position for Catholics would not necessarily be pacifism, but nor would it necessarily lead to approaching every call to arms with a strong presumption in favor of war.

Conclusion: First Things and Just War

One of the most vocal critics of TCOP and the bishops' understanding of just war theory, and especially of their claim that it begins with a presumption against war, is George Weigel. As noted previously, he alleges that this is the wrong starting place for just war theory and that "beginning at the wrong place almost always means arriving at the wrong destination."[56] For him, just war instead is "a tradition of statecraft" and "an extension of politics" that begins with "defining the moral responsibilities of governments" for protecting the *tranquillitas ordinis*, the "tranquility of order." In short, the just war tradition begins with a presumption against injustice, and it "exists to serve statesmen [*sic*]" to make "responsible" decisions concerning war.[57] In his view, the bishops' understanding of just war as starting with a presumption against war is historically, methodologically, and theologically problematic. It leads to a functional pacifism, inverts just war reasoning by placing *jus in bello* concerns over and above *jus ad bellum* ones, and emphasizes last resort over other *ad bellum* criteria such as competent authority and just cause.

While there are points on which I agree with Weigel—for example, that politics and war are human, and therefore moral, enterprises rather than "anything goes"; that a distinction needs to be kept in mind between *bellum* (armed force for public ends by public authorities) and *duellum* (armed force for private ends by private individuals); and that war is not, in itself, always immoral—I worry that his account of just war risks sliding into a functional or *de facto* "blank check" to government authorities, where the default position of most Catholics and others is, as McCormick asserted, a presumption in favor of most every call to arms. As Brian V. Johnstone has written, by regarding just war more politically than theologically, Weigel and others come perilously close to becoming "apologists" for the foreign policies of a particular nation—and less likely to use the just war tradition to evaluate any given war conducted by their nation as unjust.[58]

For Johnstone, it makes "a considerable difference" whose "tradition" and which just war theory—a more "secular tradition" of just war theory "that emerged and separated from the Christian tradition," or the "just war doctrine as it developed and is maintained within the Christian, or specifically within the Catholic tradition"—is used in interpreting and applying the criteria.[59] Like Bell, Johnstone emphasizes the importance of a tradition that conveys "not merely information, beliefs and doctrines" but is embodied "in the way of life of the community."[60] After carefully studying the "classic" thinkers, Augustine and Aquinas, Johnstone shows that the Catholic tradition of just war is linked with a virtue ethic of charity and "integrated into a life of peace and friendship with God, and one another."[61] Although he does not mention it, the liturgy of the mass coheres with Johnstone's understanding of a tradition wherein an ethic of charity, forgiveness, peace, friendship—and yes, justice, understood in light of these—are embodied in the life of the community, which, I might add, has everything to do with Catholic identity and the laity.

As James F. Keenan has insightfully written, "Liturgy is where we understand ourselves as the people we are called to become," and we "identify ourselves" by the sign of the cross that we make at the beginning and end of the mass—a gesture that "frames not only the liturgy but our lives."[62] The peace we speak of, pray for, receive and experience at mass—a peace that is more than the absence of conflict—should characterize our lives—including how we think about and put into practice the criteria and requisite virtues of the Catholic tradition of just war. From the *Gloria*—where we sing "Glory to God in the highest, and peace to God's people on earth"—to the communion rite—where the priest prays, "Lord Jesus Christ, you said to your apostles: I leave you peace, my peace I give you. Look not on our sins, but on the faith of your Church, and grant us the peace and unity of your kingdom"—peace is emphasized. The same is the case with the Lord's Prayer, when the priest adds, "Deliver us, Lord, from every evil, and grant us peace in our day," and then says, "The peace of the Lord be with you always," to which the congregation responds, "And also with you." Before receiving communion, the assembly sings the *Agnus Dei*, praying that the Lamb of God, who takes away the sins of the world, will "grant us peace." Finally, at the conclusion of the mass, the priest blesses us, "The Mass is ended, go in peace to love and serve the Lord."

While all this could indeed support a Catholic pacifist stance, if the church continues to retain its allowance for the possibility of a just war, then this recap of some of the texts and gestures of the mass reveals that peace should be the texture of the Catholic tradition of just war too. The liturgy offers a theological and traditional basis for the presumption against war or, perhaps better put, the commitment to peace. While not necessarily intrinsically evil, war requires moral justification and it must be directed toward peace. The default position of Catholics informed and formed by the liturgy should not be one that simply assumes that the wars their nation embarks upon are always justified. Rather, it should be a stance that is oriented toward and directed by the peace of Christ so that each and every criterion of the just war tradition is equally taken honestly and seriously by Catholics. Such an approach to just war would neither necessarily result in a *de facto* pacifism, nor invert the tradition and its criteria as Weigel alleges. It would instead be a tradition of just war, understood and practiced by Catholics, in which, as Kenneth Himes remarks, "the case for war should be difficult to make. Not impossible, but difficult."[63]

Notes

[1] National Conference of Catholic Bishops, *The Challenge of Peace: God's Promise and Our Response* (Washington, DC: United States Catholic Conference, 1983), par. 16.

[2] John Howard Yoder, *When War Is Unjust: Being Honest in Just-War Thinking*, rev. ed. (Maryknoll, NY: Orbis Books, 1996), 93.

[3] Drew Christiansen, S.J., "After Sept. 11: Catholic Teaching on Peace and War," *Origins* 32, no. 3 (May 30, 2002): 36. For the U.S. bishops' references to this presumption for peace and against harm or war, see *The Challenge of Peace*, 70, 80, 83, and 120.

[4] George Weigel, *Tranquillitas Ordinis: The Present Failure and Future Promise of American Catholic Thought on War and Peace* (Oxford: Oxford University Press, 1987), 257.

[5] George Weigel, "Moral Clarity in a Time of War," *First Things* 129 (January 2003): 21. A slightly revised version of this article appears as a chapter in George Weigel, *Against the Grain: Christianity and Democracy, War and Peace* (New York: Crossroad Publishing Company, 2008), 200-23.

[6] Ibid., 22.

[7] George Weigel, "The Just War Tradition and the World after September 11," *Logos* 5, no. 3 (2002): 16.

[8] Patrick T. McCormick, "Violence: Religion, Terror, War," *Theological Studies* 67, no. 1 (March 2006): 159.

[9] Due to space limitations, this essay focuses more on just war than on nonviolence, even though the bishops claim that both share a presumption against war and in favor of peace. For a treatment of the liturgy, ethics, and nonviolence, see Tobias Winright, "Gather Us In and Make Us Channels of Your Peace: Evaluating War with an Entirely New Attitude," in *Gathered for the Journey: Moral Theology in Catholic Perspective*, ed. David Matzko McCarthy and M. Therese Lysaught (Grand Rapids: Eerdmans, 2007), 281-306, esp. at 298-302.

[10] Kenneth R. Himes, O.F.M., "Eucharist and Justice: Assessing the Legacy of Virgil Michel," *Worship* 62 (May 1988): 214.

[11] Weigel, "Moral Clarity in a Time of War," 23.

[12] NCCB, *The Challenge of Peace*, 16 and 17.

[13] J. Bryan Hehir, "From the Pastoral Constitution of Vatican II to *The Challenge of Peace*," in *Catholics and Nuclear War: A Commentary on The Challenge of Peace*, ed. Philip J. Murnion (New York: Crossroad Publishing Company, 1983), 80-81.

[14] Ibid., 80.

[15] Todd D. Whitmore, "The Reception of Catholic Approaches to Peace and War," in *Modern Catholic Social Teaching: Commentaries and Interpretations*, ed. Kenneth R. Himes, O.F.M. (Washington, DC: Georgetown University Press, 2005), 493.

[16] Kristin E. Heyer, *Prophetic and Public: The Social Witness of U.S. Catholicism* (Washington, DC: Georgetown University Press, 2006), 146.

[17]John Langan, S.J., "Problems of Method and Moral Theory in the U.S. and German Catholic Pastoral Letters on Peace: A Comparative Explanation," in *Ethics in the Nuclear Age: Strategy, Religious Studies, and the Churches*, ed. Todd Whitmore (Dallas: Southern Methodist University Press, 1989), 122.

[18]Philip J. Murnion, "Introduction," in *Catholics and Nuclear War: A Commentary on The Challenge of Peace*, ed. Philip J. Murnion (New York: Crossroad, 1983), xviii; Charles E. Curran, "The Moral Methodology of the Bishops' Pastoral," in *Catholics and Nuclear War: A Commentary on The Challenge of Peace*, ed. Philip J. Murnion (New York: Crossroad, 1983), 55.

[19]Yoder, *When War Is Unjust*, 87.

[20]United States Conference of Catholic Bishops, "Statement on Iraq," *Origins* 32, no. 24 (November 21, 2002): 406-408. Subsequent statements reiterated the same questions and concerns. See the "Statement on Iraq" by Bishop Wilton D. Gregory, President of the USCCB on February 26, 2003, http://www.usccb.org/sdwp/international/iraqstatement0203.shtml (accessed June 30, 2008); "Statement on War with Iraq" by Bishop Wilton D. Gregory on March 19, 2003, http://www.usccb.org/sdwp/peace/stm31903.shtml (accessed June 30, 2008); "Statement on Iraq" by Bishop Wilton D. Gregory on June 22, 2004, http://www.usccb.org/sdwp/international/iraqstatem. shtml (accessed June 30, 2008); "Toward a Responsible Transition in Iraq" by Bishop Thomas G. Wenski, Chair of the USCCB Committee on International Policy, on January 12, 2006, http://www.usccb.org/sdwp/international/ iraqstatement0106.shtml (accessed June 30, 2008); "Call for Dialogue and Action on *Responsible Transition* in Iraq" by Bishop William S. Skylstad, President of the USCCB, on November 13, 2006, http://www.usccb.org/sdwp/ international/iraqresponsibletransition.pdf (accessed June 30, 2008). I wish to express my gratitude to my research assistant Deborah Bosworth Campbell for gathering these materials and offering her helpful insights.

[21]Similarly, a note at the end of the statement from February 26, 2003, simply provided a link to the USCCB's general website where a concerned Catholic layperson would need to take the initiative to find "liturgical and other pastoral and educational resources for dioceses and parishes as our nation prepares for possible war."

[22]NCCB, *The Challenge of Peace*, 17.

[23]Daniel M. Bell, Jr., "In War and in Peace: Implications of Just War Theory," *Christian Century* 122, no. 18 (September 6, 2005): 26.

[24]Ibid., 33. See also Daniel M. Bell, Jr., "Can a War Against Terror Be Just? Or, What Is Just War Good For?" *Crosscurrents* 56, no. 1 (Spring 2006): 34-45.

[25]NCCB, *The Challenge of Peace*, 295. Similarly, at the end of its chapter on war and peace, the recent *Compendium of the Social Doctrine of the Church* says, "In particular, the Eucharistic celebration, 'the source and summit of the Christian life,' is a limitless wellspring for all authentic Christian commitment to peace" (Pontifical Council for Justice and Peace, *Compendium of the Social Doctrine of the Church* [Washington, DC: United States Conference of Catholic Bishops, 2004], 519). Moreover, the next-to-last footnote (#1102), which is by far the longest footnote in that chapter, highlights the emphasis on peace that runs throughout the mass.

[26]These articles appeared in the *Journal of Religious Ethics* 7, no. 2 (Fall 1979).

[27]L. Edward Phillips, "Ethics and Worship," in *The New Westminster Dictionary of Liturgy and Worship*, ed. Paul Bradshaw (Louisville and London: Westminster John Knox Press, SCM Press, 2002), 167-69; and L. Edward Phillips, "Liturgy and Ethics," in *Liturgy in Dialogue: Essays in Memory of Ronald Jasper*, ed. Paul Bradshaw and Bryan Spinks (London: SPCK, 1993). For a bibliography, see Mark Searle, "Liturgy and Ethics: An Annotated Bibliography," *Studia Liturgica* 21, no. 2 (1991): 220-35. Recent treatments of this subject may be found in essays included in *The Annual of the Society of Christian Ethics* 20 (Washington, DC: Georgetown University Press, 2000), in *Theology Today* 58, no. 3 (October 2001), and in *The Blackwell Companion to Christian Ethics*, ed. Stanley Hauerwas and Samuel Wells (Malden, MA and Oxford: Blackwell Publishing, 2004).

[28]Dennis J. Billy, C.Ss.R. and James Keating, *The Way of Mystery: The Eucharist and Moral Living* (Mahwah, NJ: Paulist Press, 2006), 41.

[29]As with any typologies, these categories may overlap; also, two or more of these ways may be evident in the work of a particular theologian.

[30]Julie Hanlon Rubio, *A Christian Theology of Marriage and Family* (Mahwah, NJ: Paulist Press, 2003), 25.

[31]Don E. Saliers, "Liturgy and Ethics: Some New Beginnings," *Journal of Religious Ethics* 7 (Fall 1979): 175. This essay is reprinted in a *Festschrift* for Saliers, *Liturgy and the Moral Self: Humanity at Full Stretch before God*, ed. E. Byron Anderson and Bruce T. Morrill (Collegeville, MN: Liturgical Press, 1998), 15-35. Also see Stephen B. Wilson, "Liturgy and Ethics: Something Old, Something New," *Worship* 81, no. 1 (January 2007): 24-45.

[32]Paul J. Wadell, *Becoming Friends: Worship, Justice, and the Practice of Christian Friendship* (Grand Rapids: Brazos Press, 2002), 18.

[33]Nicholas Wolterstorff, "Justice as a Condition of Authentic Liturgy," *Theology Today* 48 (April 1991): 6-21. See also Marjorie Procter-Smith, *In Her Own Rite: Constructing Feminist Liturgical Tradition* (Nashville: Abingdon Press, 1990); Gustavo Gutiérrez, *A Theology of Liberation: History, Politics, and Salvation*, rev. ed. (Maryknoll, NY: Orbis Books, 1988), 150; and James F. White, "Worship as a Source of Injustice," *Reformed Liturgy and Music* 19 (1985): 72-76.

[34]Harmon L. Smith, *Where Two or Three Are Gathered: Liturgy and the Moral Life* (Cleveland: Pilgrim Press, 1995), x; Stanley Hauerwas, "The Liturgical Shape of the Christian Life: Teaching Christian Ethics as Worship," in *In Good Company: The Church as Polis* (Notre Dame: University of Notre Dame Press, 1995), 153-68.

[35]Smith, *Where Two or Three Are Gathered*, x.

[36]Ibid., 72-73; Hauerwas, "The Liturgical Shape of the Christian Life," 157.

[37]William T. Cavanaugh, *Torture and Eucharist: Theology, Politics, and the Body of Christ* (Malden, MA and Oxford: Blackwell Publishers, 1998), 14, 221.

[38]John Duigan, dir., *Romero* (Santa Monica: Lions Gate, 1998).

[39]See R. W. Franklin and Robert L. Spaeth, *Virgil Michel: American Catholic*

(Collegeville, MN: Liturgical Press, 1988), 105-20; and Mark Searle, "The Liturgy and Catholic Social Doctrine," in *The Future of the Catholic Church in America: Major Papers of the Virgil Michel Symposium* (Collegeville, MN: Liturgical Press, 1991). Other recent retrievals of Michel's work as a model for Catholic liturgical-moral theology include Michael J. Baxter, C.S.C., "Reintroducing Virgil Michel: Towards a Counter-Tradition of Catholic Social Ethics in the United States," *Communio* 24 (Fall 1997): 499-528; and Stephen B. Wilson, "Liturgical Life: Elements of a Contemporary Account of the Christian Moral Life Based on a MacIntyrean Read of Virgil Michel's Thought" (PhD diss., University of Notre Dame, 2000).

[40]Another Catholic figure who linked liturgical renewal with social change at that time was Paul H. Furfey; see his "Liturgy and the Social Problem," *National Liturgical Week* (1941): 181-86. Dorothy Day, cofounder of the Catholic Worker movement, was influenced by Michel and Furfey, and she also wrote some articles on the subject. See Dorothy Day, "Liturgy and Sociology," *The Catholic Worker*, December 1935, 4; and "Liturgy and Sociology," *The Catholic Worker*, January 1936, 5. Also see Mark and Louise Zwick, *The Catholic Worker Movement: Intellectual and Spiritual Origins* (Mahwah, NJ: Paulist Press, 2005), esp. chap. 4, "Dom Virgil Michel, OSB, the Liturgical Movement, and the Catholic Worker," 58-74.

[41]Virgil Michel, "The Liturgy, the Basis of Social Regeneration," *Orate Fratres* 9 (1935): 545.

[42]Virgil Michel, "Natural and Supernatural Society," *Orate Fratres* 10 (1936): 244.

[43]See Jeremy Hall, *The Full Stature of Christ: The Ecclesiology of Virgil Michel OSB* (Collegeville, MN: Liturgical Press, 1976).

[44]Virgil Michel, "With Our Readers," *Orate Fratres* 5 (1930-31): 431.

[45]Virgil Michel, "Christian Culture," *Orate Fratres* 13 (1939): 303.

[46]Michel recognized that the liturgy is not always done well by clergy or the laity, and he acknowledged that it does not automatically result in transforming worshipers' lives. He asked, "How can they do this so regularly and yet apparently remain unaffected in their daily lives, showing no improvement in the true spirit of Christ?" One might similarly ask today about why most Catholics who regularly participate in the mass apparently have, as McCormick asserted, a "presumption in favor of war." Thus Michel also stressed the importance of Christian education to foster intelligent and active participation, which would have more of an effect on the worshiper (Virgil Michel, "Frequent Communion and Social Regeneration," *Orate Fratres* 10 [1936]: 199). Similarly, Vatican II's Constitution on the Sacred Liturgy called for "full, conscious, and active participation" of "all the faithful" in the liturgy (14). I am proposing the liturgy as *a*, not the only, basis for Catholic teaching on the morality of war. Education about the liturgy and reading documents of Catholic social teaching, along with this sort of active and conscious participation in the mass, should hopefully boost both the informing and forming of Catholic lay identity and consciences concerning war and peace.

[47]Virgil Michel, O.S.B., *The Christian in the World* (Collegeville, MN: Liturgical Press, 1939), 178-88.

[48]Ibid., iii.

[49]For a more detailed treatment of what Michel writes about war and peace here, see Tobias Winright, "Virgil Michel on Worship and War," *Worship* 71, no. 5 (September 1997): 451-62.

[50]Michel, *The Christian in the World*, 178.

[51]Ibid., 179.

[52]Ibid., 181.

[53]Ibid., 183.

[54]Ibid., 182.

[55]Ibid., 186.

[56]Weigel, "Moral Clarity in a Time of War," 23.

[57]Ibid., 20-22, 27.

[58]Brian V. Johnstone, C.Ss.R., "Pope John Paul II and the War in Iraq," *Studia Moralia* 41, no. 2 (December 2003): 327.

[59]Brian V. Johnstone, C.Ss.R., "The War on Terrorism: A Just War?" *Studia Moralia* 40, no. 1 (June 2002): 43.

[60]Ibid., 44.

[61]Johnstone, "The War on Terrorism: A Just War?" 51.

[62]James F. Keenan, S.J., *The Works of Mercy: The Heart of Catholicism* (Lanham, MD: Rowman & Littlefield Publishers, 2005), 92-93.

[63]Kenneth R. Himes, O.F.M., "Intervention, Just War, and U.S. National Security," *Theological Studies* 65 (2004): 152.

Part III

THE NATURE OF AUTHORITY
IN THE CHURCH

The *Sensus Fidei* and Lay Authority in the Roman Catholic Church

Carolyn Weir Herman

The question of lay authority in the Roman Catholic Church has become an important topic of theological discussion in the aftermath of the clerical sexual abuse scandal. With the unveiling of the scandal came the unearthing of a multifaceted ecclesial crisis. Most notably, the scandal revealed the abuse of power and loss of authority by bishops and priests. In addition, it accentuated unequal ecclesial relationships, unjust institutional structures, and a pervasive clerical culture.[1]

While Catholics have responded to this crisis in a variety of ways, perhaps the most significant response has been the emergence of Voice of the Faithful (VOTF). This organization was initiated in 2002 by lay Boston Catholics who remained dedicated to the Christian faith but who were outraged and felt betrayed by their church leaders.[2] The development of VOTF has signified the desire of lay Catholics to participate more fully in ecclesial life, and this desire, in turn, has evoked many questions about the laity's role and responsibility in the church. Among these questions is the issue of lay authority, the capability bestowed on all believers in baptism and confirmation to act with a certain influence in the church and the world. This article briefly describes the theological foundations, nature, and scope of lay authority in order to argue that the VOTF is an important example of a legitimate exercise of this authority in the contemporary Roman Catholic Church.

Theological Foundations

It is my contention that lay authority has its theological grounding in the supernatural sense of faith, or *sensus fidei*. This mystical instinct or understanding of the faith is a gift given to all believers by the Holy Spirit in baptism and confirmation.[3] It enables the faithful to perceive the truth of Christian revelation and to reject erroneous opinions.[4] The *sensus fidei* exists in the individual faith-consciousness of every believer as well as in the corporate faith-consciousness of the church as a whole. This collective sense of faith is known as the sense of the faithful, or *sensus fidelium*.[5] While the *sensus fidei* is the subjective disposition of the believer, the *sensus fidelium* is the objective consciousness or understanding of the faith by the entire church.[6] The *sensus fidelium* adopts a universal character when there is complete agreement among the whole people of God on a particular matter of belief. This consensus of the faithful, or *consensus fidelium*, results from the *sensus fidei* and thereby cannot be in error.[7]

Though the specific terms were not always used, the realities of the *sensus fidei, sensus fidelium,* and *consensus fidelium* have existed with more or less emphasis throughout the church's history.[8] In general, they have had a significant and distinct place when a communion ecclesiology has been prominent and a minor and ambiguous role when a hierarchical ecclesiology has prevailed.[9] For instance, most of Catholic theology from Vatican I until Vatican II ignored these realities because of the predominant pyramidal ecclesiology and "trickle-down" theory of revelation. The church was viewed as an unequal society in which the teaching church (*ecclesia docens*), or the hierarchy, was thought to have sole possession of divine revelation, and the learning church (*ecclesia discens*), or the laity, was seen as the passive recipient of the revelation given to the hierarchy. Revelation, in turn, was regarded as a deposit of faith, which has been passed down through apostolic succession to the hierarchy who then relayed this set of propositional truths to the laity, whose task was to passively accept the hierarchy's teaching.[10]

In light of its renewed theology of church and revelation, the Second Vatican Council retrieved the notion of the *sensus fidei*.[11] Rejecting the idea of the church as an unequal society, Vatican II opted instead for a view of the church as mystery founded on the trinitarian communion. *Lumen Gentium* describes the church as "people made one with the unity of the Father, Son, and the Holy Spirit" (*LG* 4).[12] In the time between the ascension and the parousia, the church as mystery is lived out historically as the people of God. As one people, this community shares a common and equal dignity in virtue of their baptism, and all believers partake of Christ's threefold ministry of priest, prophet, and king (*LG* 12-14). Additionally, *Dei Verbum* says that the whole church has the task of "hearing the Word of God with reverence, and proclaiming it with faith" (*DV* 1). The Word of God, which has existed from the beginning of creation, was made incarnate in Jesus Christ and is now announced by the church. Vatican II rejects the idea that revelation is a deposit of faith communicated as a set of propositional truths and instead views it as a relationship, or dialogue, between God and humanity. God offers humanity the Word in love, and through the power of the Holy Spirit humanity is able to respond. By the aid of the Spirit, believers come to know and accept divine revelation. This ability to recognize and respond to God's Word is the supernatural sense of faith.[13] *Lumen Gentium* 12 states:

> The holy People of God shares in Christ's prophetic office. It spreads abroad a living witness to him, especially by means of a life of faith and charity by offering to God a sacrifice of praise, the tribute of lips which give honor to his name (cf. Heb. 13:15). The body of the faithful as a whole, anointed as they are by the Holy One (cf. 1 Jn. 2:20 and 27), cannot err in matters of belief. Thanks to a supernatural sense of faith which characterizes the People as a whole, it manifests this unerring quality when, "from the bishops down to the last member of the laity," it shows universal agreement in matters of faith and morals. For, by this sense of faith which is aroused and sustained by the Spirit of truth, God's People accepts not the word of men but the very Word of God (cf. 1 Th. 2:13). It clings without fail to the faith once delivered to the saints (cf. Jude 3), penetrates it more deeply by accurate insights, and applies it more thoroughly to life.

This text indicates that Christ imparts the truth of the Christian faith to the entire people of God and subsequently calls all believers to participate in his prophetic ministry. In order to share in this mission, the Holy Spirit anoints all the faithful with the *sensus fidei*. This mystical instinct of faith characterizes the whole of God's people; it belongs to all believers, not only to select individuals. It is evidence of the indefectibility and vitality of the entire body of Christ.[14]

Moreover, the sense of faith is of the same nature as the gift of faith; it is not something natural or acquired but something supernatural and infused, similar to the virtue of faith.[15] In addition, the sense of faith, like the virtue of faith, develops during one's life. Since the Word of God is living and dynamic, it communicates in new ways to each generation and thereby takes new forms as it roots itself in the hearts and minds of believers.[16] As *Dei Verbum* 8 asserts:

> The Tradition that comes from the apostles makes progress in the Church, with the help of the Holy Spirit. There is a growth in insight into the realities and words that are being passed. This comes about through the contemplation and study of believers who ponder these things in their hearts. It comes from the intimate sense of spiritual realities which they experience. And it comes from the preaching of those who, on succeeding to the office of bishop, have received the sure charism of truth. Thus, as the centuries go by, the Church is always advancing towards the plentitude of divine truth, until eventually the words of God are fulfilled in it.

This pneumatological perspective makes it impossible to believe that divine revelation belongs exclusively to any one group in the church, including the pope and bishops. The Word of God lives in the whole church through the Holy Spirit. Through the *sensus fidei*, the Holy Spirit enlightens all the faithful enabling them to recognize and respond to God's Word.[17] This mystical instinct of faith guides believers to make right judgments concerning matters of belief, which leads them to more "accurate insights" about Christian revelation. In this way, they reject erroneous beliefs and cling to the faith "once delivered to the saints."

Due to the *sensus fidei*, the people of God cannot err when they universally agree on matters of faith and morals.[18] That is to say, a *consensus fidelium*, or a consensus of the entire church "from the bishops down to the last member of the laity," on a matter of belief is infallible. Though this claim was believed throughout the church's history, Vatican II was the first ecumenical council to explicitly declare the infallibility of a universal consensus.[19]

Moreover, *Lumen Gentium* affirms the infallibility of a *consensus fidelium* before it deals with the infallibility of the pope, ecumenical councils, and the ordinary universal magisterium. This placement is significant because it indicates that any special exercise of infallibility is rooted in the infallibility of the believing people of God.[20] All the faithful, the laity and hierarchy alike, thereby have the right and responsibility to preserve and penetrate the faith, and when this right and responsibility leads to a universal agreement on a matter of belief, the consensus reached is infallible.[21] In sum, Vatican II's renewed ecclesiology and theology of revelation led to a retrieval of the *sensus fidei*, which, I allege, is the primary theological underpinning of lay authority in the church.

Nature of Lay Authority

Having discussed the theological foundations, we now explore the nature of lay authority. As was noted above, lay authority refers to the ability given to all believers in baptism and confirmation to act with a certain influence in the church and the world. This authority is rooted in the supernatural sense of faith and enables the whole people of God to participate in Christ's prophetic ministry. Lay authority then is *common* and *universal* among the faithful; however, it is also *diversified* by a variety of charisms. Along with the sense of faith, the Holy Spirit gives the people of God a multiplicity of spiritual gifts to be used in the service of the church (*LG* 12). These distinct charisms differentiate the common and universal authority of the baptized, and in this way enable the church to undertake its mission and ministry.

Furthermore, this authority, rooted in baptism and confirmation, is related to but distinct from the authority that is grounded in holy orders. Though the clergy share in lay authority, they also possess unique authority that comes from sacramental ordination. In addition to celebrating the sacraments and leading God's people, the clergy exercise the "official" teaching authority, or magisterium, of the church. According to Vatican II, the bishops, who receive "the fullness of the sacrament of orders" (*LG* 21), are "authentic teachers, that is, teachers endowed with the authority of Christ, who preach the faith to the people assigned to them" (*LG* 24). Priests and deacons are helpers to the bishops in teaching God's Word (*LG* 20; cf. *Presbyterorum Ordinis* 4).

Yet as we have seen, Vatican II asserts that the hierarchy are not in sole possession of divine revelation. Rather, the whole church discerns the truth in matters of faith and morals because all the baptized share the supernatural sense of faith. While the hierarchy have the task of officially naming and defining doctrine, their articulation should reflect the faith of the entire people of God. They no longer are thought to exclusively possess divine revelation, and the laity no longer are seen as the passive recipients of defined doctrine. Instead, the entire church is called to teach and to learn.[22] All the faithful are teachers, not only the clergy in the official teaching office but also the laity who mainly witness to Christ in the world. Moreover, all believers are learners; the hierarchy must learn from the laity's faith and experience in formulating doctrines, and the laity must continue to receive and be educated by magisterial teaching. For this reason, there must be collaboration and co-responsibility among all the faithful in discerning and naming new and deeper understandings of the Christian faith.

Scope of Lay Authority

The next issue to consider is the scope of lay authority. Since the laity typically are engaged in secular affairs, lay authority predominantly involves the renewal of the temporal order in light of God's reign. According to Vatican II, this renewal occurs through both *action* and *word*. Action refers to the witness of a Christian life; it means doing one's earthly duties in the spirit of the gospel (*Apostolicam Actuositatem* 6; *Gaudium et Spes* 43). As *Lumen Gentium* 38 states:

Each individual layman must be a witness before the world to the resurrection and life of the Lord Jesus, and a sign of the living God. All together, and each one to the best of his ability, must nourish the world with spiritual fruits (cf. Gal 5:22). They must diffuse in the world the spirit which animates those poor, meek, and peace-makers whom the Lord in the Gospel proclaimed blessed (cf. Mt. 5:3-9). In a word: "what the soul is in the body, let Christians be in the world."

Besides Christian witness, lay authority in the secular realm also includes the explicit proclamation of the gospel. It extends to "occasions of announcing Christ by word, either to unbelievers to draw them towards the faith, or to the faithful to instruct them, strengthen them, incite them to a more fervent life" (*AA* 6).

Though Vatican II underscores lay authority in the world, it also plants seeds for cultivating lay authority inside the church. I contend that the conciliar texts support an understanding of intra-ecclesial lay authority that includes receiving the hierarchy's teaching *and* teaching the hierarchy. *Lumen Gentium* 37, for instance, points to both of these tasks. It first signifies the laity's role in teaching the hierarchy, asserting that the laity should freely and confidently "disclose their needs and desires" to their leaders; in other words, the laity teach the hierarchy in the broad sense of informing them of their personal and communal experiences in the church, and knowing such experiences enables the hierarchy to minister more effectively. The text also indicates that lay people should bring their knowledge and experience to bear on issues affecting the larger community. It says that: "By reason of the knowledge, competence or pre-eminence which they have the laity are empowered—indeed sometimes obliged—to manifest their opinion on those things which pertain to the good of the Church." Manifesting one's opinion could be interpreted as dialoguing with the hierarchy through informal listening sessions or more established institutions like parish or diocesan councils (cf. *Christus Dominus* 27; *AA* 26); yet, it might also be interpreted as challenging or protesting the hierarchy's actions or decisions when they are unjust or fail to represent the faith of the whole of God's people.

Following these claims, *Lumen Gentium* 37 proceeds to affirm the laity's role in receiving the hierarchy's teaching. It emphasizes that, "Like all Christians, the laity should promptly accept in Christian obedience what is decided by the pastors." The laity, however, are not to be passive recipients of the hierarchy's teaching; rather, they are to be active recipients who evaluate and accept what the hierarchy teaches in light of their supernatural sense of faith.

Before concluding, *Lumen Gentium* 37 again recognizes the active role of the laity, not just in receiving teaching but in using their experience for the good of the community. This time, it reminds the clergy of the laity's authority, stating that:

> The pastors, indeed, should recognize and promote the dignity and responsibility of the laity in the Church. They should willingly use their prudent advice and confidently assign duties to them in the service of the Church, leaving them freedom and scope for acting. Indeed, they should give them the courage to undertake works on their own initiative. They should with paternal love consider attentively in Christ initial moves, suggestions and desires proposed by the laity. Moreover the pastors must respect and recognize the liberty which belongs to all in the terrestrial city.

To summarize, the scope of lay authority spans both the temporal and ecclesial arenas. It includes proclaiming the gospel in the world by witness and word; it also involves receiving the hierarchy's teaching and stating one's needs and opinions for the good of the church. Therefore, in both the secular and ecclesial realms, the laity are called to manifest the authority that comes to them through baptism and confirmation and in this way properly share in Christ's prophetic ministry.

Exercising of Lay Authority:
The Example of Voice of the Faithful

Having treated the foundations, nature, and scope of lay authority, the final issue to address is the exercise of lay authority and the notable example of VOTF. One way of exercising lay authority, as described here, is through the formation of lay movements and associations. Vatican II says that "while preserving intact the necessary link with ecclesiastical authority, the laity have the right to establish and direct associations, and to join existing ones" (*AA* 19). Canon law also affirms this right (canons 215, 216, 298, 299, 300, 301).[23]

Similar to the formation of other lay movements and organizations, VOTF began in response to a need in the church. Yet what differentiated this group was the context of its inception. Angered and betrayed by the crimes of clerical sexual abuse and the systemic cover-up by the archdiocese, Boston Catholics gathered together to process their pain and express their outrage. VOTF started as listening sessions for the Catholics of St. John's Parish in Wellesley, Massachusetts. As more and more people started to attend these sessions, this informal group evolved into a more formal social movement.[24] It emerged and grew from the "bottom up" as the laity bonded together with their collective concerns and shared stories. The movement continued to expand with its 2002 convention and as VOTF affiliates developed throughout Boston, the United States, and the world. Now with over thirty thousand members, VOTF has become an established lay organization that is dedicated to supporting victims of clerical sexual abuse, encouraging priests of integrity, and seeking structural change within the church.[25] Its mission, in brief, is "to provide a prayerful voice, attentive to the Spirit, through which the Faithful can actively participate in the governance and guidance of the Catholic Church."[26]

In my judgment, the emergence and existence of VOTF is a legitimate exercise of lay authority. Empowered by their shared sense of faith and unique charisms, lay Catholics united to take responsibility for the community. They exercised their baptismal authority by manifesting their opinion for the good of the church. In this case, they protested the sexual abuse by priests and the systemic cover-up by the bishops. Rooted in their understanding of the Christian faith, this protest ultimately seeks to stand in solidarity with victims. Additionally, VOTF rightly works to support honest priests and to reform unjust ecclesial structures. Furthermore, VOTF desires to work in collaboration with the hierarchy. It has continually sought to dialogue with church leaders, although in many cases bishops have banned conversations with VOTF members and/or have banned affiliates from meeting on church properties.[27]

It is important to note, however, that the VOTF is not *the* voice of the laity but *a* voice.[28] When looking at the demographics of the group, one hardly finds a complete picture of the Catholic laity. Sixty percent of VOTF members are women, most of whom are pre-Vatican II (born in 1940 or earlier) or Vatican II Catholics (born between 1941 and 1960). Younger Catholics are considerably absent from the group. Two-thirds of VOTF members claim Irish heritage, while Latinos and African Americans constitute only a small percentage. Almost all members are cradle Catholics who have gone through formal Catholic education. Many members are well educated, middle class, and have had professional occupations most of their adult lives.[29] Catholics who are not so committed to the institutional church are not part of the group nor are the poor members of the community. Hence, VOTF is a valid exercise of lay authority but it single-handedly does not represent the perspective of all the Catholic laity. Other voices must have an opportunity to speak and to be heard in order to discern and articulate a Spirit-led vision for how the church should proceed into the twenty-first century.

Moreover, VOTF avows that it is not seeking to change matters of doctrine but to reform the structures of the church. This claim is seen in its motto: "Keep the faith, change the church." Yet, when Vatican II discusses the *sensus fidei*, it presents it in terms of faith and morals. The supernatural sense of faith enables believers to accept truthful teachings and to reject erroneous ones; in other words, the *sensus fidei* and the lay authority rooted in it extend to matters of doctrine. Vatican II, however, does not consider the *sensus fidei* in relation to the issues of ecclesial governance that were raised in the aftermath of the clerical sexual abuse scandal; nonetheless, doctrine and church structure are integrally linked. Church structure is meant to assist doctrine. The attempt to divorce structure from church mission and doctrine is ultimately "artificial and ecclesiologically deficient."[30] By focusing only on ecclesial structure, VOTF risks falling into the same situation it critiques, "isolating and absolutizing the institutional dimensions of the church."[31] For this reason, VOTF's intention to "keep the faith" but "change the church" is theologically inaccurate. One does not change ecclesial structures without somewhat revising the faith. To change the church in response to the current ecclesial crisis is absolutely necessary, but such reform also requires an updating of the faith for the contemporary context. I propose that the scope of lay authority addresses both of these matters, and thereby it would be within the responsibility of a lay association like VOTF to consider both issues of faith and church structure in dialogue and collaboration with the hierarchy.[32]

Conclusion

The development and actualization of lay authority is an essential part of renewing the Roman Catholic Church in the aftermath of the clerical sexual abuse scandal and more importantly of be-coming the community envisioned by Vatican II. Yet, much work needs to be done to make lay authority a reality in the contemporary church, and this work must come from the collaboration of all the faithful. Ecclesial leaders must affirm the supernatural sense of faith given to all believers by the Holy Spirit and in turn must encourage the community to actively develop its faith through such means as personal prayer, scripture reflection, celebration of the sacraments, and works of social justice. In addition, they must engage in "holy conversation" with the laity and lay associations like VOTF in order to discern the *sensus fidelium*.[33] They also must articulate doctrines and make decisions that reflect a prayerful, Spirit-guided consensus. By deepening the community's sense of faith, dialoguing with groups like VOTF, and discerning the sense and consensus of the faithful, the hierarchy will be able to make more informed decisions regarding ecclesial governance and to define doctrines that reflect the faith-consciousness of the church as a whole. Furthermore, the laity must continue to demand a greater voice in the life of the church. They must seek and establish ways, like through VOTF, to exercise their authority in the church. They must continue to work in partnership with the hierarchy for the good of the community but also must challenge the hierarchy when their actions and decisions are unjust. Therefore, in this way, the entire people of God will be able to fulfill their baptismal right and responsibility to participate fully and actively in the ministry of Jesus Christ.

Notes

[1]The literature on the clerical sexual abuse scandal and the deeper ecclesial crisis is abundant. See, for example, Mary Gail Frawley-O'Dea, *Perversion of Power: Sexual Abuse in the Catholic Church* (Nashville: Vanderbilt University Press, 2007); Regina Ammicht-Quinn, Hille Haker, and Maureen Junker-Kenny, eds., *The Structural Betrayal of Trust*, *Concilium* 2004, 3 (London: SCM, 2004); Francis Oakley and Bruce Russett, eds., *Governance, Account-ability, and the Future of the Catholic Church Crisis* (New York: Continuum, 2004); Thomas G. Plante, ed., *Sin Against the Innocents: Sexual Abuse by Priests and the Role of the Catholic Church* (Westport, CT: Praeger Publishers, 2004); Peter Steinfels, *A People Adrift: The Crisis of the Roman Catholic Church in America* (New York: Simon & Schuster, 2003).

[2]On VOTF, see William V. D'Antonio and Anthony Pogerelc, eds., *Voices of the Faithful: Loyal Catholics Striving for Change* (New York: Crossroad, 2007); James E. Muller and Charles Kenney, *Keep the Faith, Change the*

Church: The Battle by Catholics for the Soul of Their Church (Emmaus, PA: Rodale, 2004); James E. Post, "The Emerging Role of the Catholic Laity: Lessons from the Voice of the Faithful," in *Common Calling: The Laity and the Governance of the Catholic Church*, ed. Stephen J. Pope (Washington, D.C.: Georgetown University Press, 2004), 209-28. See also the Voice of the Faithful website at http://www.votf.org/index.html (accessed July 13, 2007).

³Francis A. Sullivan, *Magisterium: Teaching Authority in the Catholic Church* (New York: Paulist Press, 1983), 21.

⁴Ibid., 23.

⁵Herbert Vorgrimler, "The *Sensus Fidei* to *Consensus Fidelium*," in *The Teaching Authority of All Believers*, ed. Johannes-Baptist Metz and Edward Schillebeeckx (Edinburgh: T & T Clark, 1985), 3-11 at 3.

⁶In the history of the church, the notion of *sensus fidelium* has been expressed by other terms such as *communis sensus fidei, sensus Ecclesiae,* and *sensus Christi.* See Patrick Granfield, *Limits of the Papacy* (New York: Crossroad, 1987), 136.

⁷Sullivan, *Magisterium*, 23. Since the terms *sensus fidei, sensus fidelium*, and *consensus fidelium* overlap in meaning, sometimes they are used interchangeably. Yet while they are interrelated, they clearly differ from one another.

⁸In the church's history, sometimes the *sensus fidei* has been the main focus, and other times the *sensus* and *consensus fidelium* have received the attention. Still at other times, these realities have faded into the background, though never entirely ceasing to exist. For example, patristic authors, such as Irenaeus, Tertullian, Hippolytus, and Augustine, underscored the *consensus fidelium*, while Thomas Aquinas and other scholastics emphasized the *sensus fidelium*. During the Reformation, when the church had to defend the teaching office of the hierarchy, the sense of the faithful faded into the background but was never denied. In the nineteenth century, Johann Adam Möhler, Giovanni Perrone, and John Henry Newman focused on the *sensus fidei* and the ability of all believers to know divine truth, but then Vatican I and the theological climate up to Vatican II solidified the distinction between the teaching church and the learning church. Popes exercised active infallibility by defining doctrine, whereas the rest of the church exercised passive infallibility by receiving magisterial teaching. For a detailed historical study, see Daniel Finucane, *Sensus Fidelium: The Use of a Concept in the Post-Vatican II Era* (Bethesda, MD: International Scholars Publications, 1996), especially chaps. 2-3. In addition, John Burkhard offers a brief but thorough historical survey in his article "*Sensus Fidei*: Meaning, Role and Future of a Teaching of Vatican II," *Louvain Studies* 17 (1992): 18-34.

⁹Leo Scheffczyk, "*Sensus Fidelium*—Witness on the Part of the Community," trans. Charlotte C. Prather, *Communio* 15 (1988): 182-98 at 184.

¹⁰Richard R. Gaillardetz, "The Ecclesiological Foundations of Modern Catholic Social Teaching," in *Modern Catholic Social Teaching: Commentaries and Interpretations*, ed. Kenneth R. Himes (Washington, D.C.: Georgetown University Press, 2005), 72-98 at 81.

¹¹Vatican II particularly emphasizes the *sensus fidei* though it also affirms the realities of the *sensus* and *consensus fidelium*. See *Lumen Gentium* 12.

¹²All references to the conciliar documents are from Austin Flannery, ed.,

Vatican Council II: Volume 1, The Conciliar and Post Conciliar Documents, new rev. ed. (New York: Costello Publishing Company, 1998).

[13]Gaillardetz, "The Ecclesiological Foundations of Modern Catholic Social Teaching," 82.

[14]Aloys Grillmeier, "Chapter II: The People of God," in *Commentary on the Documents of Vatican II,* vol. 1, ed. Herbert Vorgrimler (New York: Herder and Herder, 1967), 153-85 at 164.

[15]Francis A. Sullivan, "The Sense of Faith: The Sense/Consensus of the Faithful," in *Authority in the Roman Catholic Church,* ed. Bernard Hoose (Aldershot, UK: Ashgate Publishing Company, 2002), 85-93 at 86.

[16]Gaillardetz, "The Ecclesiological Foundations of Modern Catholic Social Teaching," 82.

[17]Ibid.

[18]The church's indefectibility and infallibility are connected with the ideas of the *sensus fidei* and *consensus fidelium* respectively. Indefectibility, which is the church's inability to fail in its mission of authentically teaching the gospel, is linked with the *sensus fidei.* The church cannot fail to authentically teach the gospel because the Holy Spirit bestows a supernatural sense of faith on believers, enabling the people of God to make right judgments about matters of belief. Infallibility, which is a charism that ensures immunity from error in the church's definitive teachings on faith and morals, is related to the *consensus fidelium.* Vatican II cites multiple ways in which the church exercises infallibility, and one of these ways is a universal consensus on a matter of belief (*LG* 12; see also Sullivan, "The Sense of Faith," 91). Like the *sensus fidei* and *consensus fidelium,* indefectibility and infallibility are closely related but distinct in meaning.

[19]Sullivan, "The Sense of Faith," 91.

[20]The original schema on the church did not discuss the church's infallibility until the ninth chapter. This view would have indicated that the infallibility of the church comes from the infallibility exercised by hierarchy. It also would have reinforced the differentiation between the teaching church and learning church. See Heinrich Fries, "Is There a Magisterium of the Faithful?" in *The Teaching Authority of All Believers* (see note 5), 82-91 at 84-85.

[21]Grillmeier, chap. 2: The People of God," in *Commentary on the Documents of Vatican II,* 164-65.

[22]John Burkhard, "*Sensus Fidei*: Theological Reflection Since Vatican II: II. 1985-1989," *Heythrop Journal* 34 (1993): 133.

[23]See also Mary E. Hines, "Voice of the Faithful Survey: An Ecclesiological Reflection," in *Voices of the Faithful: Loyal Catholics Striving for Change* (see note 2), 121-34 at 122.

[24]See William D'Antonio and Anthony Pogorelc, "VOTF as a Social Movement in the Catholic Church," in *Voices of the Faithful: Loyal Catholics Striving for Change* (see note 2), 11-33.

[25]For a thorough account of the emergence and development of VOTF, including its 2002 convention, see Muller and Kenney, *Keep the Faith, Change the Church.*

[26]Ibid., 62.

[27]Frawley-O'Dea, *Perversion of Power*, 208. See also Muller and Kenny, *Keep the Faith, Change the Church.*

[28]Hines, "Voice of the Faithful Survey," 121.

[29]William D'Antonio and Anthony Pogorelc, "VOTF Members: Who They Are and Why They Stay," in *Voices of the Faithful: Loyal Catholics Striving for Change* (see note 2), 50-66 at 51-52. For more demographic studies, see, for example, William D'Antonio and Anthony Pogorelc, "VOTF's Founding Leaders," in *Voices of the Faithful: Loyal Catholic Striving for Change* (see note 2), 34-49 and idem, "VOTF Members: Gender, Generation, and Region," in *Voices of the Faithful: Loyal Catholics Striving for Change* (see note 2), 67-90.

[30]Hines, "Voice of the Faithful Survey," 129.

[31]Ibid.

[32]For a similar perspective, see ibid., 131-32.

[33]The term "holy conversation" comes from Richard R. Gaillardetz, "Ecclesiological Perspectives on Church Reform," in *Church Ethics and Its Organizational Context: Learning from the Sex Abuse Scandal in the Catholic Church*, ed. Jean M. Bartunek, Mary Ann Hinsdale, and James F. Keenan (New York: Rowman & Littlefield Publishers, Inc., 2006), 57-68 at 66.

Catholic Identity, *Faithful Citizenship*, and the Laity

Angela Senander

Just days after the 2008 election of Barack Obama and Joe Biden as president and vice president respectively, the United States Conference of Catholic Bishops (USCCB) met in Baltimore for its November meeting. The bishops noted the historic significance of the election and the points of common ground where they hope to collaborate with the new administration.[1] They also discussed their concerns about Obama's promise to Planned Parenthood to sign the Freedom of Choice Act, declaring abortion a fundamental right, overturning all state and federal regulations and restrictions on abortion, and threatening the Catholic identity of the church's healthcare system.[2] They revisited the question of denying pro-choice Catholic politicians communion, an issue that resurfaced during the 2008 campaigns.[3]

Outside the meeting, Randall Terry, a recent Catholic convert, led a protest in which he tried to communicate directly to the bishops that "Faithful Citizenship makes unfaithful Catholics."[4] A month earlier he had been arrested for trespassing on church property at the cathedral in Arlington, Virginia, where he distributed his "Faithful Catholic Citizenship" brochures asserting that a vote for Obama is contrary to Catholic teaching.[5] His creation and distribution of this Catholic voter guide was contrary to *Forming Consciences for Faithful Citizenship*, a document of the USCCB.[6] Actions such as these have challenged the bishops, even as the bishops have called for lay political participation.

This essay was written with the support of a Theological Scholars Grant from the Association of Theological Schools.

Divisions among bishops and between bishops and lay political leaders have persisted despite the USCCB's effort to model and foster unity when it issued *Forming Consciences for Faithful Citizenship* in 2007.[7] John Allen rightly considers the continuation of the tradition of quadrennial statements on faithful citizenship an open question.[8] The removal of the faithful citizenship icon from the USCCB homepage underscores this question since the bishops emphasize in their document that faithful citizenship is not simply an obligation at election time.[9] To better understand the current situation, it is helpful to revisit the development of the USCCB's teaching on political responsibility.

Recent developments in Catholic teaching about political responsibility take seriously both the Second Vatican Council's teaching about the vocation of the laity and the influence of lay organizations in the conscience formation of Catholics for political life.[10] Among the ecclesial signs of the times shaping the development of the most recent U.S. episcopal statement on political responsibility were voter guides produced by two lay organizations, Catholic Answers and Catholics in Alliance for the Common Good.[11] While the statement expresses concern about voter guides, these same voter guides set much of the agenda for its first part, which introduces language and categories from fundamental moral theology and affirms the possibility of selective conscientious objection to voting in exceptional cases. This essay will consider three moments in the development of this U.S. Catholic episcopal teaching about political responsibility, and highlight the importance of faith formation for an increasingly literate and influential lay Catholic population in the United States.

The Origin of the U.S. Bishops' Teaching on Faithful Citizenship

The U.S. Catholic bishops issued their first statement on political responsibility a decade after *Gaudium et Spes* drew attention to political community as a "problem of special urgency" and called for "all citizens [to] be mindful of their simultaneous right and duty to vote freely in the interest of advancing the common good."[12] This first U.S. episcopal statement on political responsibility responded to a significant decline in voter participation from the early 1960s to the early 1970s, a decline attributed to "alienation, disenchantment and indifference."[13] In the face of governmental corruption, the bishops did not condone withdrawal from participation in society but rather advocated a responsible engagement to address problems: "We would urge all citizens to register to vote, to become informed on the relevant issues, to become involved in the party or campaign of their choice, to vote freely according to their consciences...."[14] The understanding of conscience from *Gaudium et Spes* is not articulated but presupposed.[15] Like *Gaudium et Spes*, the statement reflects on discipleship and the church's responsibilities in society.[16] Then the statement summarizes previous teaching on relevant issues to help inform consciences.

The statement's reflection on church begins with recognition that discipleship informs not only interpersonal relationships but also engagement with society. Jesus's evangelical mission to the poor (Lk 4:18), his commandment to love one's neighbor and his articulation of the works of mercy (Mt 25) provide the biblical foundation for the statement's insistence on the formative power of the life and teaching of Jesus, a power that is not limited to interactions between individuals but also invites the transformation of institutions and structures of society. This biblical vision informs the statement's ecclesiology: "The church, the people of God, is itself an expression of this love, and is required by the gospel and its long tradition to promote and defend human rights and human dignity."[17] The episcopal statement draws attention to the community's responsibility to promote human rights, to highlight the moral and religious aspects of issues in light of the gospel, and to offer a "comprehensive and consistent" concern for human rights and social justice, appreciating the complexity of the issues.[18] The range of issues is particularly notable in contrast to the focus on abortion in public debate that the bishops called for in their *Pastoral Plan for Pro-Life Activities* developed three months earlier.[19]

As the statement moves to episcopal teaching about public policy issues, including abortion, the economy, food, housing, education, and the military, its analyses reflect the natural law tradition with no explicit biblical or theological references.[20] In a document that is directed to all Americans, the public policy analyses are put forward in language that is considered accessible to all. While the list of issues has grown over the years, the statements on political responsibility have been marked by continuity, at least through 2003.[21]

The Congregation for the Doctrine of the Faith issued a *Doctrinal Note on Some Questions Regarding the Participation of Catholics in Political Life* just months before the 2003 statement on political responsibility came from the Administrative Board of the USCCB.[22] The following sections will examine first the reception of the *Doctrinal Note* by the U.S. episcopate, and second the reception of the *Doctrinal Note* by the Catholic presidential nominee and lay organizations producing voter guides.

Fall 2003: Faithful Citizenship, Conscience, and Communion

In September 2003, the Administrative Board of the USCCB approved its quadrennial statement on political responsibility, entitled *Faithful Citizenship: A Catholic Call to Political Responsibility*.[23] With the powerful image of a table as a place where basic needs are met, decisions are made, and the Eucharist is celebrated, the statement engages the imagination about Catholic political responsibility.[24] It highlights three assets that the Catholic community brings to the public square: a consistent ethical framework, direct service to the needy in society, and a diverse community.[25] The statement describes the role of the church and then shares seven themes of Catholic social teaching, which provide the basis for considering a broad range of issues.[26] While there are certainly references to the *Doctrinal Note*, the basic content and structure of the statement very much parallel that of the previous statements on political responsibility.

The same month the Administrative Board echoed the Congregation for the Doctrine of the Faith's insistence on the importance of a well-formed conscience in this statement, it also approved the formation of a task force on the *Doctrinal Note*. At the November 2003 meeting of the USCCB, this recently formed task force began its consultative work. Two quotes from the *Doctrinal Note* were offered to shape the discussion. First, "A well-formed Christian conscience does not permit one to vote for a political program or an individual law which contradicts the fundamental contents of faith and morals."[27] Second, "The Christian faith is an integral unity, and thus it is incoherent to isolate some particular element to the detriment of the whole of Catholic doctrine. A political commitment to a single isolated aspect of the Church's social doctrine does not exhaust one's responsibility towards the common good."[28] A few months later a pro-choice Catholic presidential nominee provided a concrete case to consider in relationship to these theoretical claims, raising the question of whether he would be denied communion when campaigning in St. Louis, the diocese of Archbishop Raymond Burke.

Shortly after the November 2003 meeting of the USCCB (and before his appointment to St. Louis), Burke, who was then bishop of La Crosse, Wisconsin, issued a notification to Catholic legislators in his diocese who supported abortion or euthanasia legislation that they were committing "a manifestly grave sin." They were not to present themselves for communion or be admitted to communion if they did present themselves.[29] Challenging this interpretation of canon 915, canonist John Beal has argued that the technical meaning of "manifest" refers to "an objectively sinful lifestyle" and is not met in the case of pro-choice politicians.[30]

Bishop Michael Sheridan of Colorado Springs took the communion controversy a step further by arguing that any Catholic *who votes for a candidate* who supports abortion, euthanasia, stem cell research, or homosexual marriage may not receive communion.[31] In so arguing, he neglected to consider the distinction between formal and material cooperation, which Cardinal Joseph Ratzinger, as Prefect for the Congregation for the Doctrine of the Faith, highlighted for the U.S. Catholic bishops.[32] The technical language of cooperation takes into account intentionality, the degree of causality between an individual's act and the evil act in which one cooperates, proportionate reasons for the individual's act, and the avoidance of scandal. Based on these distinctions, one could argue that a person opposed to laws supporting abortion could vote for a pro-choice candidate, despite the possibility that this politician might vote for abortion legislation that the constituent does not support, so long as there were proportionate reasons, knowing that secret ballot reduces the possibility of scandal.

While Burke and Sheridan received media attention, they were not representative of the U.S. bishops as a whole. The USCCB's task force interim report indicated that in a survey of bishops three out of four who responded opposed the denial of communion to pro-choice Catholic politicians.[33] Yet the concerns of Burke and Sheridan have led to continued reflection on eucharistic coherence

and, in the case of Sheridan, also the principle of material cooperation, for episcopal teaching about political responsibility.[34]

Kerry, Catholic Answers, and Catholics in Alliance for the Common Good

While the United States Conference of Catholic Bishops was
trying carefully to appropriate the *Doctrinal Note* for the U.S.
context, John Kerry seemed unaware of its teaching, and the
Catholic apologetic organization Catholic Answers seemed to
appropriate the *Doctrinal Note* in a selective way that would
support the other presidential nominee. John Kerry was the first
Catholic presidential nominee since the 1973 Supreme Court
decisions increasing legal access to abortion.[35] He was the center
of much controversy because his pro-choice voting record and
position conflicted with the teaching of *Evangelium Vitae* and
the *Doctrinal Note*. *Evangelium Vitae* recognizes legislators who
have supported abortion laws as responsible for contributing to a
culture of death, and Kerry's support of abortion laws was evident
in the 100 percent approval rating he received from the National
Abortion Rights Action League before the 2004 election.[36] The
Doctrinal Note rightly points to the inconsistency in divorcing
personal values from public life, noting that the church's teaching
about abortion is based on reasoned reflection on human nature
rather than strictly confessional beliefs that are necessarily dependent on faith.[37] Yet, this is precisely the strategy that Kerry used
during a presidential debate as he insisted that he was personally
opposed to abortion but could not impose an article of faith on
Americans.[38]

During the 2004 presidential campaigns, the lay apologetic
organization Catholic Answers distributed widely its *Voter's Guide
for Serious Catholics*.[39] This guide appropriates aspects of the
Doctrinal Note but in a selective way that does not do justice to
it. The *Doctrinal Note* makes reference to "non-negotiable ethical
principles,"[40] but in the voter's guide "non-negotiable" describes
not only principles and values but also issues. These issues are
further modified by the category of intrinsic evil, resulting in five
"non-negotiable issues:" abortion, euthanasia, embryonic stem-
cell research, cloning and homosexual marriage. Both the description and the length of the list differ from the *Doctrinal Note*. This

is a much shorter list than the one provided by Ratzinger as he identifies cases in which laws might compromise "fundamental and inalienable ethical demands." Ratzinger's list highlights abortion, euthanasia, rights of the embryo, family, education, protection of minors, modern forms of slavery, religious freedom, the economy and peace.[41] The Catholic Answers *Voter's Guide* neglects the vast corpus of Catholic social teaching, and it fails to convey Catholic teaching as a challenge to all political parties in the United States, as the episcopal statements on political responsibility have done.

While the *Voter's Guide for Serious Catholics* claims to be concerned about conscience formation, it fails to reflect the richness of the tradition on conscience and its formation. The only resource that the guide identifies for conscience formation is magisterial teaching. Based on the proposition that a well-formed conscience cannot differ from Catholic teaching, it advises those whose consciences are uncertain to simply follow magisterial teaching. In so doing it fails to take seriously the following statement from the *Doctrinal Note*: "Nor can a Catholic think of delegating his Christian responsibility to others."[42] Magisterial teaching certainly has an important role to play in conscience formation, but it is not a substitute for conscience formation.

The *Voter's Guide for Serious Catholics* also introduces the possibility of selective conscientious objection to voting for candidates. This goes beyond the *Doctrinal Note*, which focuses on the impermissibility of legislators voting for laws that are contrary to morality.[43] Concerned about indirect support of such laws, the guide recognizes that each candidate might support such laws, and suggests two possible courses of action: "In such a case you may vote for the candidate who takes the fewest such positions or who seems least likely to be able to advance immoral legislation, or you may choose to vote for no one." While recognizing the duty to vote articulated in church teaching, this lay organization introduces an exception to this duty.

During the 2006 midterm elections, Catholics in Alliance for the Common Good offered an alternative voter's guide: *Voting for the Common Good: A Practical Guide for Conscientious Catholics.*[44] This guide expanded the sources involved in conscience formation to include prayer.[45] It highlighted the virtue of prudence for determining how best to exercise one's responsibility for the common good of society.[46] To learn about Catholic positions and inform one's conscience for voting, it refers Catholics to *Faithful Citizenship*, the bishops' statement on political responsibility that was unacknowledged by Catholic Answers.[47] These developments from 2003 to 2006 led to a dramatic revision of the first third of the 2007 episcopal statement on political responsibility.

Innovation of a Tradition?

If the 1976 statement presupposed conscience and focused on the mission of the church, the 2007 statement presupposes the church's mission and focuses on conscience. A comparison of the titles of the two documents accurately reflects the change in emphasis. In 1976 the Administrative Board wrote "The Church's Role in the '76 Election," whereas in 2007 the full body of the United States Conference of Catholic Bishops approved *Forming Consciences for Faithful Citizenship: A Call to Political Responsibility from the Catholic Bishops of the United States*. The near unanimity with which the latter statement was approved reflects the bishops' efforts to promote ecclesial unity after the experience of divisions in recent years.

In light of the concern about conscience formation in the *Doctrinal Note* and inadequate presentations about conscience in pastoral letters from diocesan bishops and lay voter guides, the most recent statement on political responsibility explicitly reflects on the meaning of a well-formed conscience. It recognizes the role of reason, prayer, scripture, and church teaching in conscience formation.[48] Sharing Catholic Answers's emphasis on the catechism, a bishop amended the draft to narrow the scope of teaching by adding "as contained in the *Catechism of the Catholic Church*."[49] While the words narrow the range of sources of magisterial teaching to consult, the bishops' own example models a broader approach inasmuch as they quote *Deus Caritas Est*, an encyclical written after the catechism, and provide a long list of statements from their own episcopal conference as resources.

At the beginning of their statement on conscience formation the bishops indicate that they are "maintaining continuity with what we have said in the past in light of new challenges facing our nation and world. This is not new teaching but affirms what is taught by our Bishops' Conference and the whole Church."[50]

This is an important hermeneutical principle for reading the statement's description of conscience. *Forming Consciences for Faithful Citizenship* describes conscience in the following way: "[C]onscience is the voice of God resounding in the human heart, revealing the truth to us and calling us to do what is good while shunning what is evil."[51] This appears to be an unfortunate paraphrase of *Gaudium et Spes* no. 16, which states: "Conscience is the most secret core and sanctuary of a man. There he is alone with God, whose voice echoes in his depths."[52] *Gaudium et Spes* does not identify conscience with the voice of God as the statement on political responsibility does. This is significant because an identification of conscience with the voice of God calls into question both the purpose of conscience formation and the possibility of an erroneous conscience. In order to support the purpose of *Forming Consciences for Faithful Citizenship* and its own stated intention not to introduce new teaching, it is important to retrieve the teaching of the bishops of the Second Vatican Council on conscience.

The debates about the legitimacy of cooperation that arose during the communion controversy, the use of the category of intrinsic evil for identifying issues in one voter guide, and the use of the virtue of prudence in another shaped the bishops' extended reflection on fundamental moral theology. The statement warns against making no ethical distinctions, on the one hand, and using ethical distinctions as a way of avoiding responsibility, on the other.[53] Articulating the possibility of selective conscientious objection to voting for candidates under exceptional circumstances, *Forming Consciences for Faithful Citizenship* states:

> When all candidates hold a position in favor of an intrinsic evil, the conscientious voter faces a dilemma. The voter may decide to take the extraordinary step of not voting for any candidate or, after careful deliberation, may decide to vote for the candidate deemed less likely to advance such a morally flawed position and more likely to pursue other authentic human goods.[54]

In terms of both structure and content, the statement on political responsibility attempts to respond to ecclesial needs in new ways.

Conclusion

In 1976, the first statement on political responsibility highlighted the compatibility between discipleship and citizenship,
as it encouraged all Americans including Catholics to vote. In
2007, the bishops recognized the potential conflict between discipleship and citizenship that a voter could encounter. In such a
situation, they recognize that a disciple's responsibilities as citizen
might lead to legitimate material cooperation, or that a citizen's
responsibilities as disciple might prevent one from voting when
all candidates support an intrinsic evil. A rich understanding of
conscience from *Gaudium et Spes* 16 will be essential for proper
discernment in such a situation. Arguably, the most significant
new contribution resulting from *Forming Consciences for Faithful Citizenship* is an on-line resource to accompany the statement
which introduces people to methods of prayer that inform political
participation.[55]

A Catholic identity of discipleship requires a deep prayer life.
This prayer life can be informed by the example of communal
prayer before Catholic Common Ground Initiative dialogues
about polarizing issues, the recognition of prayer as essential to
conscience formation by Catholics in Alliance for the Common
Good, and the nine methods of individual prayer about the needs
of our world on the USCCB's Faithful Citizenship website. Some
of the methods on the website begin with a social issue, encouraging intercessory prayer for those affected by the issue and asking
God's guidance in responding to the issue. Others begin with
the parables or the prophets and let God's word speak, engaging
the imagination. Still others focus on activities, such as serving,
journaling, and listening, as opportunities to engage in conversation with God. These methods invite an engagement with God
in which one grows in love of God and neighbor. This prayer life
bears fruit in charity toward others as the disciple becomes more
Christ-like.

This formation takes place in a community of faith that is a
sacrament of Christ. The tradition of this community is a source
of God's revelation, which explains both the concerns over interpretations of the tradition and the need for a deep knowledge of
the tradition. There is a danger in appropriating concepts from

the tradition in a superficial way that does not do justice to the tradition, whether the concept is conscience or intrinsic evil. There is also a danger of mistaking a part for the whole when a narrow range of issues is used as the criteria of Catholic identity. In political life, sharing the tradition in a meaningful way fosters a deeper appropriation of Catholic identity by the laity.

Notes

[1] Francis Cardinal George, *Plenary Session Address*, November 10, 2008; available at http://usccb.org/meetings/2008Fall/address_george_plenary.shtml [accessed November 29, 2008], and *Statement of the President of the United States Conference of Catholic Bishops*, November 12, 2008; available at http://usccb.org/comm/archives/2008/08-174.shtml [accessed November 29, 2008].

[2] *Statement of the President of the United States Conference of Catholic Bishops*.

[3] John Allen, "USCCB: No Retreat on Abortion, But No New Communion Ban," John L. Allen Jr. Daily's Blog on NCRCafe.org, November 11, 2008; available at http://ncrcafe.org/node/2272 [accessed December 3, 2008].

[4] "Pro-lifers Prophecy at USCCB"; available at http://video.aol.com/video-detail/pro-lifers-prophecy-at-usccb/2305843011944910595 [accessed November 30, 2008].

[5] Michael Humphrey, "Catholic Vote: Group Targets Parishes with Anti-Obama Flier," *National Catholic Reporter,* October 31, 2008; available at http://ncronline3.org/drupal/?q=node/2285 [accessed November 30, 2008].

[6] USCCB, *Forming Consciences for Faithful Citizenship: A Call to Political Responsibility from the Catholic Bishops of the United States*, 2007, nos. 8 and 15; available at http://www.usccb.org/faithfulcitizenship [accessed July 1, 2008].

[7] See, for example, Steve McConnell, "Bishop Stresses Abortion View at Political Forum," *Wayne Independent,* October 20, 2008; available at http://www.wayneindependent.com/news/x270972980/Bishop-stresses-abortion-view-at-political-forum [accessed December 3, 2008].

[8] John Allen, "USCCB: It Ain't Easy Being a Bishop, Especially after the '08 Elections," *National Catholic Reporter,* November 9, 2008; available at http://ncrcafe.org [accessed November 29, 2008].

[9] The faithful citizenship icon of flag and cross had appeared in the left column of the USCCB homepage (http://www.usccb.org) and functioned as a link to http://www.faithfulcitizenship.org, the bishops' website dedicated to sharing their teaching through a variety of resources created for different constituencies [accessed November 29, 2008]. The bishops teach that political participation goes beyond casting a ballot, and to demonstrate that point it would have been wise to maintain the link from their homepage. For this teaching, see USCCB, *Forming Consciences for Faithful Citizenship*, no. 7.

[10] Second Vatican Council, *Gaudium et Spes*, no. 43, in *Catholic Social*

Thought: The Documentary Heritage, ed. David J. O'Brien and Thomas A. Shannon (Maryknoll, NY: Orbis Books, 1992).

[11]USCCB, *Forming Consciences for Faithful Citizenship;* Catholics in Alliance for the Common Good, *Voting for the Common Good: A Practical Guide for Conscientious Catholics;* available at http://www.catholicsinalliance.org/files/Voting-for-the-Common-Good.pdf [accessed July 1, 2008].

[12]*Gaudium et Spes,* title of Part II (between nos. 45 and 46) and no. 75.

[13]Administrative Board of the U.S. Catholic Conference, "The Church's Role in the '76 Elections," *Origins* 5 (February 26, 1976): 567.

[14]Ibid.

[15]*Gaudium et Spes,* no. 16.

[16]Ibid., nos. 1, 43.

[17]Administrative Board of the U.S. Catholic Conference, "The Church's Role in the '76 Elections," 567.

[18]Ibid., 567-68.

[19]National Conference of Catholic Bishops, "Pastoral Plan for Pro-Life Activities," *Origins* 5 (December 4, 1975): 372.

[20]Administrative Board of the U.S. Catholic Conference, "The Church's Role in the '76 Elections," 569-70.

[21]This conclusion is the result of a line by line comparison of the U.S. Catholic bishops' documents on political responsibility.

[22]Congregation for the Doctrine of the Faith, *"Doctrinal Note on Some Questions Regarding the Participation of Catholics in Political Life,* 2002; available at http://www.vatican.va/roman_curia/congregations/cfaith/documents/rc_con_cfaith_doc_20021124_politica_en.html [accessed April 20, 2008]; henceforth referred to as *Doctrinal Note.*

[23]Administrative Committee of the United States Conference of Catholic Bishops, "Faithful Citizenship: A Catholic Call to Political Responsibility," *Origins* 33 (October 23, 2003): 321, 323-30.

[24]Ibid., 323.

[25]Ibid., 324-25.

[26]Ibid., 325-30.

[27]John Ricard, "Task Force Report on the Church and Catholic Political Leaders," *Origins* 33 (November 20, 2003): 416.

[28]Ibid., 416-17.

[29]Raymond Burke, "Catholics and Political Responsibility," *Origins* 33 (January 29, 2004): 557, 559. For an explanation of his position, see his articles "Prophecy for Justice: Catholic Politicians and Bishops," *America,* June 21, 2004, 11-15, and "Canon 915: The Discipline Regarding the Denial of Holy Communion to Those Obstinately Persevering in Manifestly Grave Sin," *Periodica De Re Canonica* 96 (2007): 3-58.

[30]John Beal, "Holy Communion and Unholy Politics," *America,* June 21, 2004, 16-18.

[31]Michael Sheridan, "The Duties of Catholic Politicians and Voters," *Origins* (May 20, 2004): 6.

[32]"Ratzinger Advises U.S. Bishops on Principles for Denying Communion and Voting," *America,* July 19, 2004, 4.

[33]William Cardinal Keeler, "Summary of Consultations from Interim

Reflections of the Task Force on Catholic Bishops and Catholic Politicians," *Origins* 34 (July 1, 2004): 106.

[34]To follow the episcopal conversation on eucharistic coherence and political life, see the following: Synod of Bishops (2005), "Overview of the Synod's Propositions," *Origins* 35 (November 3, 2005): 348; Cardinal Theodore McCarrick, "Final Report: Bishops and Catholic Politicians," *Origins* 36 (June 29, 2006): 97, 99-100. United States Conference of Catholic Bishops, "'Happy Are Those Who Are Called to His Supper': On Preparing to Receive Christ Worthily in the Eucharist," *Origins* 36 (November 30, 2006): 393.

[35]In 1973 the Supreme Court ruled in *Roe v. Wade* that a restrictive abortion law was unconstitutional on the basis of a woman's right to privacy. This decision allowed no regulation of abortion during the first trimester, regulation only to protect the health of the pregnant woman during the second trimester, and the possibility of regulation to protect a viable fetus unless this affected the life or health of the pregnant woman during the third trimester. The companion case, *Doe v. Bolton*, found Georgia's reformed abortion law unconstitutional. Based on this decision's broad definition of health, the fetus receives no protection at any point during pregnancy. See *Roe v. Wade* 410 U.S. 113 (1973) and *Doe v. Bolton* 410 U.S. 179 (1973).

[36]John Paul II, *Evangelium Vitae*, 1995, no. 59; available at http://www. vatican.va/ encyclicals [accessed April 20, 2008].

[37]Congregation for the Doctrine of the Faith, *Doctrinal Note*, no. 5.

[38]See the transcript of "The Third Bush-Kerry Debate," October 13, 2004; available at http://www.debates.org/pages/trans2004d.html [accessed December 3, 2008].

[39]Catholic Answers, *Voter's Guide for Serious Catholics*.

[40]Congregation for the Doctrine of the Faith, *Doctrinal Note*, no. 3.

[41]Ibid., no. 4.

[42]Ibid.

[43]Ibid.

[44]Catholics in Alliance for the Common Good, *Voting for the Common Good*.

[45]Ibid., 4.

[46]Ibid., 5.

[47]Ibid., 8.

[48]USCCB, *Forming Consciences for Faithful Citizenship*, no. 17, identifies the role of reason and magisterial teaching in conscience formation. Scripture and prayer are added to the list in no. 18.

[49]Compare the draft provided to the media with the approved statement.

[50]USCCB, *Forming Consciences for Faithful Citizenship*, no. 3.

[51]Ibid., no. 17.

[52]*Gaudium et Spes*, no. 16.

[53]USCCB, *Forming Consciences for Faithful Citizenship*, nos. 28 and 29.

[54]Ibid., no. 36.

[55]USCCB, *New Ways to Pray*; available at http://www.faithfulcitizenship. org/youth/deeper/pray [accessed July 1, 2008].

"Save Our Church!"

Resistance to Parish Restructuring as Practical Ecclesiology

William A. Clark

In May 2004, after months of increasingly contentious discussions and anxious waiting, the Archdiocese of Boston finally announced the names of over sixty parishes, around a fifth of its total number, that would be closed during the following year. The parishes named were located throughout the archdiocese, in inner-city neighborhoods and in affluent suburbs, some dating from the nineteenth century, others only a few decades old.[1] In some of the affected parishes there were resigned sighs, as what had come to be seen as the inevitable end of a long process of decline finally came to pass. And in many parishes there were stories of what the parishes had meant to their members over the years or even generations; there were sad farewells, and lots of tears—tears of grief, certainly, but also of anger at the loss of something held dear. In these parishes, too, there was resignation, the sense that however right or wrong the decision, nothing could be done to change it.

In a few cases, however, the tears of anger were accompanied by voices of protest and ultimately by acts of resistance, up to and including the occupation of church buildings in desperate attempts to prevent the closures. Today, four years after the initial announcements, five Boston churches remain occupied, twenty-four hours a day, by lay members of the former parish communities. Although a panel of the Apostolic Signatura in the Vatican has recently ruled against the canonical appeals filed by some of the protesting lay groups,[2] and so has clearly signaled what the official verdict on this resistance will be, still pending is the final appeal to the full Signatura, as well as final rulings in a variety of civil suits (preliminary rulings that have not been favorable for the resisters). The resisters have made it clear that they will push their cases to the final possible legal appeals, both canonical and civil.[3] Meanwhile, in the wake of increasing clergy shortages and financial shortfalls, rumors abound of another round of closure announcements.[4]

The case of the Archdiocese of Boston is admittedly the most dramatic and difficult example of parish restructuring in the U.S. Catholic Church in recent years. It came directly on the heels of the first large-scale settlement of sexual abuse cases,[5] in what had come to be acknowledged as the epicenter of the abuse crisis. The wholesale restructuring was carried out quickly, with what most people experienced as a very short and restricted process of public consultation. Parish representatives—not chosen by any uniform or necessarily open process—met by geographical "clusters" (which in many cases included communities not previously used to cooperating with each other) and were told simply and bluntly to decide which one or two parishes in their cluster should be recommended for closure. Once the recommendations were vetted by diocesan officials, parishes that a few months previously would have been on no one's "endangered" list outside of the chancery heard their suppressions decreed.

All this took place amidst the still-raw wounds of the abuse crisis, the resignation of the previous cardinal archbishop, and the birth of the lay reform group Voice of the Faithful. Under these circumstances resistance of some sort is hardly surprising. Nonetheless, even if the circumstances are acknowledged as exceptional, the fact remains that, on a smaller scale, resistance to similarly comprehensive diocesan plans for restructuring has occurred in a variety of other places in the country, and a national network of resisters, through such organizations as Boston's "Council of Parishes," has begun to grow.[6] Though by no means evenly distributed or uniformly practiced across the country, the phenomenon of resistance to parish restructuring is a significant "sign of the times" in the U.S. church today.

As a sign, the resistance can be read through various lenses, including Catholic and American history, politics, and culture, as well as those provided by each of the other social sciences. For a variety of reasons, on the other hand, discussion of the phenomenon to date has not included much attention to its theological aspects. In part, this is due to the fact that much of the reporting and commentary that has been attempted has taken place in the secular media. Lay persons directly involved in the resistance have not, by and large, included trained theologians (although there are certainly exceptions to this general trend). Church officials, apart from employing a few stock popular phrases with an ecclesiological ring (such as, "the church is the people, not the buildings") have generally approached the whole issue as a management problem rather than a theological one. Much can and should be learned from the ecclesiological assumptions of those who have planned the restructuring, and of those parishioners who have willingly cooperated with the planners. This essay, however, will focus on those who have resisted the restructuring and, more specifically, discuss whether the resistance itself might be a form of practical theological activity.

The Nature of Practical Theology

Practical theology was presented in the first half of the nineteenth century by the German Protestant thinker Friedrich Schleiermacher as what he called "the crown of theology," in which the various theological sciences attained their ultimate purpose in directing the ministerial life of the church. However, practical theology never really attained this "crowning" status, but instead came to be seen as a largely technical pursuit focused on the skills of professional ministry that barely retained its credentials as a genuine academic discipline. In recent decades, both Don Browning[7] and Alistair Campbell[8] have examined the reasons for this failure. Chief among them, they claim, were Schleiermacher's own conception of the discipline as deductive from the formal study of scripture and doctrine, and his explicit linking of it to the formal membership of the church. These features ensured that practical theology would generally be conceived merely as an application of academic theology to an increasingly narrow field of human activity.

Retrieval of a conception of practical theology as an intellectually rigorous discipline deserving of a place with, and capable of influencing, the more traditional branches of theological study, had to await the emergence of more inductive methods across the theological spectrum in the last half of the twentieth century. Numerous theological methods and approaches since that time have contributed to the possibility of what Browning has called a *fundamental* practical theology.[9] These include such varied enterprises as clinical pastoral education and community-based learning on the pedagogical side, and on the side of research, engaged scholarship, liberation theology, political theology, Christology and ecclesiology from below, and countless types of contextual theologies. The particular contributions of each of these approaches could be profitably traced, but more important for the present article are the characteristics of the rich concept of practical theology toward which they all point. In the brief synthesis that follows, my primary guides are Browning's *A Fundamental Practical Theology*, Stephen Bevans's *Models of Contextual Theology* (particularly the chapter called "The Praxis Model"),[10] and the excellent essays collected in James Woodward and Stephen Pattison's *Blackwell Reader in Pastoral and Practical Theology*, in particular those essays by Alistair Campbell, Elaine Graham,[11] and Edward Farley.[12] All of these authors draw deeply on foundational philosophical and theological work by such figures as Hans-Georg Gadamer, Jürgen Habermas, Johann Baptist Metz, David Tracy, and others.

From an academic point of view, the most notable thing about practical theology may be its *engagement* with the situation of the church and the world. This is not an intellectual pursuit that can afford to pretend that it is somehow "objective" and independent of either the object of its study or the subjectivity of its scholars.[13] Practical theology, in fact, seeks to be "transformational," write Pattison and Woodward, in that "both in terms of process and outcome it aims to make a difference to people, understandings, and situations in the contemporary world."[14] It must therefore be highly responsive to particular circumstances. It thereby resists the impulse toward systematization, preferring instead a continual open-endedness toward the changing circumstances of concrete living within a theological tradition. A meaningful and influential connection of this approach to more traditionally rigorous theological pursuits relies on development of the idea, by philosophers such as Gadamer and many others, that theory and practice are not two separate enterprises, the latter illuminated by the application of the former, but in fact depend on and determine each other in essential ways. Christian practice is already "theory laden," to use Browning's phrase,[15] and what is not yet articulated inevitably shapes previously articulated doctrine and theology. For this reason, practical theology does not focus merely on the analysis and evaluation of the theological tradition itself, but equally on the understanding of the contemporary situation of the community that maintains and is challenged by that tradition.

The method of practical theology, therefore, like the contextual methods of various other types of contemporary theology, correlates elements of the tradition and of the present cultural situation. It begins in a descriptive mode that analyzes the context of a particular question and the community within which it is raised—what Edward Farley calls "the situation"—which is further broken down into components such as characteristic features, history, setting within larger contexts, and demands made by those contexts.[16] Such an analysis will inevitably shape the initial question and raise new ones as familiar modes of understanding and explaining are put in dialogue with the changing features of a new situation. Practical theology is therefore required to be critical and self-critical, as the origins and limitations of every previous approach are brought to light in the face of the dynamic needs of the community. Following methodologies of this type, practical theologians are invited to become the "reflective practitioners" of Christian tradition.

Browning draws this descriptive phrase from the title of the 1983 book, *The Reflective Practitioner: How Professionals Think in Action*, by Donald Schön.[17] If we are to extend this image into the realm of practical theology, however, who should "count" as a "professional Christian"? Some help on this point comes from practical and pastoral theologian Elaine Graham, who writes that "the proper object of the discipline is ... the *practice of intentional communities.*"[18] The question before us here is a variation of Graham's definition: Could the resisters to parish restructuring— "practitioners" of Christian action within communities that they have deliberately and publicly chosen to sustain—themselves be legitimately understood as both the objects *and* the subjects of the discipline of practical theology? Under what circumstances might they be so understood? If in fact they are understood as engaged in genuine practical theology, what does their engagement bring to

our understanding of this discipline, and indeed to our understanding of the church itself? I have encountered such questions over
and over again while following developments among resisters in
the Archdiocese of Boston, both in the public media and through
personal contacts, including ongoing correspondence and dozens
of observations, interviews, and focus groups.

Public Resistance in Boston

Effective public resistance to the wave of parish restructurings
has taken a variety of forms, including forms not always as blunt
as the physical occupation of church buildings. In many parishes,
staff members and ordinary church-goers gathered on the day appointed for announcing the closure decisions in order to pray and
support one another as they waited to learn of their communal
fate. Immediately after the announcements, with at least some
time left to react (since closures were staggered over three, six,
and twelve months), Save Our Parish committees were formed in
a number of places. The lay group Voice of the Faithful, having
gathered first as a locus for lay dissatisfaction with the hierarchy's
treatment of the abuse crisis, began through its Boston affiliate to
bring together representatives of the affected parishes to strategize.
Concerned lay people began to educate themselves on the theology,
canon and civil law, and church politics necessary to comprehend
what was happening. They discussed public relations and organizing tactics. They planned and held a media day at which several
parishes were represented at booths with displays, brochures,
petitions, and ardent supporters. Out of these early meetings and
activities grew a new organization that came to be known as the
Council of Parishes, taking as its mission the coordination and
support of efforts on behalf of threatened parishes.

As the time drew near for the first official closures to take
place, the activities grew more radical. Groups began to publicly
confront chancery officials and the new archbishop. Civil lawyers
among the resisters began preparing suits challenging the archdiocese's assumption of unrestricted rights over parish property.
Canon lawyers were engaged to prepare canonical appeals of the
suppression decrees. State and town officials—some of whom
were themselves members of threatened parishes—were drawn
into the discussion based on the potential public impact of the

closures, the loss of community services, and the sale of properties.[19] It was the ultimate move of several groups, however, that attracted the most attention: parishioners who ran out of time for all these other activities and found themselves sitting in the "final Mass" of their parish simply refused to leave. In the face of understandable reluctance on the part of the archdiocese in most cases to remove the squatters forcefully (particularly with appeals and civil suits pending), the strategy moved from a spontaneous event to a carefully planned one, and as many as a dozen parishes ultimately held what came to be called a "vigil." Four years after the initial events that sparked them, at least some of these "24/7" occupations are still in progress.

Whatever form their actions have taken, the resisters have generally seen themselves, at least initially, as simply asking for their fair say in managerial decisions that affect their parish, to which they claim a right by reason of their various competencies and their history of involvement and financial support. They were not, they believed, demanding any doctrinal or theological authority in the church. Such early disclaimers, however, may already have proven a bit too modest. Effective resistance is not done alone: it has virtually always resulted in the more or less spontaneous creation of new forms of communities of believers.

These communities of resistance have found the cooperation necessary to sustain a 'round-the-clock presence in their churches, in several cases for years. Far from merely clinging to a physical location, they have also worked hard to sustain the basic functions of a Christian community, maintaining group worship, education, and community outreach. Such communities are new because they draw together certain parishioners—by no means all—with a different and more focused purpose than those same parishioners have had previously. The new mission requires different kinds of organization and alters relationships with an array of other communities and sub-communities, from the clergy to the surrounding secular community to non-resisting fellow parishioners. Such changes present enormous challenges, but when experienced by spiritually aware people they also open new perspectives for understanding themselves and their relationship with God. The result has often been a community that, while organically and fiercely linked to the previous parish community that it intended to defend, possesses a clearer and more urgent sense of its own identity than the broader parish community ever had in recent memory. The creation of such a distinctive form of community, and by members who make it clear again and again that they consider themselves faithful Catholics, surely carries ecclesiological and not just managerial consequences. It also demonstrates in a variety of ways the analytical, dialogical, and critical functions of practical theology mentioned earlier.

The Nature of Boston's Resistance Communities

These communities of resistance, by virtue of their determination to save their particular parishes from closure, offer an attention to the *localness* of church—its essential tie to place and to relationships—that is often missed by officials of what is usually called the "local church"—the church at the diocesan level. This is demonstrated in the Boston case by the very contrast between the restructuring plans and the resistance to them. On the one hand stands the sweeping and ultimately bureaucratic nature of the chancery procedures: the input of cluster representatives was limited to a response to a question posed by the planners, and the final decisions were sent to the parishes by FedEx from the chancery on the date and time chosen by them for the entire archdiocese. On the other hand is the resisters' stubborn and energetic focus on their shared history, networks of relationship, and knowledge of neighborhood society and local politics; this made possible such tactics as the enlistment of local politicians and city planners in the fight to block archdiocesan plans. While archdiocesan officials have continually called on the people to think first of the good and continued strength of an archdiocese that includes five counties, two million members, and three hundred parishes, resisters have focused instead on the church evoked by recognizable faces, familiar names, retold stories, and neighborhood organizing efforts.

There is certainly great potential for such an intense local focus to produce isolation and short-sightedness. Many official pronouncements on the resistance, including the recent negative ruling of the Apostolic Signatura panel, cite this "parochialism" specifically as a reason for rejecting the parishioners' appeals.[20] Yet, paradoxically, there is also potential for the resisting communities to be *less* narrowly circumscribed than their diocesan counterparts, given their frequently very detailed concern for the whole social context of the parish. For example, one resisting community consisted of members from several different ethnic groups historically associated with the parish; they have a wide variety of understandings of the church from "traditional" to "progressive" and a correspondingly wide range of motivations for resisting the closure plans. Nonetheless, they succeeded in building not only a strong "inner core" of organizers, but also an impressively large group of followers and ultimately a neighborhood coalition that went far beyond the church membership, and they managed to pass town zoning ordinances that attempted to limit the archdiocese's ability to market the parish's real estate.[21]

In other cases, such as in those of recent immigrants, resistance groups have been more homogeneous and aloof both from internal church politics and external neighborhood organizing. Nonetheless, they have utilized their communities' strong cultural cohesion, shared self-understanding, and networks of related communities to find ways of surviving changes they could not control. There was, for example, a Vietnamese community that had been gathering for many years in one of the parishes subsequently slated for closure. Although not many of them joined actively in the resistance campaign organized by "Anglo" members of the parish, Vietnamese members were heard to comment more than once on their astonishment at finding that, in the U.S. as well as in Vietnam, churches were arbitrarily closed by the authorities! The resistance of such groups often seems more passive, but to understand it as support for restructuring is a frequently made mistake. Like other underestimations of the resistance, it results from a too narrow view of the meaning of church community and of its relationship to the other foundational structures of people's lives.

The resistance communities have been what Robert Bellah or Johann Baptist Metz might call "communities of memory."[22] One of the most striking features of most of the communities' gatherings, and of the cases they make for rejecting the restructuring plans, is the prominence of *story* in their discourse. They carefully recount the founding of their parishes. They recall family narratives centering on the church that may go back generations. They tell about personally memorable events, beloved former pastors, and previous struggles for survival, growth, or redefinition. They also appeal to what seems to them to be "common sense"—for example, why should a church offering active and successful social programs to a large needy population be sacrificed in favor of a seemingly more traditional and less dynamic parish? Slowly, however, they begin to realize that their reasoning about such matters is based on a communal experience that the decision-makers have not necessarily shared. Their common treasury also includes, of course, those shared values, beliefs, and practices that bind them to the Catholic tradition in the first place. Under the new circumstances in which the resistance communities live, though, these traditional practices have sometimes had to undergo some communal development. Thus, consecrated hosts for a well-attended Sunday communion service at one occupied church are supplied by an anonymous priest or priests referred to with a grin as "Deep Chalice." Yet in all of this there is a palpable recognition that the wider Catholic culture and tradition, even when locally preserved in what might seem rather unorthodox ways, is an absolutely essential part of the identity the groups are struggling to preserve.

The resistance communities, clearly, do not merely preserve memories and traditional values. They are also *interpretive* communities, dealing with a wide variety of what might be called "contemporary texts" in addition to Catholic Christian doctrine and practice. Their relationship to American civic values and expectations is quite obvious in the methods and style with which they have pursued their cause, which includes everything from public rallies to civil lawsuits as well as an approach to canon law that often seems to treat it as a rather less efficient Roman means to very American ends. (In addition to the suppression appeals, the ultimate failure of which is almost certainly guaranteed by the recent ruling already referred to, much earlier in the struggle there was also a well-publicized Vatican ruling against the archdiocese's handling of the assets of the suppressed parishes.[23]) As both observers of and participants in contemporary shifts in American communal culture, the resisters look for ways of preserving individualist goals and community support alike. Witnesses to increased cultural pressure on the very notion of religious commitment, they worry about how to pass on to their skeptical children the faith practice that has been a key part of their own identities. Partakers in the paradoxical cultural longing for spiritual depth, they cling to what has been helpful in the past and marvel at what they have discovered even in their very acts of resistance and community-building.

Their experience with all these dimensions and more gives resisting parishioners new perspectives on the tradition that they are defending in such unusual ways, and it raises questions that were not on their horizons before the restructuring was announced. To deal with these questions, many of the resisters have become voracious readers and scanners of internet and news media on questions both church-political and directly theological. They seek resources for better understanding from experts in history, canon law, ecclesiology, social ethics, and other fields. They listen avidly to what is offered, but are always ready to question the relevance and application of received wisdom to their own situation. In all of this, communities of resistance are continually fashioning a new self-description and understanding. This activity is *not* "objective" in the usual modern academic sense, but is becoming more and more informed and constructive—in a word, "engaged."

Is it too much to say that these diverse groups of lay persons, most without any formal theological education, are engaged in a process of practical theology that can teach and raise important questions for professional theologians, and the church at large? Of course, there are important obstacles to the theological enterprise that not every resistance group has succeeded in regularly overcoming, but the question is not misplaced—so long as it is asked sincerely and in each particular situation—if it asks whether the resisters seek a new synthesis or, rather, simply an opportunity to demonstrate unflinching loyalty to local custom. This is the question of whether what is called "tradition" is a living, developing thing or merely a snapshot from the past. How one is likely to read the evidence on this question depends a lot on how one focuses on a particular group, issue, and time. It is also worth wondering whether a "mythos of resistance" is developing in some quarters—a pride, energy, and identity drawn from the simple fact that organized resistance has been able to endure so long. Such a sensibility could cause people subtly to begin to value the very impasse they face with diocesan officials, and so become just as much an obstacle to effective Christian praxis as the narrow bureaucratic vision of some chanceries.

Despite such potential limitations on their theological freedom, communities of resistance have been forced to respond to a new situation for their faith, and have often been able to create and sustain dialogues with others where no dialogue was previously encouraged. Previously so deeply and unreflectively embedded in the church's structure that they were unable to examine it, they have been jolted into reflection by a sudden loss of this "embeddedness." Their new habit of reflection has begun in many cases to produce a vision of church that suggests that its authors are bearers and interpreters of much of the rich practical wisdom (and so also a measure of the authority) of the church itself. Even when they are unable to see the wider context from which their own actions spring and to which they contribute, communities of resistance are providing new questions for professional theologians, for other communities, and for the church as a whole.

One of the first sources of such fruitful questioning has been the groups' own astonishment at the vitality revealed by their actions of resistance. Measures of "success" in this regard should not focus so much on reversing a closure decision that they miss other indicators of vibrant Christian community that accompany many of the resistance communities. The numbers of people responding to appeals for help, the variety of concerns and talents that they represent, and the complexity of the efforts that groups have undertaken have in themselves raised a new series of reflective questions within the communities: What are the values that have called us together? Where did these values originate? Are we truly supporting them—and how—in this entirely new setting? If *this* also—and not merely what we used to experience in the parish—is church, then what exactly *is* "church"? Unexpectedly creating a new form of parish community, the resistance groups have found themselves reflecting on ecclesiology without ever having planned to do so.

Conclusions

This experience is already shouting volumes to the church at large, if it is willing to hear. Communities that were deemed apt material for closure and merger with other communities are demonstrating a resilience and adaptability that no one among the official decision-makers seems to have anticipated. So called "ordinary parishioners" are making it clear by their actions that a truly honest assessment of the realities of parish life requires giving an active voice to these members of local church communities. They are demonstrating an age-old truth that various ecclesiologists have specifically pointed out since the Second Vatican Council—that local communities are centers of ministerial energy that are essential to the church's identity and the effective pursuit of its mission. Therefore, even when particular communities are struggling or dying and in unavoidable need of change, they cannot be dealt with as if they were merely dispensable administrative conveniences rather than embodiments of much of what is sacred in the church. Much less should this be the case when the communities in question are in fact vital enough to carry on in the face of strong official opposition.

The reassertion of local community and lay initiative represented by the resistance communities also calls for a more serious discussion of how such energies can serve the church at large in ways that often seem to be systematically ignored by some church officials. The severe and worsening shortage of available priest-pastors is usually presented as the most urgent reason for parish restructuring (although finances often play an important role, as they have in Boston). Yet, continual amalgamation and "multi-parish pastoring" cannot be an ongoing solution in itself unless we are willing to accept clerical overwork and lay alienation as the long-term norm in the U.S. church. The resistance communities give us a demonstration of how hard active lay Catholics are willing to work to preserve their worship communities, once it becomes clear to them that their contributions make an essential and valued difference to the survival and the shape of the community. Making this truth clear is not so much a matter of verbal persuasion and cajoling, as it has often seemed to be in the past, but rather of recognition of and respect for the gifts and dedication of the laity. Clerics, trained theologians, and other church professionals have an opportunity in the face of the resistance communities to ask questions of their own regarding their mission vis-à-vis the laity. To what extent might their own resources be offered for clarifying the analysis, focusing the questions, promoting the dialogue, and encouraging the critical task of "reflective practitioners" of Christianity, such as those found among the resisters to parish closure? Understood from within the discipline of practical theology, the activities of the resistance communities are theological in character, and the entire church could benefit from participation in the theological dialogue that they have begun.

Notes

[1]Mac Daniel, "Amid Prayers, Vows to Appeal Parish Closures," *Boston Globe*, May 27, 2004, B7.

[2]Michael Paulson, "Vatican Tribunal Hands Loss to Eight Local Groups on Closings," *Boston Globe*, June 11, 2008, B1.

[3]Ibid.

[4]For example, a confidential e-mail that I received in May 2008 from a parishioner involved in a resisting group, stated in part: "A close friend ... has reported that at an off-the-record meeting with diocesan officials, it was stated that 40 to 50 more parishes will be closed in the near term."

[5]Michael Paulson, "Accept Pain of Closings, Letter Says; Archbishop Prepares Parishes for Decisions," *Boston Globe*, January 10, 2004, B1.

[6]Paulson, "Vatican Tribunal Hands Loss to Eight Local Groups," B1.

[7]Don S. Browning, *A Fundamental Practical Theology: Descriptive and Strategic Proposals* (Minneapolis: Fortress Press, 1991), 43, 57.

[8]Alistair Campbell, "The Nature of Practical Theology," in *The Blackwell Reader in Pastoral and Practical Theology*, ed. James Woodward and Stephen Pattison (Malden, MA and Oxford, UK: Blackwell, 2000), 78-80.

[9]Browning, *A Fundamental Practical Theology*, 7-8.

[10]Stephen B. Bevans, *Models of Contextual Theology*, rev. and exp. ed. (Maryknoll, NY: Orbis Books, 2002), 70-87.

[11]Elaine Graham, "Practical Theology as Transforming Practice," in *The Blackwell Reader in Pastoral and Practical Theology*, ed. James Woodward and Stephen Pattison (Malden, MA and Oxford, UK: Blackwell, 2000), 104-17.

[12]Edward Farley, "Interpreting Situations: An Inquiry into the Nature of Practical Theology," in *The Blackwell Reader in Pastoral and Practical Theology*, ed. James Woodward and Stephen Pattison (Malden, MA and Oxford, UK: Blackwell, 2000), 118-27.

[13]Browning, *A Fundamental Practical Theology*, 38.

[14]Stephen Pattison and James Woodward, "An Introduction to Pastoral and Practical Theology," in *The Blackwell Reader in Pastoral and Practical Theology*, ed. James Woodward and Stephen Pattison (Malden, MA and Oxford, UK: Blackwell, 2000), 13.

[15]Browning, *A Fundamental Practical Theology*, 6.

[16]Farley, "Interpreting Situations," 119-21.

[17]Donald Schön, *The Reflective Practitioner: How Professionals Think in Action* (New York: Basic Books, 1983).

[18]Graham, "Practical Theology as Transforming Practice," 109.

[19]Stephen Kurkjian, "Archdiocese Rebuffs Pleas on Closings," *Boston Globe*, March 6, 2004, A1.

[20]Paulson, "Vatican Tribunal Hands Loss to Eight Local Groups," B1.

[21]Erica Noonan, "City Joins Church's Battle; Plan Would Toughen Zoning of Parish Site," *Boston Globe,* June 6, 2004, 1.

[22]See Browning, *A Fundamental Practical Theology,* 2.

[23]Michael Paulson, "Vatican Stops Diocese in Taking Parish Assets," *Boston Globe*, August 11, 2005, A1.

Snapshots of Laity in Mission

Consciousness of Responsibility for Ministry and Identity

Zeni Fox

Recently a colleague observed that we are experiencing "an unprecedented transfer of responsibility to the laity."[1] I think that is precisely the heart of the change in the Catholic Church in our time—not simply that laity are participating in the work of the church, but that they have assumed responsibility for so much of that work. Of course, this change is far from complete. While responsibility has often been delegated, and certainly assumed, official authority has been granted to a far lesser extent. The following "snapshots" offer evidence of this change.

Parish Ministry

Today our parishes visibly represent this change each Sunday in the entrance procession for the liturgy. Lectors, eucharistic ministers, and acolytes enter with the priest. In a way, they represent the many other laity involved in ministry in the parish—leaders of children's church and of the Rite of Christian Initiation of Adults, catechists and youth ministers, pastoral council members, and small Christian community leaders, to name only some. The *Notre Dame Study of Catholic Parish Life* stated that an average of 208 parishioners provided 810 hours of service a month in our parishes.[2] (While those statistics from the 1980s are dated, they are the most recent available; I expect that the numbers are greater today.)

Often, individual parishioners identify a need and then ask the pastor if they may begin a ministry to meet that need. Bereavement ministries, youth ministries, retreat ministries, food pantries, thrift shops, outreach to migrant workers, and services for new immigrants are just some of the initiatives undertaken through the leadership of individuals.[3] As once vowed religious began new ministries to meet new needs, today parishes are often the locus of such endeavors. This engagement in ministry indicates the consciousness of men and women of their responsibility for the work of the church. It flows from their consciousness of *being church*, a fruit of Vatican II.

Another development in ministry is the increasing number of lay men and women serving on parish staffs in roles such as directors of religious education, coordinators of youth ministry, directors of liturgy or social concerns, and pastoral associates. These roles began to emerge in the mid-1960s; by 1992, the first study to project numbers estimated that about twenty thousand lay men and women were serving twenty hours or more on parish staffs,[4] and by 1997, the number had grown to almost thirty thousand, a 35 percent increase.[5] In 2000, the number of lay ecclesial ministers (LEMs) on parish staffs surpassed the number of priests in parish ministry.[6]

An important point to note about this growth is that, unlike the restored permanent diaconate, lay ecclesial ministry did not emerge because of a decision by Rome or by local bishops. Rather, it sprang up like dandelions in spring, seemingly everywhere, simultaneously, without a master plan. And, like dandelions, there was a tenacity about these new ministers: relative to their education and experience, they were not that well paid; their positions did not have job security, as attested by the frequently circulated stories of new pastors firing long-time ministers; and in a hierarchical system that emphasized the roles of clergy and vowed religious, they had little status. And yet research, beginning with my own in 1985 and continuing with studies in 1997 and 2005, indicated that many desired to make a life-time commitment to their ministry, though there is no official avenue for that.[7]

The United States bishops first commented on these new ministers in 1980 in their document *Called and Gifted*. At that time, they noted that professionally prepared ecclesial ministers were a gift to the church, a first step in recognizing this new reality.

However, it was another twenty-five years before a second document was approved that gave official recognition to the new parish ministers. The subtitle is significant: *A Resource for Guiding the Development of Lay Ecclesial Ministry*. The document is not a particular law and therefore is not binding on any individual bishop. Nonetheless, the title *Co-Workers in the Vineyard of the Lord* has given considerable support to LEMs.[8]

As the bishops developed this document, a process that took over ten years, they first struggled with the entire spectrum of lay ministry: volunteers, "professionals," and "ministry in the world" (the language of the 1980 bishops' document *Called and Gifted*). Over time, they decided to focus on what they would eventually call lay ecclesial ministry. As they did so, they determined that a delineating characteristic is leadership, and that LEMs exercise leadership in a particular area of ministry in a parish. Hence, a director of religious education (DRE) is an LEM, but a catechist is not.[9] This focus officially recognizes that, indeed, laity share in the responsibility for ministry.

Another development in lay ecclesial ministry provides a snapshot of the concern these lay ministers have for Catholic identity. Starting in the late 1980s, associations of lay ministers began conversations about standards for certification in ministry. The National Federation for Catholic Youth Ministry (NFCYM) developed competency-based standards that were approved by the United States Catholic Conference Commission on Certification and Accreditation (USCC/CCA) in 1990. These standards include many focused on the skills and knowledge needed to work with youth and to develop a parish youth ministry. But they also focus on spirituality (for example, "Understanding of the necessity for ongoing spiritual formation, a personal prayer life and an awareness of God's redeeming activity in one's experiences, ministry and lifestyle"); on ministry ("Understanding of parish structures and one's role as a pastoral staff member); and on Catholic theology (" formed in the Catholic theological tradition; ... knowledgeable in Sacred Scripture, Christology, Ecclesiology, Catholic Doctrine, Sacramental and Moral theology.")[10] The National Association for Lay Ministry (NALM) has developed competency-based standards for pastoral ministers, pastoral associates, and parish life coordinators, and the National Conference for Catechetical Leadership (NCCL) has done so for professional parish directors of religious education. Subsequently, after dialogue with leaders of graduate programs in ministry, the three organizations have cooperated in developing common formation goals for ministry, rooted in competency-based standards. It is worth noting that the initial publication of standards predates the publication of *Co-Workers* by fifteen years, and that of the common formation goals by five years. The valuing of Catholic identity, indeed, the active fostering of it by lay leaders in ministry, is certainly clear.

Foundations and Donors Interested in Catholic Activities

The organization called Foundations and Donors Interested in Catholic Activities (FADICA), a consortium of private funders, is another striking example of lay involvement. People with wealth have always been an important part of the church's story, but in recent centuries they have responded generally to the initiatives of bishops, vowed religious, or pastors, serving more as helpers than planners, more assistants than deciders. FADICA, on the other hand, exercises leadership in determining needs and ways to respond. It works together with ordained church leaders in a participatory style, and its initiatives demonstrate this new mode of participation by those whose wealth is put at the service of the church's mission and ministry.

Begun three decades ago, FADICA's central office assists individual donors and foundations in understanding the needs of the church today. It convenes an annual educational forum to explore current trends and realities in the church. In recent years, topics have included leadership for Catholic institutional ministries (education, health care, and social services/charities) and lay leadership in parishes. Earlier in its history, FADICA was the impetus behind the annual collection for retired religious and the outreach to the churches of Eastern Europe after the fall of communism. Recently it has assisted eight congregations of women religious in New Orleans to rebuild their ministries in that devastated city. The president of FADICA, Frank Butler, said that members of the organization have a strong sense of their own baptism and a sense of responsibility for the church. When they gather, they do so in a context of prayer, they share their faith, they ponder the exercise of their stewardship, and they weigh the signs of the times. Of his own work, Frank said: "You know this as well as I do: it's a

vocation. My small gifts fit this organization very well."[11] Frank
Butler and the other members of FADICA share a consciousness
that they are the church and that they must participate in its mission and ministry. They recognize that they have a responsibility
to use their gifts and their wealth to serve others.

The National Leadership Roundtable on Church Management

Another organization reflective of the consciousness of the laity of its responsibility for the church is the National Leadership
Roundtable on Church Management. Formed in July 2005, in
the wake of the clergy abuse crisis, its impetus derived not from
the abuse as such, but from the way the situation was managed.
A number of Catholic philanthropists realized that it was not
enough to carefully weigh which projects to fund, but that it was
also necessary to attend to how the church conducts its temporal
affairs. They recognized that they needed to exercise their own
due diligence as they worked to serve the needs of the church.
Therefore, they convened Catholic leaders from the worlds of
business, religion, and non-profit organizations to discuss ways
to strengthen the "structures of participation, consultation and
shared responsibility" in our parishes, dioceses, and national
office.

At the first conference, bishops, Catholic college presidents,
parish priests, lay ecclesial ministers, leaders of Fortune 500
companies and of major secular and religiously oriented foundations discussed helpful practices emerging in parishes and dioceses
regarding management, finances, and human resource issues. Their
concluding recommendations focused significantly on the role of
the laity and how best to use their talents.[12]

One result of the conference was to initiate the Roundtable.
Kerry Robinson, its executive director, stated that its mission is "to
promote excellence and best practices in the management, finances
and human resource development of the Catholic Church in the
U.S. through greater incorporation of the expertise of the laity."
The organization has developed resources on parish planning,
ethics, and accountability, and now offers training for parishes.
In addition, the Roundtable is assisting the church through con-
sultancy work. The first major effort was in New Orleans after
Katrina. Bishop Hughes welcomed this offer of help and asked

that the first focus be the Catholic school system, so central to the recovery of the city. A staff member from the Roundtable went to New Orleans for four months. Working in concert with a leader of a major consulting firm, they were able to tap many individual consultants to participate in the recovery effort. It is estimated that this effort provided $900,000 in pro-bono work.[13] The sense of responsibility for the life of the church, and for the needs of the larger community, is evident in this work.

Catholic Institutional Ministries

One of the great legacies of the Catholic Church in the United States is the extensive development of Catholic institutional ministries in health care, social services, and education. While laity have been part of the birth and growth of these institutions, today the leadership positions of presidents, CEOs, board members, and sponsors are increasingly held by lay persons. These men and women have a notable consciousness of their responsibility, and many different initiatives have contributed to this deepening awareness.

One striking example is the Congregation of St. Agnes, a small community of sisters in Wisconsin. The congregation's sponsored ministries include a college and two health care facilities. About ten years ago, it sponsored a forum, similar to a twenty-four-hour retreat, for its trustees, CEOs, and executive leaders, along with its General Council. Sr. Mary Noel, who directs this effort, explained that the goal was to help participants understand the importance of lay ministry and to grow in their understanding of the role of laity as bearers of the tradition. Sr. Noel said that the gathering has fostered a sense of community among the lay and vowed religious who gather, and that it has deepened their sense of mission and of participation in the healing and teaching ministry of Jesus. The intention is that these understandings be integrated into strategic planning and operational work in the institutions in which the members serve.[14]

In my conversations with a number of participants at this year's forum, the fruit of these efforts was evident. The lay men and women had a strong commitment to the mission of their institutions and to the core values that informed them. For example, James Moore, who recently accepted a position as dean of Marian College, explained that what first drew him to Marian was the mission of the school and its core values, which matched his personal values. When he visited the campus, he noted that "the mission and core values of the president, faculty, staff and sisters" permeated the educational mission of the school. He wanted to be part of the institution and its mission. Moore has spent his entire professional life in Catholic colleges and universities; at each school, he said he found support for the personal spiritual growth of faculty and administrators.[15] The Catholic educational community influenced Moore, the Congregation of Saint Agnes influenced the leadership at Marian College, and the leadership at Marian College created an institution whose values permeate the life of the college. In multiple ways, the church and its varied communities contribute to the changed consciousness of the laity and to the reshaping of our institutional ministries.[16]

Laity in Ministry and the Signs of the Times

I will briefly explore the interplay between three societal developments and the snapshots I have presented. The first is virtually a truism: throughout the world, the status of women is changing. Belief in and commitment to the equality of men and women affects the way women are treated interpersonally and under the law, it influences the roles that women are able to hold, and it challenges structures that exclude women. In our parishes, 80 percent of the lay ecclesial ministers are women, as are the great majority of lay ministers. The faithful work of these women as co-workers with clergy, and the press of societal change, has led to efforts on the part of many bishops to appoint women to every role that canon law permits. It is surely this lived experience of the church that led to the emphasis by Pope John Paul II on the importance of using the gifts of women in the church to the fullest extent possible. The women involved in ministry are a leaven in the church, bringing change.

Second, in the United States, and in much of the Western world, society has become increasingly secularized. I do not use that term in a negative sense, but rather as a way to describe how religion and religious leadership are regarded as one aspect of political life, and certainly not the most dominant. In a secularized culture, the task of transforming the culture must be primarily *from within*, not by the authoritative action of religious leadership. Laity active in church ministry are also part of society, not set apart in rectories or convents, but present to all dimensions of contemporary life. They are able to be leaven, as Vatican II emphasized, working to transform the social order. Furthermore, these men and women are signs to the wider community of the role of laity as leaven. We could say that just as a primary function of vowed religious among us is to be a sign that all are called to holiness, so a primary function of lay ministers is to be a sign that all are called to prepare the way for God's reign.

Third, our society is increasingly comprised of complex institutions. Think for a moment of a visit to a doctor's office, usually a practice with several doctors. The doctors work with nurses, perhaps a mid-wife or nurse practitioner, lab technicians, book-keepers, and receptionists. And the complexity of the medical practice is dwarfed by that of a hospital. On the one hand, this complexity serves the task of healing—each part of the whole contributes something to the task. On the other hand, within complex systems, it is harder to maintain attention to individuals, which the dignity of the human person calls us to do. It is also hard to maintain a focus on the mission of the institution so that it permeates every part of the whole. Catholic institutional ministries are increasingly intentional about their focus on mission, which includes a focus on individual persons. This includes those who serve, those who are served, and even the larger community of which the institution is a part. The effort today to re-define the meaning of the Catholic identity of our institutions embraces this task of working out policies, practices, and institutional cultures that seek to transform the temporal order and that seek to reflect more fully "God's design for the world."[17] Most of those who serve within our institutions are lay people; they are assuming responsibility for this new aspect of mission, creating institutions that, as institutions, embody our values and serve as signs of the coming of God's reign.

Higher Education

The increasing role of the laity has three implications for professors of theology. First, theological work is needed to more fully understand these new developments in the light of our tradition and to determine the ideological and structural changes needed to fully incorporate the new realities into our life as a community. Varied theological disciplines are needed for this task.

Second, the story of these changes in the life of the church needs to be explored with students, simply as commentary, and also to seek meaning, to discern God's action within our communities today. The implications for whatever work our students will undertake and the responsibility of the laity for church *and* world can be drawn from the stories of laity active in the mission of the church today. The function of witness is powerful in the classroom.

Third, students need to know that there are many avenues open to them for work within the church. A number of years ago a study of Catholic college students found that most had no knowledge of options for them in church ministry.[18] The fact that the median age of lay ecclesial ministers is now fifty-two reflects that LEM positions are not drawing significant numbers of younger adults.[19] College students today need to hear the stories of lay involvement that can be visible role models for their lives.

Conclusion

In conclusion, I would again affirm that the laity have an increased consciousness of their responsibility for ministry and for Catholic identity today. This is true of individuals and groups in diverse settings, focused on a myriad of ministerial functions, who participate in the life and mission of the church.

Notes

[1]Patrick Marrin, editor of *Celebration*, conversation on May 17, 2008.

[2]A picture of the arenas of involvement is offered in David Leege, Report No. 8, "Parish Organizations: People's Needs, Parish Services, and Leadership" (Notre Dame: University of Notre Dame, July 1986).

[3]A sense of the multitude of ministries in parishes can be gained through the work of Paul Wilkes, *Excellent Catholic Parishes: The Guide to Best Places and Practices* (Mahwah, NJ: Paulist Press, 2001).

[4]Philip J. Murnion, *New Parish Ministers: Laity and Religious on Parish Staffs* (New York: National Pastoral Life Center, 1992), v.

[5]Philip J. Murnion and David DeLambo, *Parishes and Parish Ministry: A Study of Parish Lay Ministry* (New York: National Pastoral Life Center, 1999), iii.

[6]*The Study of the Impact of Fewer Priests on the Pastoral Ministry*, docu-

mentation for the Spring General Meeting of the United States Conference of Catholic Bishops, June 15-17, 2000, 14 and 29.

[7]Zeni Fox, *New Ecclesial Ministry: Lay Professionals Serving the Church*, rev. ed. (Kansas City: Sheed & Ward, 2002), 70-71; Murnion and DeLambo, *Parishes and Parish Ministry*, 63; David DeLambo, *Lay Parish Ministers: A Study of Emerging Leadership* (New York: National Pastoral Life Center, 2005), 142.

[8]Washington, DC: United States Conference of Catholic Bishops, 2005.

[9]*Co-Workers in the Vineyard of the Lord: A Resource for Guiding the Development of Lay Ecclesial Minsitry* (Washington, DC: United States Conference of Catholic Bishops, 2005), 10-11.

[10]Joseph Merkt, ed., *Common Formation Goals for Ministry* (Washington, DC: USCCB [NALM, NCCL, NFCYM], 2000), 202-15.

[11]Francis Butler, telephone interview by author, April 15, 2008.

[12]National Leadership Roundtable, *Report of the Church in America: Leadership Roundtable 2004 at the Wharton School*, Philadelphia, July 9-10, 2004; annual reports available at www.nlrcm.org.

[13]Kerry Robinson, telephone interview by author, April 25, 2008.

[14]Sr. Mary Noel, interview by author, April 18, 2008.

[15]James Moore, interview by author, April 25, 2008.

[16]At the College Theology Society convention, a participant raised an important point: we read of times when Catholic institutions violate Catholic social teaching. Certainly, the developments I am commenting on here do not permeate all of our institutions, but represent examples of the cutting edge, the desired direction.

[17]Many institutions are striving to meet such goals. For an example in a college, see Sean Peters, C.S.J., "Embodying the Spirit of Those Who Came Before," in *Called and Chosen: Toward a Spirituality for Lay Leaders*, ed. Zeni Fox and Regina Bechtle, S.C. (Lanham, MD: Sheed & Ward, 2005), 113-26.

[18]The study was commissioned by Aquinas Institute, in St. Louis. A marketing firm surveyed students in select Catholic colleges.

[19]DeLambo, *Lay Parish Ministers*, 46.

Lay? Ministry?

Christian Mission in a Pluralistic World

Edward P. Hahnenberg

In reflecting on his own contribution to a theology of church and ministry, Yves Congar once remarked that the door by which we enter into a question often determines how we come out of it.[1] In approaching lay ministry in our present context, it seems there are at least two "doors" in. We can come into the question through a *theology of laity* that seeks to locate lay ministry within the context of the distinctive vocation of the layperson in the world. Or we can come in through a *theology of ministry* that places lay ministry amid various other ministries in the church. Will we enter through the "laity" or through the "ministry"? These are two different points of entry that take us in two different directions.

If we choose Door #1, and enter through the lay vocation, we will be ushered into the corridor of Vatican II's teaching on the secular character of the laity. We will be led to reflect on the laity's call to be Christ's presence "in the world," and we will be asked to explain lay activity both in the church and in the world in light of that secularity. On the other hand, if we choose Door #2, and go in through the idea of ministry, we will be brought down the hallway of Vatican II's teaching on the nature and mission of the church. We will be invited to think about how various ministries flow out of the whole church community and its mission in the world. And we will be asked to clarify the distinctions among the many and diverse ministries in the church.

I do not want to suggest that these two approaches are mutually exclusive. If you go in one door, you will still run into people and have things to talk about with people who came in the other door. Neither approach denies the ecclesial dimension of lay ministry, nor its "worldly" context. Still, "lay" and "ministry" are two different starting points, and these starting points determine the direction of the theology that follows.

This essay argues that Door #2 is a better way in. The reality we refer to as "lay ministry" is best understood from the perspective of a comprehensive theology of ministry, rather than from the perspective of a theology of laity for two reasons: (1) It is more faithful to the best of our theological tradition and (2) it is more relevant to our contemporary situation. That is, it is an approach truer to our understanding of the church and to our view of the world. The following paragraphs touch on these two points and then suggest three implications for ministry today.

The Theological Tradition

I can treat the theological rationale for preferring Door #2 quite quickly, largely because I believe that the theological case has already been made.

Almost forty years ago, in a 1969 essay titled "A Theology of the Laity," Richard McBrien began:

> I should regard this essay a success if it becomes the last article ever written on the theology of the laity. Otherwise, I shall have contributed one more item to a body of literature which, as a systematic theologian, I can find little reason to justify. The topic itself betrays an understanding of the Church which is simply untenable; namely, that the non-ordained constitute a special segment of the Body of Christ whose vocation, dignity, and mission are somehow regarded as a limited aspect of the total vocation, dignity, and mission of the church.[2]

McBrien was alerting his readers to the fact that—despite all the positive things Vatican II had to say about laypeople—the category of layperson itself is basically negative. It is a remainder concept, a left-over term. It names something over against something else: the laity are not clergy. Although he does not cite it, McBrien could very well have pointed to the 1891 edition of Wetzer and Welte's multi-volume *Kirchenlexikon* as evidence of this negative view. This encyclopedia's entry on "Laity" read simply: "See clergy."[3]

In 1969 McBrien was adding his voice to a chorus of European and North American theologians already raising questions about the theology of the laity that had been so influential before the council. The chorus included such giants as Edward Schillebeeckx and Yves Congar, scholars who had helped promote the theology of the laity and who were later reevaluating their positions.[4] In light of the broader ecclesiological revolution confirmed by the Second Vatican Council, these theologians had begun to question the value of building a theology on a basic and non-biblical distinction between two groups in the church: clergy and laity.

Congar, in the 1971 essay cited above, acknowledged that his early work on the laity had distinguished things "too nicely," thus leading to a linear scheme in which "Christ makes the hierarchy and the hierarchy makes the Church as community of faithful."[5] Despite his efforts to promote the laity, Congar recognized that, simply by the way he framed the question, he had inadvertently perpetuated a theological subordination of laity to clergy and thus of baptism to ordination. He then suggested that the decisive pair for a truly post-conciliar theology of ministry was no longer "clergy-laity" but "ministries-community."[6] In that line, Congar captured the fundamental sea change taking place in the theology of church and ministry after the council: a shift from a linear model putting clergy over against laity to a model of two concentric circles, where various ministries are seen within the whole church community and its mission in the world.[7] This insight was Congar's way of naming the turn from Door #1 to Door #2.

Congar was joined by a host of voices who advocated this turn to ministry, and who did so on specifically theological grounds. They appealed to Vatican II's theology of baptism, its teaching on the universal call to holiness, its vision of the church as the People of God, and its claim—heard strongly in the Pastoral Constitution *Gaudium et Spes*—that it is not just the laity, but the whole church that has a mission and responsibility in the world. On this last point, it is important to note that this turn to ministry cannot be reduced to a turn inward, or cast as a preoccupation with the internal affairs of the church to the detriment of its external mission. Rather, on a theological level, the focus on ministry emerged within the context of a renewed recognition that the external mission of the church is a responsibility of the whole community, clergy and laity alike.

The Contemporary Situation

The theological case has already been made. The context, however, keeps shifting. And we see the world differently than we did forty or fifty years ago. One way of characterizing this difference, in a very general way, is in terms of a shift from the interpretative framework of secularization to that of pluralization. If the categories were not so contested, we might think of this as the movement from a modern to a postmodern mentality. I prefer the first pair, however, because these categories highlight a parallel between the contextual shift from secularization to pluralization, on the one hand, and the theological shift from laity to ministries, on the other.

The pre-conciliar theology of the laity that shaped the treat-ment of the layperson in the documents of Vatican II, and gave rise to *Lumen Gentium*'s claim that "To be secular is the special characteristic of the laity," was crafted in Europe in the middle decades of the twentieth century.[8] It took shape at the precise moment that the secularization thesis—proposed by intellectuals since the Enlightenment—had reached its broadest academic and popular appeal.

The thesis is simple: modernization spells trouble for religion. In its classic form, the secularization thesis argues that the more the world modernizes, the less religion will hold. It presumes the two exist in a kind of zero-sum game, unable to live alongside one another. Eventually, proponents of the thesis argued, science, rational thought, and human emancipation will push the supersti-tious and backward world of religion off the stage.[9]

That is the thesis. And for a good part of the modern period, the Roman Church bought into it. Seeing modernization as a threat, the church fought it tooth and nail. But by the middle of the twentieth century, some Catholic thinkers sought a more nuanced response. People such as Congar, Schillebeeckx, Gustave Thils, and others struggled to articulate a theology of worldly realities that would engage these broader currents.[10] Taking secularization seriously, they crafted a theology that affirmed both the ecclesial identity of the laity and their activity in the world.

Congar, for example, began his magisterial study on the laity by agreeing with proponents of secularization that the church's confiscation of temporal realities over the course of the Middle Ages was problematic. He called the modern secularization process a movement, after centuries of clerical tutelage, "to recapture rights in second causes."[11] Against such paternalism, and along with the mid-century proponents of secularization, Congar argued for the proper autonomy of the secular. Throughout his book, Congar tried to make space for the laity, for the world, for the free activity and interplay of secondary causes. His Thomistic background allowed Congar to grant independence to these secondary causes—without minimizing the presence and activity of the first cause, God. It is here that Congar parted company with the secularization thesis. For Congar, the one first cause and the various secondary causes cannot exist in a zero-sum game, because the world is always permeated by the active presence of God. But while Congar came to a very different conclusion, his early work shared a certain affinity or orientation with the classic secularization thesis. Because he was pushing off of medieval Christendom more than the Enlightenment, the force of Congar's argument is toward autonomy. His theology of the laity took shape in this dialogue with secularization.

And then, much to the surprise of secularization theorists, a funny thing happened. Religion didn't go away. Indeed, over the past forty years, religion seems to have enjoyed a resurgence, gaining new strength and popping up everywhere—from the Religious Right to traditionalist Catholics to the Latin American evangelical explosion to various and sometimes violent forms of fundamentalism around the globe. It's enough to drive a good secular humanist crazy![12]

Religion didn't go away. And the force of that fact burst open a torrent of commentary and debate about the meaning of secularization. Early proponents of the thesis, including Peter Berger and David Martin, revised their positions,[13] while others, like Karel Dobbelaere, Talal Asad, José Casanova, and Charles Taylor have painted a more nuanced, complex picture of the various phenomena gathered under the umbrella of secularization.[14] This debate has important consequences for Catholics thinking about lay ministry today. At a minimum, it brings this realization: If we are going to repeat *Lumen Gentium*'s claim that "To be secular is the special characteristic of the laity," then we have to recognize that the concept of the secular has been significantly complicated since those words were written. Either we have to incorporate this more complex picture into our efforts to do a theology of laity,[15] or we have to shift the way we come into the question.

We find this new way in by noticing that, in the ongoing debates over secularization theory, what stands out is not so much the relative strengths and weaknesses of the arguments advanced. Rather, what stands out is a more fundamental shift in the way in which the conversation is framed. The old binary opposition of belief and unbelief has faded in front of a multifaceted appreciation of plurality and perspective. *Duality* has given way to *difference*. Lieven Boeve captures this shift when he argues that the religious world of Europe and North America can no longer be imagined as a simple continuum ranging from "churched Christians" at one end to "atheistic humanists" on the other. Such a view simply perpetuates the zero-sum game of the classic secularization thesis. What has emerged instead is a more complicated picture, namely that of a "plural arena of interacting religious positions." For Boeve,

> [I]t is not the presupposed discontinuity or continuity between the Christian and the secular that determines today's spectrum of fundamental life options but rather the multiplicity of conceptions of humanity and the world, the plurality of religions and other convictions, of which the Christian faith and radical Enlightenment thinking (in their own variety) have evolved into but two positions among the many.[16]

Pluralization has become the lens through which to view the emergence of the modern (and now postmodern) worldview. As Harvey Cox—an early proponent of secular theology—put it more recently: "The fact is that atheism and rationalism no longer constitute (if they ever really did) the major challenge to Christian theology today. That challenge comes not from the death of God but from the 're-birth of the gods' (and the goddesses!)."[17] Or, to borrow a phrase from Fareed Zakaria, it is not so much the fall of "us," but the "rise of the rest" that challenges believers today.[18]

Today, what needs explanation is not the absence of religion, but the enormous diversity of worldviews and fundamental life options that have come to stand alongside traditional religious belief. That is the fuel that fires Charles Taylor's recent and rich book, *A Secular Age*. How did we in the West, Taylor asks, move from "a society in which it was virtually impossible not to believe in God, to one in which faith, even for the staunchest believer, is one human possibility among others"?[19] The answer can only come through a thick historical narrative that illustrates the many layers at which secularization works. Taylor points out that secularization is usually charted according to the public space of religious institutions or the private realm of belief and practice. But he suggests a third way of talking about secularization, namely, as a basic shift in the background conditions of belief that relocates religion within a cultural context full of alternate and compelling accounts of the meaning of life—different ways of thinking that cannot be easily dismissed by believers. Thus our "secular age" is not one in which belief has been replaced by unbelief (in other words, the secularization thesis has failed). Rather, our age is one in which belief has been repositioned within a boggling diversity of other beliefs. For Taylor, secularity itself needs to be seen within the context of plurality.

Implications for Ministry Today

What might this new contextual appreciation for plurality mean for our understanding and practice of ministry? Three sets of implications follow.

Theologies of Ministry

First, an appreciation for plurality helps us refine some of the theological accounts of ministry that have been current since the Second Vatican Council. In *A Secular Age*, Taylor repeatedly rejects what he calls the "subtraction stories" of modernity.[20] These are accounts of the modern world that present secularization as simply the sloughing off of religion and the confining horizons that go along with it. According to such subtraction stories, once we kick off the crust of religious superstition, what we find underneath is something like pure human nature—a rational, Enlightenment individual, who was there all along, just waiting to be set free. What these stories miss, according to Taylor, is the fact that Western modernity cannot simply be explained in terms of the perennial features of human existence (as if "our" way of looking at the world is the natural default mode of all people from all times). Instead, modernity emerges as the result of new constructions, new self-understandings, new forms of life and assumptions about the world.

Is there a parallel in the theologies of ministry of the post-conciliar period? Are there certain "subtraction stories" going on here as well? Do we tend to see the post-conciliar renewal as simply the shaking off of medieval or tridentine forms? Do we assume that all we have to do is scrape off the barnacles from the bark of Peter, and thus free ourselves from centuries of clericalism and custom, in order to uncover underneath it all something like pure ministry—just like it existed in that Golden Age of the first Christian communities?

Insofar as we tell the story in this way we flirt with a Harnack-ian narrative of post-apostolic decline: early charism good, later institution bad. Few Catholic theologians slip all the way down this slope of universal devolution. Instead, our weakness seems to be a linear narrative of ups and downs, a kind of sine wave story that charts broad periods of advance and broad periods of decline. But history suggests a more scattered screen, a story in which there are gains and losses all along the way.

A more significant concern is the way in which such subtraction stories too easily overlook the radical newness in ministry that has emerged in recent decades. If we take our local context in the United States, for example, and think about the rise of professionally prepared, more-or-less full-time, long-term lay ministers working in parishes (what the U.S. bishops are calling "lay ecclesial ministers"[21]), we see something that has not really existed in this form and on this scale before. We are not just uncovering ministerial forms that were there at the beginning. The evolving shape of lay ecclesial ministry is the result of new constructions, new self-understandings, new forms of church life and assumptions about our ecclesial identity. These ministers are offering new ways of talking about vocation, new ways of pursuing formation, new ways of relating to ecclesial authority. And we have a lot to learn from their stories.

This realization does not make the biblical witness or that early experience insignificant. But what we gain from the early evidence is not a model to imitate, but a witness to diversity in ministry that ought to free us for new forms today.

Ministerial Identity and Collaboration

A second implication has to do with ministerial identity and collaboration. The continuation of an approach to lay ministry that begins with Door #1 is favored by some for its emphasis on clear boundaries and distinct realms of responsibility. According to such a view, lay ministry ought to be seen always in light of the lay vocation "in the world." For advocates, only a clear distinction between the secular orientation of the laity and the sacred ministry of the clergy will protect against the danger of what Pope John Paul II called "the clericalization of the laity and the laicization of the clergy."[22]

To argue for an approach that enters through Door #2 is not to ignore questions about identity among ministers or to dismiss distinctions among ministries. But when such distinctions presuppose a zero-sum game of ministerial identity, we have a problem. Even though our theology rejects it, and our pastoral experience by and large does not bear it out, still there are some who see raising lay ministry as lowering the ordained. For some, that is just how it feels. Limited, sinful human beings that we are, we often fear that attention to anyone—even my closest confidant or co-worker—will take attention away from me. As Gore Vidal put it so sadly, "Whenever a friend succeeds, a little something in me dies."

Here we don't need a theologian, we need a therapist. And so my contribution in this area is limited. There are deep psychological dynamics at work, issues of personal identity, socialization, and structures of power that need careful attention. But I think we make a mistake when we reduce the difficulty of collaboration and the conflicts over identity to a power struggle between two groups or centers of authority. It is not that the laity are trying to push the clergy off the stage or take over their roles. The insecurity out there comes not from confrontation, but from co-existence.

Not long ago in this country, the priest was for many Catholics the principal source of spiritual wisdom and sanctifying grace. Now he is one voice among many. It's not getting bumped off the stage that is the problem, it's having to share it. The dynamic recalls the words of the anonymous evangelical theologian who said, "What we like about postmodernity is that it has given us a place at the table. What we don't like is that it is *just* a place."

What some clergy (especially younger priests[23]) may be struggling with is a question of identity that faces the whole Christian community: Who am I, who are we, in a world marked by the "rise of the rest"? Thus questions of ministerial identity—both for priests and lay ministers—will be fruitfully addressed only if they are folded within a larger conversation about Christian identity and engagement in our pluralistic, postmodern world.

Ministerial Diversity

My last comment on pluralism and ministry is probably the one most of us think of first, namely the pluralism that we meet in the midst of cultural, ethnic, and generational diversity.

The most recent study of professional lay ministers working in parishes reveals that these lay ecclesial ministers are overwhelmingly white, female, and older than the median age of adult Catholics in the United States.[24] Moreover, most recent theologies of ministry (my own included) rely on a canon of figures and texts almost exclusively European in origin. What is missing in all of this? The short answer is: most of the church.

Our new consciousness of pluralism has in recent years opened us up to conversations we did not know we were missing—a tendency to overlook "the other" that particularly plagues those of us who fit comfortably within dominant cultures. In terms of numerical growth, institutionalization, and theological attention, lay ecclesial ministry as we have come to know it in this country has reached a kind of stasis—poised and waiting for what comes next. My expectation is that the next great stage in the ongoing evolution of ministry will come out of mutual dialogue with "the other" within our own faith community—a conversation that promises the kind of "interruption" needed to deepen and expand our thinking about the mission of Christ in our pluralistic world.

Notes

[1]Yves M.-J. Congar, "My Path-Findings in the Theology of Laity and Ministries," *The Jurist* 32 (1972): 169-88, at 176-77. This essay originally appeared in *Ministères et communion ecclésiale* (Paris: Cerf, 1971).

[2]Richard P. McBrien, "A Theology of the Laity," *American Ecclesiastical Review* 160 (1969): 73-85, at 73.

[3]Heinrich J. Wetzer and Benedict Welte, *Kirchenlexikon, oder Encyklopädie der katholischen theologie und ihrer hülfswissenschaften*, vol. 8 (Freiburg im Breisgau: Herder, 1891), 1323. This telling entry appears to have been first noticed by R. Müller in "Der Laie in der Kirche," *Theologische Quartalschrift* 130 (1950): 184-96. Congar often cited the entry, and it even made its way into the debates on the laity at the Second Vatican Council in an address by Bishop Stephen László of Austria. See Hanjo Sauer, "The Council Discovers the Laity," in *History of Vatican II*, ed. Giuseppe Alberigo and Joseph A. Komonchak, vol. 4 (Maryknoll, NY: Orbis Books, 2003), 256.

[4]At a 1966 symposium on Vatican II, Abbot Christopher Butler observed: "I should like to suggest that this question of the definition of the laity is a completely false problem. There is no definition of laity. There is a definition of a Christian. We have a definition of a priest or of a minister in holy orders. There is no third definition of the laity. A member of the laity is very simply a Christian" (in *Vatican II: An Interfaith Appraisal*, ed. John H. Miller [Notre Dame: University of Notre Dame Press, 1966], 269). See Congar, "My Path-Findings," and Edward Schillebeeckx, *The Church with a Human Face: A New and Expanded Theology of Ministry*, trans. John Bowden (New York: Crossroad, 1985), 157.

[5]Congar, "My Path-Findings," 174-75.

[6]Ibid., 176. The English translation of this passage obscures Congar's point. His phrase *"ministères ou services-communauté"* becomes "ministries/modes of community service," instead of "ministries or services/community." The emphasis in the original is not to distinguish ministries from services, but to place a variety of ministries and other services within the context of the church community.

[7]Congar's model of concentric circles was developed and fruitfully applied to the North American context by Thomas F. O'Meara, *Theology of Ministry*, rev. ed. (New York: Paulist Press, 1999, orig. 1983). See Edward P. Hahnenberg, *Ministries: A Relational Approach* (New York: Crossroad, 2003), 7-38.

[8]*Lumen Gentium*, 31 (in *Vatican Council II: The Basic Sixteen Documents*, ed. Austin Flannery [Northport, NY: Costello Publishing, 1996]).

[9]An updated, and carefully qualified, defense of the secularization thesis is found in Steve Bruce, *God Is Dead: Secularization in the West* (Oxford: Blackwell, 2002).

[10]See two early articles by Yves Congar, "Sacerdoce et laïcat dans l'Église,"

Vie Intellectuelle 14 (1946): 6-39 and "Pour une théologie du laïcat," Études 256 (1948): 42-54, 194-218, and his classic study Jalons pour une théologie du laïcat, Unam Sanctam, vol. 23 (Paris: Cerf, 1953); ET: Lay People in the Church: A Study for a Theology of Laity, trans. Donald Attwater (Westminster, MD: Newman Press, 1965). See also Gustave Thils, Théologie des réalités terrestres, 2 vols. (Paris: Desclée, De Brouwer, 1949).

¹¹Congar, Lay People in the Church, 22.

¹²Jay Tolson, "Why God Won't Die," Wilson Quarterly 32 (2008), http://www.wilsoncenter.org/index.cfm?essay_id=369424&fuseaction=wq.essay (accessed May 23, 2008).

¹³See Peter L. Berger, "The Desecularization of the World: A Global Overview," in The Desecularization of the World: Resurgent Religion and World Politics, ed. Peter L. Berger (Grand Rapids: Eerdmans, 1999), 1-18, and "Secularization Falsified," First Things 180 (2008): 23-27; David Martin, "The Secularization Issue: Prospect and Retrospect," British Journal of Sociology 42 (1991): 465-74, and Tongues of Fire: The Explosion of Protestantism in Latin America (Oxford: Blackwell, 1990).

¹⁴See Karel Dobbelaere, "Secularization: A Multi-Dimensional Concept," Current Sociology 29 (1981): 1-216; José Casanova, Public Religions in the Modern World (Chicago: University of Chicago Press, 1994); Talal Asad, Formations of the Secular: Christianity, Islam, Modernity (Stanford: Stanford University Press, 2003); Charles Taylor, A Secular Age (Cambridge: Belknap Press, 2007). Another helpful "complication" is Grace Davies, Religion in Modern Europe: A Memory Mutates (Oxford: Oxford University Press, 2000).

¹⁵One of the more substantive attempts at a renewed theology of the laity is Paul Lakeland's The Liberation of the Laity: In Search of an Accountable Church (New York: Continuum, 2002), esp. 149-85.

¹⁶Lieven Boeve, God Interrupts History: Theology in a Time of Upheaval (New York: Continuum, 2007), 8; see also 26-28.

¹⁷Harvey Cox, "The Myth of the Twentieth Century: The Rise and Fall of 'Secularization,'" in The Twentieth Century: A Theological Overview, ed. Gregory Baum (Maryknoll, NY: Orbis Books, 1999), 135-43, at 140.

¹⁸Fareed Zakaria, "The Rise of the Rest," Newsweek (May 12, 2008), http://www.newsweek.com/id/135380 (accessed May 16, 2008).

¹⁹Taylor, A Secular Age, 3.

²⁰Ibid., 22.

²¹U.S. Conference of Catholic Bishops, Co-Workers in the Vineyard of the Lord: A Resource for Guiding the Development of Lay Ecclesial Ministry (Washington, DC: USCCB Publishing, 2005).

²²A strong concern for the distinction between ordained and lay ministers appears in the 1997 Vatican instruction "On Certain Questions Regarding the Collaboration of the Nonordained in the Sacred Ministry of Priests," Origins 27 (November 27, 1997): 397-409.

²³Several studies have charted generational trends within the U.S. clergy. See Katarina Schuth, Seminaries, Theologates, and the Future of Church Ministry: An Analysis of Trends and Transitions (Collegeville, MN: Liturgical Press, 1999), and her "A View of the State of the Priesthood in the United States,"

Louvain Studies 30 (2005): 8-24; Dean R. Hoge and Jacqueline E. Wenger, *Evolving Visions of the Priesthood: Changes from Vatican II to the Turn of the New Century* (Collegeville, MN: Liturgical Press, 2003).

[24]David DeLambo reports that in 2005, the median age for a layperson (excluding women religious) employed in parish ministry was 52, compared to the median age of 44 for adult Catholics in the United States. See David DeLambo, *Lay Parish Ministers: A Study of Emerging Leadership* (New York: National Pastoral Life Center, 2005), 44.

Lay Ecclesial Ministry in Theological and Relational Context

A Study of Ministry Formation Documents

William H. Johnston

Lay ecclesial ministry represents a new and significant form of lay involvement in church leadership since the Second Vatican Council. This essay explores its emerging place in the ministerial life of the church by investigating a specific set of sources: church documents directing formation for ministry. Other documents and secondary literature provide context and illustration. Formation documents generally offer theological reflections on the ministry to which they pertain, as well as detailed objectives on formation for that ministry; both components (the "theological" and "curricular") inform this study. The primary resource for this essay will be *Co-Workers in the Vineyard of the Lord*, the 2005 statement of the U.S. Catholic bishops on lay ecclesial ministry.[1] Further, since *Co-Workers* notes that examining relationships with all who serve in "public ministries" in the church can help us "arrive at a better appreciation of the specific place of lay ecclesial ministers in an ordered, relational, ministerial community" (*Co-Workers*, 21), I will draw on formation documents for priests and permanent deacons as well as lay ecclesial ministers.[2]

This study proceeds in three main parts. First, a comparison of the curriculum components of the various formation documents yields selected indicators of how the different ministries relate. Then, in view of challenges to positive relations among ecclesial ministers, we focus on the theology section of the formation documents, noting in particular how attention to the sacraments, which are a basis for ministerial distinctions, can also be a basis for mutual ministerial respect. Finally, since actually building and maintaining such respect requires not only a theological basis but also the cultivation of appropriate dispositions, the study concludes by briefly suggesting attitudes or dispositions that can promote effective relations and mutual support among all the church's ministers.

Formation Documents: The Curricular Components

A notable feature of the formation documents is the considerable degree of overlap in their listing of curriculum elements. As formational topics or goals, for example, all the documents specify the ability to relate well with others, affective maturity, good moral character, a balanced lifestyle, a healthy sense of boundaries, deep prayer life, relationship with Christ, importance of word and sacrament, the *Catechism of the Catholic Church* as a doctrinal baseline or touchstone, knowledge of scripture and tradition, moral and social teachings, theological anthropology, liturgy and sacraments, facility in a wide range of pastoral skills (such as listening and communication, leadership, collaboration, change management, conflict management, planning skills), appreciation of many cultures, understanding of family dynamics, and so on.

All the documents also acknowledge the pastoral orientation of formation, encourage the practice of theological reflection, promote efforts to integrate the four dimensions of formation (human, spiritual, intellectual, pastoral[3]), and emphasize the need for ongoing formation. This shared curriculum could or should constitute a foundation for a shared ministerial culture to develop among priests, permanent deacons, and lay ecclesial ministers working together in ministry.

In addition, all the documents call for high standards of formation, although they differ regarding accommodations to those standards. For priests, the master of divinity is the "recognized standard" before ordination (PPF, nos. 231f.), although seminaries may show some flexibility regarding admission standards.[4] No degree is required for diaconal ordination, but formation is to last "at least three years" (BNFPD, no. 49) and comprise at least 1,000 clock hours of theological formation (BNFPD, no. 82). For lay ecclesial ministers, "a master's degree, or at least a bachelor's degree ... is preferable" (Co-Workers, 34), but this, as all the provisions in Co-Workers, is only proposed and recommended, not mandated or binding. Further, while a bishop is to set "high standards for the sake of excellence in ministry, expecting and assisting lay ecclesial ministers to meet such standards," he is also to recognize "special situations in his diocese where exceptions may be called for" (52). In addition, processes "for certifying the qualifications of candidates [for lay ecclesial ministry] should include a provision for accepting experience in lieu of course-work for those whose service predates education and formation requirements" (60).

Formational standards for lay ecclesial ministers are, as this comparison indicates, lower than for ordained ministers. The explanation may be that lay ecclesial ministry is simply newer, and support structures (such as financial assistance) to sustain high standards are not yet sufficiently developed. Also, the bishops recognize that persons enter lay ecclesial ministry by different pathways, which the bishops did not wish to close by insisting too stringently on academic standards.[5] Other considerations may also have a bearing. Priests and permanent deacons are considered "official" church ministers in a way lay ecclesial ministers are not; they are understood to "represent" the church in a way lay ecclesial ministers (though they "serve publicly in the local church" [Co-Workers, 10]) do not; they promise stability in ministry while lay ecclesial ministers (even those who make a career of it) do not. Such factors help explain why lay ecclesial ministers do not receive financial and other assistance to the degree seminarians and even permanent deacon candidates do.

So while the considerable overlap in formation topics could foster bonds of connection, commonality, and equality among all these ministers, the greater allowance for lay ecclesial ministers to achieve lesser standards of excellence can position them "lower" (because less professionally qualified) in the configuration of min-istries—even though individual lay ecclesial ministers can, because of their own competence and qualifications, be highly regarded and even better qualified than their ordained colleagues.

Further distinctions among these ministries may be noted in the formation documents—for example, regarding apostolic obedi-ence, ministerial spirituality, and pastoral charity.

Apostolic Obedience

Apostolic obedience is that form of obedience clergy owe their bishop, based on the vow of respect and obedience made to the bishop at ordination.[6] Lay ecclesial ministers are expected to be faithful to the church (*Co-Workers*, 40f.), but they are neither asked nor given the opportunity to commit themselves to this form of obedience with a binding vow.[7] This fact constitutes a distinct difference between ordained and lay ecclesial ministers. It invites reflection on the theological, juridical, and practical significance of the vow of permanence and stability in ministry made by the ordained, and on how better to recognize the kind of commitment to ministry (sometimes life-long) that lay ecclesial ministers currently make by practice, not vow. It invites further reflection on how to invite and recognize forms of promise, which some lay ecclesial ministers may be willing and wish to make, to a degree of stability in their ministry—for a given period of time,[8] perhaps, even if not permanently (as in a kind of incardination). Should this happen, would the church's pastoral leaders be willing to accept such a promise, with the reciprocal commitments on their part that might entail? Openness to and recognition of different forms of ministerial commitment could allow the church's ministerial life and structures to develop in ways responsive to contemporary circumstances and in continuity with other eras of ministerial evolution and innovation.[9]

Ministerial Spirituality

Ministerial spirituality represents another facet of formation that distinguishes ordained and lay ecclesial ministers. *Co-Workers* intentionally does not develop a spirituality specific for lay ecclesial ministers; the other formation documents, in contrast, call for cultivation of a distinctively priestly or diaconal spirituality, grounded first in baptism and then further in sacramental ordination.[10] Priests, for example, are encouraged to conform themselves to the image of Christ the Good Shepherd, and deacons to Christ the Servant.[11]

Should *Co-Workers* have offered some aspect of the life and ministry of Jesus as paradigmatic for the spirituality of lay ecclesial ministry?[12] Would a distinctive spirituality help clarify or establish the "place" of lay ecclesial ministers in the church's ministerial community? Does such a spirituality authentically emerge from their roles or responsibilities? If so, what is it?

Pastoral Charity

Pastoral charity refers to a priest's "total gift of self to the Church" (PDV, no. 23) in imitation of Christ's "shepherding" love.[13] A corresponding element in deacon formation is *diakonia* and the role of being "servant" to others in imitation of Christ the Servant (ND, nos. 28, 29, 37, 39).[14] *Co-Workers*, in contrast, offers no image to give direction and unity to the ministry of lay ecclesial ministers. What might such an image be?[15] And to take the question a step further: What, corresponding to "pastoral charity," would give unity to both the ministry *and life* of lay ecclesial ministers?[16] Or would searching for that unity *of life* and ministry be a kind of category error, since lay ecclesial ministers do not typically, or as such, *identify* with their ministry in the same way as priests (or, perhaps, deacons)? A priest, for example, can say, "I am a priest," and a once-a-month lector can say, "I am a lector"; the syntax is similar but the meaning is different. The priest is saying something more comprehensive—*being* a priest is more a core, defining identity for that person than *being* a lector is for the other (PPF, nos. 23, 25). In view of this difference we can then ask: On a Likert scale between these two points, where do lay ecclesial ministers fall? Where do deacons fall? Asking and answering such questions can contextualize and shed light on the relation and distinction of ordained and lay ecclesial ministries.[17]

While shared core curricular elements, then, could provide a basis for unity among all the church's ministers, other factors highlight differences—based, for example, on the vows of permanence in ministry made by the ordained, on the extent of formation required (or, rather, not required) for lay ecclesial ministers, or on the greater clarity of the ecclesial-ministerial identity of ordained as compared with lay ecclesial ministers.[18]

This brief indication of ministerial relations as described or implicit in certain curriculum components of formation documents gives rise to a subsequent question: What about actual ministerial relations as lived out in the parish setting? Evidence is mixed. On one hand, lay parish ministers report experiencing a "very high" level of support from staff as well as parishioners, and a "very high" level of satisfaction in their work.[19] On the other hand, collaboration can be "very difficult," lay ecclesial ministers see their work as undervalued and underappreciated, and they report "interactions with clergy" as among the aspects of being a lay parish minister most needing improvement.[20]

These more negative factors provide a context for understanding a challenge posed by the U.S. bishops in *Called and Gifted for the Third Millennium*. At the end of that document's section on "The Call to Mission and Ministry," the bishops name several challenges, concluding with this statement:

> One challenge undergirds all [the others]. It is the need to foster respectful collaboration, leading to mutual support in ministry, between clergy and laity for the sake of Christ's Church and its mission to the world. This is a huge task requiring changes in patterns of reflection, behavior, and expectation among laity and clergy alike.[21]

The bishops' challenge invites reflection. It invites ordained ministers to consider their commitment to supporting the ministry of lay ecclesial ministers, and to respectful collaboration with them in ministry *as lay persons*, as people baptized, called by Christ, gifted by the Spirit, and "entrusted by God with the apostolate" (CCC, no. 899). If lay ecclesial ministers consistently experienced positive affirmation and support in the words, actions, and attitudes of the clergy of their diocese, then whatever fear, insecurity, or resentment they may have of clerical power and authority could dissipate, along with the need to be defensive or aggressive about their own role as laity.

The same challenge from the document invites lay ecclesial ministers to consider their commitment to supporting the ministry of priests and permanent deacons, and to respectful collaboration with clergy *as clergy*, as people ordained, called by Christ, gifted by the Spirit, and sent "to serve in the name and in the person of Christ the Head [or Servant] in the midst of the community" (CCC, no. 1591). If clergy consistently experienced positive affirmation and support in the words, actions, and attitudes of the lay ecclesial ministers of their diocese, then whatever fear, insecurity, or resentment they may have of lay influence, competence, or advancement could dissipate, along with the need to be defensive or aggressive about their own role as clergy.[22]

What factors could foster this kind of positive response to the challenge posed by the bishops? The following section explores this question through examination of the theology of ministerial roles offered in ministry formation documents.

Formation Documents: The Theological Component

The formation documents offer concise articulations of a theology of their particular ministry. All such statements are grounded in the Trinity, in communion and mission, in Christ and Spirit, and the sacraments. This study explores one of these elements: the sacraments.

A passage from *Co-Workers* gives us that document's view of the sacramental relation and distinction between lay and ordained ecclesial ministers.

Within this broad understanding of ministry [as *diakonia*, service], distinctions are necessary. They illuminate the nature of the Church as an organic and ordered communion.

The primary distinction lies between the ministry of the lay faithful and the ministry of the ordained, which is a special apostolic calling. Both are rooted in sacramental initiation, but the pastoral ministry of the ordained is empowered in a unique and essential way by the Sacrament of Holy Orders (*Co-Workers*, 20).

So, all ministerial roles and relations are grounded in the sacraments of initiation (see also *Co-Workers*, 21); ministerial distinctions illustrate ordered communion; the distinction of lay and ordained is primary; and that distinction is based in sacraments (of initiation and orders).

An aspect of the sacraments that most of the documents work with and build on is the notion of sacramental "character," much debated in the Middle Ages and still part of church teaching (see CCC, no. 1121, 1272ff.). *Co-Workers*, for example, says the unique ministerial role of the ordained "is a distinction based on the sacramental character given by the Holy Spirit" (21). Exploring this topic can lead to deeper understanding of the sacraments in general, and of ministerial relations of lay and ordained ecclesial ministers.

The Council of Trent said baptism, confirmation, and ordination imprint "a certain spiritual and indelible mark" on the soul.[23] What does this defined teaching mean? Trent did not explain, theologians before and since have not agreed,[24] and the topic is wide open, making it a good catalyst for theological reflection today.

That reflection needs to be characterized by what Frank Quinn has called "the note of metaphoric surprise"[25]—the ability to let a familiar way of speaking communicate in new ways. How can this metaphor of sacramental character surprise us, yielding new insights into baptism-confirmation and ordination, and the ministries based on them?

Relational Ontology v. Substance Ontology

One example is the theory of a "relational ontology" of ministry, as proposed by Wood, Gaillardetz, Hahnenberg, and others.[26] In contrast to what has been called a "substance ontology" of ministry,[27] a relational ontology sees the impact of the sacramental character of holy orders to be found not in the person or *being* of the minister (in the tradition of "ontological change") but in his *relationships*, with Christ and the church.

Relational ontology is a fruitful theological development and a good example of creative fidelity with tradition. It accords with various patristic analogies used to explain the biblical image of *sphragis* or "seal"[28] that contributed to the development of the concept of sacramental character; it is well rooted in the theology of the Trinity; it lessens the tendency to make too absolute the distinction between clergy and laity; and it supports a more nuanced and comprehensive way of perceiving and describing the diverse positions and relationships among persons in ministry today—for example, the "concentric circles" model.[29]

There is still benefit, though, in seeing this development as a complement to and enrichment of, not a replacement for, a substance ontology approach—to think it helpful but on its own incomplete. Consider this sentence, for example: "The metaphors of an indelible 'mark' or 'seal' may be mistakenly identified as effecting a change in a person apart from the ecclesial and christological relationship when the change effected is precisely that relationship."[30] That sacramental character (the "mark" or "seal") is a metaphor is well said.[31] So, too, that the "change effected" by the character is misunderstood if separated from the minister's relationship with Christ and church. But that "the change effected is precisely that relationship" is, I think, only partly right; what changes is the relationship, and more.

What is the *more*? It is the change, not just in the person's relations, but in the *person*—who is changed not only in one's relations with Christ and church, but also by them, and by events (such as through the sacraments). What is the change in the person? That is the substance ontology question—which sacramental theology is diminished by not asking (subsuming it instead into and explaining it by relational ontology), and which can be explored creatively when pursued in search of "metaphoric surprise."

This approach invites a line of reflection on the effect of the sacraments—and of Christ and the Spirit who act in the sacraments—on persons. We might look for comparisons to explore how persons can be fundamentally changed. We might turn to the New Testament language of Paul, who said, "I no longer live, but Christ lives in me" (Gal 2:20), or who spoke of those in Christ becoming a "new creation" (2 Cor 5:17; see Gal 6:15), or of being "changed into his likeness from one degree of glory to another" (2 Cor 3:18). We might think of a mystic describing the transforming effect of the indwelling of the Trinity;[32] of a soldier home from war, traumatized, and now "a different person" than before; of the way events (for example, the Depression) can permanently "mark" the members of a whole generation; or even, from the realm of fiction, of a difference such as that between Gandalf the Grey and Gandalf the White—different examples of change, not only in relationships but in persons themselves. How fundamentally can people be changed? What kind of transformation does God—through events, relationships, sacraments—bring about in persons? How does this affect church ministry?

Such questions will be pursued one way in terms of relational ontology and another in terms of substance ontology—and each is useful. Just as light behaves like a wave and also a particle and needs to be interpreted as both, so both forms of "ontology" when used together can expand the range of our reflections on different aspects of sacramental and ministerial realities. By keeping the language of "ontological change" in play and exploring it with a spirit of metaphoric surprise, we may discover new ways God acts in sacraments for people, and in people through sacraments.

If that kind of thinking then prompted lay ecclesial ministers to new insight into and appreciation for just how powerfully ordination can affect a priest or deacon personally, in his deepest self, with the transforming touch and enduring mark of the Spirit, this could lead to a "change in patterns of reflection" and "behavior," fostering greater "respect" for clergy, and thus building up "mutual support in ministry" (CGTM, 18).

Respect and Mutual Support in Ministry

What about clergy respect for lay ecclesial ministers? Here, too, we can look at the impact of the sacraments of baptism and confirmation. A fruitful text for this purpose is section three in chapter one of the Second Vatican Council's *Decree on the Apostolate of Lay People*.[33] This passage speaks of the place and role of the laity in general; from this starting point, "laity" is the genus of which "lay ecclesial ministry" is a species—both of them within the "family" of the People of God.[34] If we read the passage not only as a doctrinal text but also as a piece of rhetoric that communicates theologically in and through its rhetorical dynamics, its meaning emerges still more powerfully.

Further nuances emerge when we approach the text from two perspectives simultaneously: from the perspective of today, looking for implications for lay ecclesial ministry and, at the same time, from the perspective of November 1965, when the document was approved, reading it in light of the church's views on laity at that time. New ideas then were stirring: Pius XII had said the laity "are" the church,[35] and the movements were striving for greater involvement of laity in the church's worship and life. Yet we would still be imbued with over half a century of Catholic Action, and thus would understand lay persons active in the church to be participating in an apostolate of the hierarchy.[36] With this perspective in mind, what we will find in reading AA, no. 3, is that, sentence by sentence and phrase by phrase, the Catholic Action framework is dismantled and replaced with a different foundation for the place and work of laity in the church.

In AA, no. 3, we first read that the laity are "apostles" and that this "derives from their union with Christ their head"—not, as in Catholic Action, from the hierarchy. This role is then called a "right," something within the laity's own prerogative to exercise, not merely with the permission of others. It is also called a "duty," something they are bound to exercise, despite what others think, judge, or wish. Continuing, we read that "it is by the Lord himself that they are assigned [or "deputed," *deputantur*] to the apostolate"—again, not by the mediation of the apostolic ministry of the ordained, but immediately, directly, personally by Christ. This solid christological basis for the apostolate of the laity is rooted in its sacramental grounding: the laity are "inserted ... in the mystical body of Christ by baptism and strengthened by the power of the holy Spirit in confirmation." All of this is familiar from the 1964 *Constitution on the Church*,[37] which says the same things in nearly the same words (no. 33).

The last paragraph of AA, no. 3, develops a pneumatological grounding for the laity's ministry. The paragraph begins and ends with explicit reference to the role of the ordained; what happens in between reconfigures, even revolutionizes, that role. The paragraph opens by recalling LG, no. 12, and affirming that "the holy Spirit sanctifies the people of God" not only "through the ministry [of the ordained] and the sacraments" but also directly, giving "the faithful special gifts besides (cf. 1 Cor. 12:7)," for the apostolate. The Spirit does this in freedom, " 'allotting them to each just as the Spirit chooses' (1 Cor 12:11)."[38]

The reception of these charisms gives the faithful "the right and the duty to use" them. Here, as before, we find the strong language of "right" and "duty"—before, grounded in Christ's personal deputation, and here, in the Spirit's gift of charisms. These charisms can be exercised anywhere: "in the church and in the world," and thus provide a warrant for lay *ecclesial* ministry.

Then comes a fascinating affirmation, a simple phrase that rhetorically crowns this concatenation of theological points. It is not only the Spirit that has freedom in giving these gifts; *recipients* have a *like* freedom in using them—they can exercise them "in the freedom of the holy Spirit who 'blows where it will' (Jn 3:8)." Not just in the freedom of the Spirit, but the Spirit specifically as the one who, like the wind, "blows where it will" (Jn 3:8)—a powerful scriptural image for the Spirit's utterly free, divinely sovereign, humanly unconfinable scope of action. It is *that* degree of freedom the laity have when using their gifts and charisms, whether in world or church. The rhetorical image makes the underlying theological point all the more emphatic and compelling. We are a long way from Catholic Action.

But the Spirit brings harmony and peace, not competition and chaos. So after emphasizing the laity's right, duty, and freedom to use the charisms received, the paragraph goes on to say this happens "at the same time in communion with the sisters and brothers in Christ. . . ." This is a major point that, in the interests of space, will only be mentioned here: the discernment of callings and charisms is essentially, necessarily, an ecclesial activity. No one person determines the authenticity of charisms—not the person receiving them, and not the community's pastor acting on his own; rather, the whole community has a part to play in what has been described as the church's "ecclesiology of call" or "vocational ecclesiology."[39]

Then the final point: charisms are discerned in communion with the whole community, "and with the pastors especially." This responsibility is well noted in priestly formation documents.[40] Here in AA, no. 3, this deciding role of the pastor is supported with an often-quoted reference to 1 Thessalonians: He is "to pass judgment on the authenticity and good use of these gifts," doing so "not certainly with a view to quenching the Spirit but to testing everything and keeping what is good (cf. 1 Thes 5:12, 19, 21)."[41]

Fulfilling this role takes not just the pastoral skill of making decisions but the spiritual gift of discernment. It calls a priest to be "alert to the internal movements of the Holy Spirit" in himself, and to work "in communion with others." It consists in "deciphering how the gifts of the Spirit are at work in individuals and through individuals in the Church at large. Once discerned, the gifts of the Spirit at work in the parish can be affirmed, celebrated, and encouraged" (BPOFP, 71).

The pastor has a pivotal role in the discernment of charisms because of his leadership function in the community, but all traces of unilateral and authoritarian exercises of power should, in fidelity to AA, no. 3, be exorcised and replaced with a sacred appreciation for Christ's deputation of the faithful to their apostolates, and with "a prompt and heartfelt esteem for all the charisms and tasks which the Spirit gives believers for the building up of the Church" (PDV, no. 74). These charisms and tasks surely include the role of lay ecclesial ministry, upon which the U.S. Catholic bishops as a body have already passed judgment, discerning it to be a work of the Spirit in the church today (see *Co-Workers*, 14, 26). In all this we find multiple reasons for "changes in patterns of reflection" (CGTM, 18) that can lead clergy to deeper respect and stronger support for laity in ministry.

Cultivating Dispositions

Acknowledging theological grounds for mutual support in ministry is a necessary but not sufficient basis for implementing such support in the pastoral ministry setting. Making it a pastoral reality requires effective methods and the right spirit and dispositions as well. What dispositions? Let us briefly consider two for clergy and two for lay ecclesial ministers.

Pastors

For pastors, the well-known passage from Augustine is instructive: "When I am frightened by what I am for you, then I am consoled by what I am with you. For you I am the bishop; with you I am a Christian. The first is an office, the second a grace; the first a danger, the second salvation."[42] Notice, in particular: "frightened," and "danger." Neither rhetorical flourish nor hyperbole, these words are best taken literally; Augustine is terrified of a peril he finds himself in as a bishop/pastor. Our study of AA, no. 3, helps us appreciate the peril: that of having to "pass judgment" on the authenticity of the charisms of the faithful, with the risk of getting it wrong and becoming a barrier between Christ the Head and Shepherd and one of his flock. In doing so a pastor can hinder a person's exercise of a right bestowed and duty imposed by the Lord himself, or prevent the use of a charism given directly by the Spirit to benefit the whole community.

The possibility of being such a barrier to God's purposes should cause a holy fear among conscientious clergy. Too much fear could engender pastoral paralysis and the hobbling of a pastor's genuine authority. But if something like it never entered his mind when making decisions about the roles of Christ's faithful in the community, that would indicate a failure both to grasp the full scope of the theological teaching of the Council on the laity and to feel the full weight of his pastoral responsibility of "passing judgment."

A second disposition that follows from the first was well expressed by Pope Benedict XVI responding to an interview question about the role of women in the church today. After recalling parameters for discussing the question, he then said, "and we will have to listen to God so as not to stand in their way"—a good pastoral application of "do not quench the Spirit," and echoing as well the advice of Gamaliel in Acts 5:34—39.[43]

Lay Ecclesial Ministers

What dispositions are relevant for lay ecclesial ministers? One is the willingness to speak up and make known their insights and proposals for the pastoral good of the community. Lay silence is an abdication of responsibility for the common good and manifests reluctance to collaborate with clergy; "lay voice" is a right, even a responsibility, noted in both Council documents and canon law.[44] A second disposition is that "Christian obedience" articulated in the same two sources[45]—a lay form of obedience correlative to the "apostolic obedience" of the ordained. The intricate interplay these sources describe, of mutual speaking and listening and of discerning and doing, is meant to characterize a faith-filled community in which the Lord's voice is heard in the voices of all the faithful, in such a way that the community is "strengthened by all her members" (LG, no. 37).

Conclusion

Much of this need for respect and mutual support was concisely and well summarized by Zeni Fox: "There is a priority of charism, but a necessity of order, which is also an action of grace"[46]—an action of healing, affirming grace when carried out with a healthy mix of holy fear (of obstructing the Lord's work), pastoral responsibility (to make good decisions), confident hope (in the Spirit's help), respectful appreciation (for people's gifts), and willingness to minister in the manner of Christ who came to serve.

If these dispositions are to grow and flourish, whether in ordained or lay ecclesial ministers, it will require the combined force of all four dimensions of formation: human formation to cultivate the affective maturity to embrace these dispositions; spiritual formation for the nourishment of prayer, word, and sacrament to sustain them; intellectual formation to recognize their theological basis; and pastoral formation to gain the skills to implement them.

When such formation bears fruit, grounded in a sacramentally and charismatically informed appreciation for the calling of each and all in ministry, and flowering in dispositions of esteem for ministerial "co-workers," the conditions will be in place to sustain the "changes in patterns of reflection, behavior, and expectation among laity and clergy alike" that the U.S. bishops think necessary "to foster respectful collaboration, leading to mutual support in ministry" (CGTM, 18). The more this vision and practice take hold among those in church ministry, both lay and ordained, the freer they will be to devote themselves to their necessary but subsidiary task[47] of serving the church's people and *their* primary mission of evangelization, worship, and justice—which is the whole point of clarifying positions and fostering good relations among the church's ministers.

Notes

[1]U.S. Catholic Bishops, *Co-Workers in the Vineyard of the Lord: A Resource for Guiding the Development of Lay Ecclesial Ministry* (Washington, DC: USCCB, 2005), 21 (cited in text as *Co-Workers*).

[2]Documents include: Congregation for Catholic Education and Congregation for the Clergy, *Basic Norms for the Formation of Permanent Deacons* and *Directory for the Ministry and Life of Permanent Deacons* (Vatican City: Libreria Editrice Vaticana, 1998) (cited in text as BNFPD and DMLPD, respectively). John Paul II, *I Will Give You Shepherds* (Washington, DC: USCC, 1992) (cited in text as PDV, for *Pastores Dabo Vobis*). U.S. Catholic Bishops, *The Basic Plan for the Ongoing Formation of Priests* (Washington, DC: USCC, 2001) (cited in text as BPOFP). U.S. Catholic Bishops, *National Directory for the Formation, Ministry, and Life of Permanent Deacons in the United States* (Washington, DC: USCCB, 2005) (cited in text as ND). U.S. Catholic Bishops, *Program of Priestly Formation*, 5th ed. (Washington, DC: USCCB, 2006) (cited in text as PPF). Also, *Catechism of the Catholic Church*, 2nd ed. (Washington, DC: USCC, 1997) (cited in text as CCC).

[3]These are the four dimensions of formation as presented in PDV and used in the PPF (5th ed.), ND, and *Co-Workers*.

[4] PPF specifies admission standards (no. 50: "a bachelor's degree or its equivalent," as well as 30 credit hours of philosophy and 12 of theology), but also allows for flexibility (see nos. 49 and 183).

[5]Thanks to Zeni Fox for this observation.

[6]The formation documents describe apostolic obedience as, for example, "a surrender of one's own will for the sake of the larger mission" of the church (PPF, no. 110); it is expressed and nourished by "the practice of regular prayerful submission to what is asked" (BPOFP, no. 34).

[7]Nor do lay ecclesial ministers make a formal profession of faith or take the oath of fidelity, as do priests (upon becoming deacons, PPF, no. 283) and permanent deacons (ND, no. 236).

[8]See Elissa Rinere, "Canon Law and Emerging Understandings of Ministry," in *Ordering the Baptismal Priesthood: Theologies of Lay and Ordained Ministry*, ed. Susan K. Wood, Michael Downey, Zeni Fox, and Richard R. Gaillardetz (Collegeville, MN: Liturgical Press, 2003), 81: "In lay ministry developments, we see the need for recognition of charisms that might not be life-long...." See also Edward P. Hahnenberg, *Ministries: A Relational Approach* (New York: Crossroad, 2003), 134, and Zeni Fox, *New Ecclesial Ministry: Lay Professionals Serving the Church*, rev. ed. (Franklin, WI: Sheed & Ward, 2002), 330. This suggestion is comparable to the new forms of relationship John Paul II has recognized between laity and religious communities (see *Vita Consecrata*, no. 56), including arrangements where lay persons "share fully for a certain period of time the Institute's community life" and mission (full membership, temporary term).

[9]Thomas F. O'Meara, "The Metamorphoses of Ministry" (chap. 3), *Theology of Ministry*, rev. ed. (New York: Paulist Press, 1999), provides a helpful account of ministerial changes through the centuries.

[10]*Co-Workers*, 38; PDV, nos. 20, 45ff.; PPF, no. 109f.; BPOFP, 31; BNFPD, nos. 11, 72; DMLPD, no. 44; ND, nos. 62-65, 112, 246.

[11]For priests, see PPF, no. 109; BPOFP, no. 18; PDV, no. 20. For deacons, see ND, no. 62; DMLPD, no. 45.

[12]The 1993 *Guide for Catechists* from the Congregation for the Evangelization of Peoples articulated features of a distinctive catechist spirituality (nos. 6-10), including "openness to God's word, to the Church and to the world; authenticity of life; missionary zeal; and devotion to Mary" (no. 6).

[13]"Shepherding" love means, for example, feeding the flock, calling each by name, going in search of lost sheep, binding up wounds (see PDV, no. 22). Pastoral charity is meant to direct "every moment and every one of [a priest's] acts toward the fundamental choice to 'give his life for the flock,'" and in so doing to "unify" his life and activities (PDV, no. 23). See also PDV, nos. 30, 40, 70; PPF, no. 25 (citing Vatican II, *Presbyterorum Ordinis*, no. 14); BPOFP, no. 31.

[14]For a critique of this theology of the diaconate, see Richard R. Gaillardetz, "On the Theological Integrity of the Diaconate," in Owen F. Cummings, William T. Ditewig, Richard R. Gaillardetz, *Theology of the Diaconate: The State of the Question* (Mahwah, NJ: Paulist Press, 2005), 72ff.

[15]Consider, for example, Michael Downey's suggestion to see lay ecclesial ministers as "an *icon of the Church ad-vent-ing*" and, with reference to the Emmaus passage, as "accompanying other disciples on the road." See Downey, "Ministerial Identity: A Question of Common Foundations," in Wood et al., *Ordering the Baptismal Priesthood*, 21.

[16]Note that the U.S. bishops' national deacon directory deals with their formation, ministry, *and life*, and Vatican II wrote a decree on the ministry *and life* of presbyters.

[17]For example, Hahnenberg notes the "ambiguity" (*Ministries*, 100), "asymmetry" (146), or "imbalance" (194) in the present situation where it can happen that full-time and perhaps better prepared and more experienced lay ecclesial ministers receive less formal ecclesial recognition than part-time, less prepared, and less experienced permanent deacons.

[18]On this last point, see Fox, *New Ecclesial Ministry*, 35ff., 323ff.

[19]On staff support see David DeLambo, *Lay Parish Ministers: A Study of Emerging Leadership* (New York: National Pastoral Life Center, 2005), 113. On satisfaction in ministry see Fox, *New Ecclesial Ministry*, 53.

[20]On the difficulty of collaboration see Fox, *New Ecclesial Ministry*, 38, 41. On feeling undervalued and underappreciated see Fox, 50, 308f. On interactions with clergy needing improvement see DeLambo, *Lay Parish Ministers*, 141 (this item was second on a list of 14; the first was salary).

[21]U.S. Catholic Bishops, *Called and Gifted for the Third Millennium* (Washington, DC: USCC, 1995), 18 (cited in text as CGTM).

[22]On clerical fear or insecurity regarding the gifts of the laity, see Bishop John M. D'Arcy, "The Call to Communion and the Road to Priestly Maturity: 'Circles of Communion,'" in *Priests for a New Millennium: A Series of Essays on the Ministerial Priesthood by the Catholic Bishops of the United States*, ed. Secretariat for Priestly Life and Ministry (Washington, DC: USCC, 2000), 19. Bernard Sesboüé believes that lay ecclesial ministers will not become well recognized and integrated into the church's ministerial life as long as "the priests in a diocese perceive [them] as a threat to their own identity" (see "Lay Ecclesial Ministers: A Theological Look into Their Future," *The Way* 42, no. 3 [July 2003]: 71; also BPOFP, no. 23).

[23]Trent, *Decree on the Sacraments*, Canons on the Sacraments in General, no. 9.

[24]See David Foxen, *The Dogmatic Interpretation of Sacramental Character According to the Discussions and Documents of the Council of Trent* (Shelby, OH: n.p., 1975), chap. 4, esp. 314, 316. Also J. Galot, "Le caractère sacerdotal selon le Concile de Trente," *Nouvelle Revue Theologique* 93, no. 9 (November 1971): 941-43.

[25]Frank Quinn, "Ministry, Ordination Rites, and Language," in *The Theology of Priesthood*, ed. Donald J. Goergen and Ann Garrido (Collegeville, MN: Liturgical Press, 2000), 47.

[26]See Susan K. Wood, *Sacramental Orders* (Collegeville, MN: Liturgical Press, 2000), for example, 72-74; Richard R. Gaillardetz, "The Ecclesiological Foundations of Ministry within an Ordered Communion," in *Ordering the Baptismal Priesthood*, 38-41; Edward P. Hahnenberg, *Ministries*, chap. 2, esp. 92-97. All three authors reference the work of John D. Zizioulas; see his "Ordination—A Sacrament? An Orthodox Reply," in *The Plurality of Ministries*, ed. Hans Küng and Walter Kasper (New York: Herder & Herder, 1972), 33-40, and his *Being as Communion: Studies in Personhood and the Church* (Crestwood, NY: St. Vladimir's Seminary Press, 2002), esp. chap. 6, "Ministry and Communion," 209-46.

[27]See Gaillardetz, "The Ecclesiological Foundations," 40; Hahnenberg, *Ministries*, 92.

[28]See Ephesians 1:13 and 4:30 and 2 Corinthians 1:22 (where the verb *sphragizein* is used). See also Gerald Austin, *Anointing with the Spirit* (New York: Pueblo Publishing, 1985), 9-10; Austin refers to the more extensive treatment of *sphragis* in chap. 3 of Jean Daniélou's classic, *The Bible and the Liturgy* (Notre Dame: University of Notre Dame Press, 1956), 54-69.

[29]For patristic analogies (in particular, relational analogies of belonging— of sheep to their particular shepherd, soldiers to their army unit or general, slaves to their master) see A.-M. Roguet, "La théologie du caractère et l'incorporation à l'église," *La Maison-Dieu*, no. 32 (1952): 76f. For theology of the Trinity see Hahnenberg, *Ministries*, chap. 2. For the concentric circles model see, most extensively, Hahnenberg, *Ministries*, chap. 3 and passim; also O'Meara, *Theology of Ministry*, for example, 6, 157ff., 183; O'Meara, "The Ministry of Presbyters and the Many Ministries in the Church," in *The Theology of Priesthood*, 80ff.; Thomas Groome, "The Future of Catholic Ministry: Our Best Hopes," in *Priests for the 21st Century*, ed. Donald Dietrich (New York: Crossroad, 2006), 169, 184.

[30]Wood, *Sacramental Orders*, 74.

[31]Aquinas called it the same in *Summa Theologiae*, III.63.2 ad 1. Juan de Lugo in the seventeenth century referred to it as a "way of speaking [*modus loquendi*] of the councils and the Fathers"; cited in Foxen, *The Dogmatic Interpretation of Sacramental Character*, 328.

[32]For example, John of the Cross, *The Living Flame of Love*, Prologue.

[33]*Apostolicam Actuositatem* (cited in text as AA).

[34]Paul Lakeland raised the question at the 2008 College Theology Society annual meeting during discussion of this paper: Why not consider ministry, instead of laity, as the genus? This is a good point, and articulates the preferred approach today. Yet following the path of laity as genus continues, I think, to hold potential; moreover, it accords with the context provided by the Council's decree on the laity (developed here), and also with *Co-Workers*, which speaks first of "The Call to All Believers" (6ff.), and within that, as a subset, "The Call to the Lay Faithful" (8ff.), and within that, as a further subset, "The Call to Lay Ecclesial Ministry" (10ff).

[35]Pius XII, Address on February 20, 1946, cited in CCC, no. 899.

[36]The classic definition of Catholic Action as formulated by Pius XI was: "the participation of the laity in the apostolate of the hierarchy." See, for example, his Letter to Cardinal Bertram of 13 November 1928, in *Acta Apostolicae Sedis* 20 (1928): 385 (English translation in *The Lay Apostolate: Papal Teachings* [Boston: St. Paul Editions, 1961], 289). For further reading, see Fernand Lelotte, *Fundamental Principles of Catholic Action* (Montreal and South Bend: Fides Publisher, 1947); Arthur Alonso, *Catholic Action and the Laity* (St. Louis: B. Herder Book Co., 1961); "Catholic Action," in *New Catholic Encyclopedia*, 2nd ed. For a more specialized study, presented at the 2005 College Theology Society annual meeting, see Christopher D. Denny, "The Laity and Catholic Action in John Courtney Murray's Vision of the Church," in *Vatican II: Forty Years Later*, ed. William Madges (Maryknoll, NY: Orbis Books, 2006), 55-77.

[37] *Lumen Gentium* (cited in text as LG).

[38] Compare Karl Rahner's remark that "charism does not owe its ecclesial character to hierarchical blessing"—another allusion, it seems, to Catholic Action. Karl Rahner, *Theology of Pastoral Action* (New York: Herder & Herder, 1968), 60.

[39] Edward Hahnenberg, "The Vocation to Lay Ecclesial Ministry," *Origins* 37, no. 12 (August 30, 2007): 181. See also Paul Lakeland, *The Liberation of the Laity: In Search of an Accountable Church* (New York: Continuum, 2002), 225, on discernment as "a work of the whole community."

[40] See PDV, nos. 26 (par. 6), 40, 59 (par. 3), 74 (par. 2); BPOFP, 23, 71, 111.

[41] AA, no. 3; see LG, no. 12. *Presbyterorum Ordinis*, no. 9, roots the same task in 1 Jn 4:1. Carolyn Osiek, in her scripture-based study of AA, no. 3, draws the conclusion that "AA's procedure of leaving it to the pastors to 'make a judgment about the true nature and proper use of these gifts' is an incomplete appropriation of the Pauline vision of community." See "Relation of Charism to Rights and Duties in the New Testament Church," in *Official Ministry in a New Age*, ed. James H. Provost (Washington, DC: Canon Law Society of America, 1981), 57. Without disputing this exegetical conclusion, I hope to indicate the possibility of "judgment" being exercised in the church in a genuinely communal manner that can be duly mindful of rights and duties.

[42] Augustine, Sermon 340; cited in part in PDV, no. 20; in full, in LG, no. 32. Translation here as in Richard R. Gaillardetz, "Mission and Ministry," in *Lay Ministry in the Catholic Church: Visioning Church Ministry Through the Wisdom of the Past*, ed. Richard W. Miller II (St. Louis: Liguori, 2005), 55.

[43] "Not to stand in their way" is cited in Phyllis Zagano, "The Question of Governance and Ministry for Women," *Theological Studies* 68, no. 2 (June 2007): 367. "Do not quench the Spirit" is from 1 Thes 5:19; see *Co-Workers*, 23; AA, no. 3; LG, no. 12.

[44] LG, no. 37; Canon 212, §3. The phrase "lay voice" is from Lakeland, *The Liberation of the Laity*, 213.

[45] LG, no. 37; Canon 212, §1.

[46] Fox, *New Ecclesial Ministry*, 318.

[47] Paul Lakeland rightly calls the role of the clergy—and in the context of this paper, I would extend this description to ecclesial ministers generally, both the ordained and the lay ecclesial ministers who work with them in pastoral ministry—"indispensable but ancillary," in *The Liberation of the Laity*, 255.

PART IV

THE FUTURE CHALLENGES
FOR THE LAITY

Maturity and the Lay Vocation

From Ecclesiology to Ecclesiality

Paul Lakeland

Reflecting on a lifetime of involvement in Catholic theology, Yves Congar once opined that "Today it is the case ... that the clergy need to be defined in relation to the laity."[1] Congar's mature work on the role of the laity in the church, expressed in three key articles written in the 1960s, seemed in some ways to close the circle, to return the church to the healthier understanding of what it is to be a Christian that had prevailed in the first centuries.[2] Before the specialization of "priestly" roles and the advent of monasticism had reduced the laity to what Congar called "negative creatures," everyone was part of the *laos*. But later people came to be defined by what they were *not*, in other words, not religious professionals and not professionally holy. Now, thought Congar, after the great work of the Council, upon which he had been so influential, and indeed in the light of his later thinking that could not have been part of the conciliar vision, it was evident that the layperson was the standard Christian. Perhaps today he would have used the phrase "default Christian." Since Congar, many others have taken up the conciliar rediscovery of baptism and recognized that it is through baptism that we become a new creation, that baptism is our entry into the priestly and apostolic character of the whole faithful people, that baptism is entry into Christian mission.[3] As Cardinal Suenens never tired of saying, "The proudest moment in the life of a pope is not his coronation as supreme pastor, his consecration as bishop or his ordination as a priest, but his baptism as a Christian."

This essay explores some elements of the "full circle" that we have traversed, in my view, from the first centuries of the church to the present day. In the beginning, the involvement of the whole faithful people in responsibility for their community was palpable. Today we have reached a point, at least in so-called "first world" Catholicism, where the emergence of an educated lay Catholic community providentially coincides with the appearance of challenges to the survival of our church. To deal with these enormous challenges it will not be enough to harness the energies of clergy and laity, for the very division between these two groups is much of what has occasioned the problems in the first place. It will be necessary, perhaps, to abandon the very terms themselves, to retranslate *laos tou theou* as "the faithful," and to rebuild a church on Congar's model of "different ministries."

I am dividing this essay into five brief sections. The first will present some of the particular challenges in and to American Catholicism today, focusing on my view that "the laity" are infantilized by oppressive ecclesial structures. Second, I will very briefly recall three familiar ideas from Vatican II that are especially germane to this inquiry. Third, I want to make the case that the emergence of an educated laity requires a shift in how we think about what the church is—in my terms, from "ecclesiology" to "ecclesiality." Fourth, I want to see what sociological data has to offer to fill out this picture of the life of faith. Finally, I will offer one example of the way in which this shift might be undertaken.

Essentially I argue that a thick description of the life of faith is the way to "do" what has traditionally been called ecclesiology. This more inductive approach implies that polity or church organization is much more important than Catholics have traditionally thought and, in particular, that it leads to an ecclesiology that emerges from the consciousness of the believing community rather than one that is imposed from above as some abstract and essentialist representation of "the mind of Jesus" or "the plan of God." Moreover, this must be how ecclesiological understanding emerged in the early church; first the community, then reflection upon it. To anticipate: ecclesiality precedes ecclesiology and is, therefore, determinative of it.

The Crisis in American Catholicism Today

While Dietrich Bonhoeffer was sitting in prison awaiting his fate at the hands of the Nazis, not so far away Yves Congar languished in a German prisoner of war camp. They were both about the same age, both ecumenically minded, both deeply concerned about the role of the church in the modern age. It would be wonderful to have an exchange of letters between them, but we don't. It would be exciting to read the comments of one upon the other, but there are none. If I were a novelist I would imagine some, but I am not. Yet I think it is safe to say that, had they met, their conversation would sooner or later have turned to the idea of "coming of age." Bonhoeffer's notion of "the world come of age" is what anyone who knows anything at all about him knows he wrote, and Congar's work on the role of lay people in the church effectively addressed the question: how shall the church be, now that the laity have come of age? Congar was of the opinion that the very idea of "laity" as a distinct group in the church only emerged when the Enlightenment canonized the separation of the sacred and the secular. For Congar, "the secular" begat "the laity." Admittedly, Congar would not have gone along with Bonhoeffer's contention that Catholics were too closely allied with their church rather than the world, but there is much common ground in their different calls for a new way of being the community of faith, one that mirrors the world come of age.

There is a well-worn story of the famous preacher whose annotated sermon notes were left in the pulpit one day and found to have the marginal comment, "argument seems weak here, so speak louder." The story of the post-Tridentine Catholic Church and especially the church of the nineteenth century sometimes seems like the preacher's desperation stratagem writ large. From Gregory XVI's 1832 encyclical letter *Mirari Vos*, condemning Lammenais in particular and the obscenity of "freedom of conscience" in general (the same pope famously banned railroads from the Papal States on the grounds that they were a dangerous innovation, *"chemin de fer, chemin d'enfer"* or "the iron road, the road to hell"), to Pius IX's 1864 "Syllabus of Errors" condemning freedom of religion, to Vatican I's dogmatic definition of papal infallibility, the less the church was listened to, the louder it shouted. Modernism was banned and Pius X told the laity that their "one duty" was "like a docile flock, to follow their pastors."[4] But Vatican II still happened and its spirit, while under stress, continues today. The message of Esdras by way of Thomas Jefferson might be a good antidote to the beleaguered preacher or the beleaguered church: "Truth is great and it will prevail, if left to itself."[5]

While the church through the Modernist crisis and to a degree still today has been expending energy resisting change of all sorts, the developing complexion of the Catholic laity escapes ecclesiastical control. Even allowing for the impact of the extraordinary influx of Catholic immigrants in recent years, the American Catholic community today is one of the most successful religious groups measured both by affluence and education. It is also by far the largest division of American Christianity, some 65 million people, about the same size as the next twelve denominations combined. Yet the entirety of competent professional lay Catholics in today's church continues to have absolutely no formal role or voice in any governance or leadership positions. Where they are invited and even encouraged to participate in situations like parish pastoral councils or parish or diocesan finance councils, the last word—indeed the only executive word—is that of the pastor or bishop.[6] There is one canonical structure that could encourage a measure of shared responsibility, the diocesan synod in which canon law mandates significant lay representation. However, the 1984 revision of the Code of Canon Law removed the requirement that a synod be convened every seven years, probably because no one was paying any attention to it anyway, and replaced it with the stipulation that it should convene whenever the bishop deems it opportune. That does not seem to be very often. If Catholicism in America ever needed a synod to address a crisis, the early years of the twenty-first century surely qualify. The combined impact of declining numbers of clergy, growing numbers of Catholics, declining levels of church attendance, the fall-out from the sexual abuse scandal and the financial challenges that have led to five dioceses, to date, declaring bankruptcy ought to encourage a prudent bishop to pool our collective Catholic wisdom. To my knowledge, no diocesan synod has yet taken place in this century.

American Catholicism today is thus in a somewhat explosive and distinctly frustrating situation. Many educated lay professionals have countless gifts to lend to the church but no formal avenue through which their voices and expertise can be brought to bear independently of the invitation from the clerical leaders of a hierarchical institution in which they have no voice whatsoever. Thus, to use my own term, they are "infantilized" by oppressive structures. This situation will end only when the laity themselves take steps to bring it to an end, and while this is not yet occurring in numbers sufficiently large to get the attention of bishops, the response to the scandal of clerical sexual abuse has brought it closer. Anger can often lead to courage. On the other hand, one well-documented alternative avenue of response to oppression is depression. The much-noted passivity of the laity is a fact. The energies of relatively few are driving movements for ecclesial reform and, if they remain the work of a few, they will eventually languish. Lay passivity needs to come to an end, but it is hard to overcome centuries of theology and pastoral practice that have induced layfolk to embrace their own oppression.

Theological Principles: Consent, the "Sense of the Faithful," Secularity

Three important ecclesiological notions deserve fuller treatment than I can give them here, but a summary should suffice. They are (1) the "principle of lay consent" stressed so forcefully in Congar's *Lay People in the Church*; (2) the conciliar rediscovery of the *sensus fidei*; and (3) the assertion that the true defining characteristic of the laity is their secularity.

First, I am persuaded that it is important to recover the ancient principle of lay consent for our adult Catholic Church of today. Lay consent was and is the means by which what is taught as true actually comes to life in the community of faith. Or not, of course. It also was—and should be again—an actual mechanism through which the whole community chose or assented to the nomination of a new bishop or pastor. Second, then, the principle is revived in *Lumen Gentium*'s treatment of the *sensus fidei*, especially as glossed in *Dei Verbum*. Third, the "secularity" of the laity makes sense as a statement about the way in which the mission of the church occurs in the world, not internally to the community of faith, so that it is the laity, not the clergy, who are primarily responsible for that mission. In this sense, the church itself is secular.

We simply cannot overstate the importance of *Dei Verbum*'s assertion that the Holy Spirit guides tradition in several ways, including "through the contemplation and study of believers who ponder these things in their hearts" and "from the intimate sense of spiritual realities which they experience."[7] The vehicle of the *sensus fidelium* and the engine of reception/rejection is nothing other than the faithful sociality of the whole believing community. It cannot, of its very nature, be assigned to the voice of authority or the teaching office of the magisterium. In the final analysis, the long-term effective rejection of a teaching by the whole body of the faithful, which is precisely the exercise of the *sensus fidelium*, must be determinative of the magisterium, and not the other way around. Of course we can argue at length about how long-term is long-term, and what constitutes wholesale rejection, but the principle is sound because the magisterium is, in the final analysis, a dimension of tradition, and not tradition itself. A teaching that has not been received can only be explained in one of three ways, as bad teaching that is not the work of the Spirit, as good teaching that is being poorly taught, which is a wake-up call to the magisterium, or as good teaching well-taught that the sinfulness of the human condition resists accepting. The longer the resistance to reception continues and the more widespread it is, the less likely is it that the third option can be invoked.

From Ecclesiology to Ecclesiality

The most significant change in recent years within the intellectual tradition of Catholicism has been its shift from a deductive to an inductive approach to theological reflection. It was probably the Canadian Jesuit theologian Bernard Lonergan who was the first to be clear about this shift, writing in 1968 that theology has "become largely an empirical science" and that "Scripture and Tradition now provide not premises, but data."[8] In the end, in the Catholic Church, real change will always involve a theological component, and the move to an inductive method (and its corollary, historical sensitivity) has enormous implications for the practice of ecclesiology. Seeking an inductive ecclesiology or an "ecclesiology from below" means attending to the actual practices and beliefs of Catholics, to what I have elsewhere called "faithful sociality"[9] and that here I am designating by the term "ecclesiality." Ecclesiality, the community's life of faith, must be determinative of ecclesiology, which is second-order reflection. Ecclesiology is theological knowledge that is at least as much descriptive as it is prescriptive.

Ecclesiology, like theology in general, can be conducted deductively or inductively. *Deductive* ecclesiology can be oriented prescriptively and proscriptively. Oriented *prescriptively*, deductive ecclesiology proposes theoretical models or derives models from scripture and the tradition and employs them to make normative claims about what the church is, who is part of the church and who is not, what its mission and destiny are, and how it is related, if at all, to the wider world and to the extended family of other Christian and non-Christian religious communities. This is the accepted mode of ecclesiology even today, and while its preference for models over an earlier orientation to definition is a distinct improvement, it remains a fundamentally deductive enterprise.

Oriented *proscriptively*, ecclesiology takes the normative claims of prescriptive ecclesiology and sanctions those who do not accept the canonized models. In centuries gone by, normative ecclesiology would stoke the pyres prepared for heretics whose sin, in the end, was always defiance of authority, hence always ecclesiological apostasy. Prescription usually leads to proscription, and proscription to sanctions. Then you were burned at the stake; now you are relieved of your responsibilities. Inductive ecclesiology, on the other hand, is always descriptive; it is, indeed, a "thick description" of ecclesiality or faithful sociality that not merely describes practices and patterns but that places them in a larger context, for example, within power relations. It makes its task a faithful account of the *sensus fidelium* in a particular time and place. It locates "church" wherever the living Spirit is at work in the community, and it derives ecclesiological principles from the grassroots context of faith in the life of the believing community.

To the distinction between deductive and inductive ecclesiology and the nuances of prescriptive, proscriptive, and descriptive forms of attention we can add three further pairs of characteristics. First, ecclesiology that is deductive is of its nature elite, while inductive ecclesiology is more popular. Second, inductive ecclesiology will be pluralistic, since there are many concrete ecclesial contexts out of which it will emerge, while deductive ecclesiology is bound to lean toward the univocal and the putatively universal.[10] Finally, while deductive forms of reflection are more abstract and theoretical, inductive approaches tend toward concreteness. In sum, then, the distinction is between a form of ecclesiology (deductive) that is derived from the texts and history of the tradition's reflection upon them, and a form of ecclesiology (inductive) that begins from a thick description of actual ecclesial life. If this form of ecclesial reflection eventually uses the terminology of the tradition, it is because those images and concepts seem to fit the ecclesiality under consideration.

This approach to ecclesiology leads to a new understanding of the priority of the community's faith experience over the more abstract determinations of the deductive approach. This is evident from the role of censor that ecclesiality plays relative to received ecclesiologies. To take one obvious example, the longstanding definition of the church as an institution or "perfect society," most commonly associated with the sixteenth-century Jesuit Cardinal Robert Bellarmine, has been sidelined in current ecclesiology.[11] Of course the church bears certain institutional elements, but while the model was displaced for a number of reasons, the clinching argument is that it does not correspond to ecclesial reality. The faithful as a whole do not accept that the church needs nothing beyond itself and that those outside the church are beyond salvation, still less that the mechanical application of church attendance and reception of the sacraments says the last word on faithfulness.

In any stand-off between the *sensus fidelium* and theological concepts or teachings, the last word must go to the *sensus fidelium* because the other ecclesial *loci* of the work of the Holy Spirit—episcopal collegiality and papal primacy—require for their legitimacy that they reflect the "faith of the church" and therefore that they are in the last analysis in service to that faith. Of course, collegiality and primacy have an important role in correcting evident and severe aberrations, though this service to the church is more a matter of discerning where the Spirit is truly at work in ecclesial life than in identifying deviations from some theoretical norm. In the four hundred years between the Council of Trent and Vatican II, the institutional church willfully misunderstood a series of efforts within Catholicism for the reform of the church. Jansenism, liberal Catholicism and the work of the Catholic Tübingen School, Americanism, Modernism, the twentieth-century theological renewal movement of *la nouvelle théologie*, the worker-priest movement in France, and the emergence of liberation theology were all resisted and mostly swept aside. The great pioneers[12] of the French "new theology" were subject to severe ecclesiastical sanctions under the papacy of Pius XII, only to be subsequently rehabilitated. Three of them were later named to the College of Cardinals. When the bishops at Vatican II recognized the theological importance of "reading the signs of the times" (an inductive impulse *par excellence*), the valuable insights of all these movements became clearly etched in the conciliar documents.

If the best example of inductive ecclesiality available to us is the church of Latin American liberation theology, one closer to home to which we need to attend is that of the contemporary Roman Catholic Church in the United States. Borrowing from John Thiel's typology of senses of tradition for my ecclesiological purposes, I want to examine the American church as an example of "incipiently developing" ecclesiality.[13] Such a designation is, it seems, arguable if the American church offers an occasion for truthful novelty that with the passing of time may gain the recognized authority of tradition. Among significant changes in the American church at the present time that provide a context for truthful novelty are an aging and numerically declining parochial and religious clergy; a rapidly growing work force of lay ecclesial ministers; significantly declining concern for weekly mass attendance among self-professed Catholics, missing generations of "millennials," Generation Xers, and some of their parents; a somewhat lower valuation of episcopal leadership; and a noticeable increase in interest in prayer and spirituality. To this we can add a discernible shift on the part of some more affluent and some more conservative Catholics, though the move is perhaps temporary, away from traditional Democratic political identification toward the Republican Party. But the more significant social and political shift may be that increasingly Catholics are indistinguishable from Americans in general in terms of their positions on political, socioeconomic, and personal ethical questions. On abortion, stem cell research, immigration, capital punishment, same-sex civil unions and marriages, premarital cohabitation, welfare programs, and so on, Catholics mirror American public opinion in general.

Since the Catholic Church in its traditional teaching role has very clear positions on most if not all ethical questions that concern Americans today—some of them, like immigration, remarkably radical, and some, like the question of same-sex unions, very conservative—the fact that Catholics are all over the map on precisely these issues makes it safe to say that the hold of church teaching authority over the ethical and political consciences of contemporary Catholics is rapidly weakening. On the issue of ecclesial authority alone, contemporary ecclesiality is obviously at odds with received ecclesiology. As a consequence of the arguments above about the role of the *sensus fidelium* and the priority of faith life over pronouncements of the church leadership, we cannot assume that the views of American Catholics are wrong where they conflict with official church teaching. Nor can all their views be correct, if they are as divided as seems to be the case. Resolving this issue requires us to turn our attention to some hard data on the state of American Catholicism.

Public Opinion, Gallup Polls, and the "Sensus Fidelium"

While the importance of the *sensus fidelium* is well attested in *Lumen Gentium*, actually gauging the way in which it forms, shifts, and develops is quite another matter. Since the understanding of the tradition and even of major doctrines is subject to historical development in the view of the Catholic tradition, the practical awareness of authentic faith must also be on the move, however imperceptibly, if only to reiterate by its continuing practice the unchanging truth beneath changing historical conditions. Once again it makes sense to read *Lumen Gentium*'s words on the sense of the faithful through the more dynamic, process-oriented references of *Dei Verbum* where it is "through the contemplation and study of believers who ponder these things in their hearts" and "from the intimate sense of spiritual realities which they experience" that the sense of the faithful remains a living reality. Attesting to the reality of the sense of the faithful is one thing, but delving more deeply into it will require some reliable means for measuring how teaching is being received and how practice is, or is not, attesting to its truth.

One very common approach in today's world to the problem of obtaining data about human behavior and beliefs is through responsible polling. There seems no reason in principle to imagine that somehow this kind of method would not work when we are asking people about their religious beliefs and practices, and in recent years much work has been done in this area. For our purposes here, we will restrict ourselves to the investigations of a small group of sociologists of religion: William V. D'Antonio, James D. Davidson, Mary L. Gauthier, and Dean R. Hoge. In four books published over the last fifteen years—namely, *American Catholic Laity in a Changing Church* (1989), *Laity, American and Catholic: Transforming the Church* (1996), *American Catholics: Gender, Generation, and Commitment* (2001) and *American Catholics Today: New Realities of Their Faith and Their Church* (2007)—they have produced extensive data and analysis that lead to conclusions both reassuring and challenging.[14] Their work uses the best Gallup Poll methods and is likely to be as reliable or as unreliable as polling in any other area of questioning. While the data is certainly not the last word on anything, it provides us with the best available information about the shape of American Catholic ecclesiality as a whole, and over the twenty years a fairly reliable picture of how that ecclesiality might be shifting in one direction or another.

Among the many fascinating findings in the latest book (*American Catholics Today*), some bear directly upon our questions about ecclesiality. The first has to do with Catholic identity. Of all of those questioned, 85% said that being Catholic was "a very important part" of who they were, 78% thought it important that younger generations of their families grew up as Catholics, and 70% said they couldn't imagine "being anything but Catholic." When the data was analyzed by generation it showed, not surprisingly, that only 7% of millennials rate Catholic identity high, as compared with 25% of Vatican II Catholics, and 47% of the younger generation rated it low, as compared with 31% of those from the Vatican II era.

The second revealing set of data emerges when the authors produce a list of twelve prominent teachings and practices and ask which were most important to the respondents. The four receiving the most positive response were helping the poor (84%), belief in Jesus' resurrection from the dead (84%), the sacraments such as the eucharist (76%), and Catholic teaching about Mary as the Mother of God (74%). These replies prompted Jim Davidson, one of the participant sociologists, to quip when making a presentation at Fairfield University, "So, what are the bishops worried about?"

What they are worried about, however, may be clearer when we look at the four items that received the lowest grades for importance. Only 44% rated church teachings opposing abortion, followed by Vatican teaching authority (42%), church teaching opposing the death penalty (35%), and a celibate male clergy (29%). All four of these items represent direct challenges to recent proclamations of the magisterium, and while the authors of the survey may be right in concluding that the laity "may simply be taking seriously Vatican II teachings on freedom of conscience informed by reason and faith,"[15] it seems highly unlikely that the U.S. bishops or Rome would see it in quite the same way. The present pope would also be very disquieted to hear that although a small majority of those questioned (53%) agreed that Catholicism has "a greater share of truth than other religions," a whopping 86% said that "if you believe in God, it doesn't really matter which religion you belong to."[16]

One further set of questions looks at the local parish. Here we find those questioned strongly believing that on the whole pastors do a good job (91%), though most expect laity to be "just followers" (53%). Some 40% believe Catholic parishes are too big and impersonal, and 63% think "Catholic church leaders are out of touch with the laity." In an area in which lay Catholics have no canonically recognized role, it is very instructive that they believe overwhelmingly that lay people should have a say in how parish and diocesan income is spent (89% and 84% respectively), in deciding about the increasingly common and difficult issue of parish closings (80%), and in the selection of priests for their parish (71%). On the question of the role of women in leadership in the church, those asked support their place as parish administrators caring for a parish in the absence of a resident priest (93%), as deacons (81%), and even as priests (63%).

Assessing the significance of these and the many other items of information that can be gleaned from these fascinating books is by no means easy. However, one or two tentative conclusions can be offered. First, one can say that Catholics as a whole seem to be firm on basic doctrines of the church, though they are more tolerant than they used to be of those who may in conscience dissent from one or other, and they certainly do not believe that regular mass attendance is any indicator of being a good Catholic. Second, it is clear that more and more Catholics are asserting the primacy of their consciences over church teaching in most if not all fundamental ethical issues. This seems to be true whether or not church teaching is perceived to be too conservative (birth control, abortion, extra-marital sex) or too liberal (capital punishment). Third, lay Catholics are increasingly discontented with their historic and still mostly *de facto* positions as somewhat passive recipients of the grace and favor of the clergy and the institutional church.

What these conclusions mean for our consideration of ecclesiality is even more complex. Clearly, there is no <u>*consensus fidelium*</u> where there is no real overwhelming agreement on this or that doctrine or practice. However, where prayerful discernment is taking place, there surely is *sensus fidelium* exactly as *Dei Verbum* described it. The probable response of the bishops to this kind of data would be to dismiss the opinions as ill-informed, disobedient, dissenting, or skewed by the inclusion of many people who are "not really practicing Catholics." Much of this, however, begs some questions, the most important being *who* determines the relationship between being Catholic and attending church on a regular basis. You or I may think it is valuable, even important, to worship in the faith community, but the deeper question is this: who is Catholic?

The charges of dissent also seem insecure when the numbers are as large as they apparently are. My local bishop refuses to talk with members of the lay organization Voice of the Faithful (VOTF)[17] in his own diocese on the grounds that they hold unacceptable views on hot-button issues like mandatory celibacy, the ordination of women, and the selection of bishops. The data presented here suggest that even if this is true, their "unacceptable" views are more or less mainstream.

Finally, if the opinions are dismissed as ill-informed, this invites two responses. The first would be that the *sensus fidelium* is the voice of the Spirit acting independently of the magisterium, always in process of formation, and that difference from current magisterial teaching can in some circumstances be an appropriate corrective to outmoded theological approaches. The second is to point out that if indeed numbers of this magnitude merely represent ill-informed people's opinions, then the effectiveness of church teaching, especially in ethical areas, is far from acceptable. If people "dissent" from church teaching, then shouting louder is not the answer. The responsibility clearly lies with the magisterium if faithful Catholics moved by the Holy Spirit and acting in conscience do not "receive" their teaching. The teaching authority needs to ask itself: are we teaching poorly, or are we teaching the wrong thing? Or is sinfulness really *so* pervasive? If prayerful and sincere people apparently cannot receive the teaching, can it really be possible that church authority is fighting a rearguard action on behalf of the Holy Spirit against the sinfulness of the (mostly lay) majority?

All of the above discussion suggests a very different inductive ecclesiology from the dominant deductive version. "Communion," "mystical body of Christ," "sacrament," "institution," and even "people of God" are certainly suggestive models for understanding ecclesial reality, but they are helpful only if they coincide with and are appropriately supportive of the actual life of the church as it is being lived today. The American Catholic Church of today is increasingly made up of much larger numbers than those who attend church regularly. Both those who do and those who don't continue to affirm basic beliefs like resurrection and the real presence of Christ in the eucharist. However, they are also much less likely to take their cues on ethical issues from church authority, and they are more and more unlikely to listen to the magisterium uncritically. All of this is entirely consistent with the demographic shifts with which we began that have produced a mostly middle-class and increasingly affluent, well-educated, and professional laity who affirm the cultural values of the American public square. The laity are come of age. The bigger question is whether the "parents" are ready to recognize it. True, some laity need incentive to develop critical approaches to the practices of their faith, and some still seem to be waiting for ecclesiastical permission, but the data suggests that these are far fewer than we might imagine. Unfortunately, if the "parents" cannot welcome and affirm these developments, more and more will take wing and never come home again.

Whole-body Ecclesiology

What, then, will a focus upon ecclesiality suggest as an appropriate ecclesiological model? An inductive approach can have no *a priori* preference for one received model over another, but will act to filter out models that are unhelpful. First to go is the model of "institution," closely followed by any models that seem to suggest a subordinationist understanding of hierarchy. Chapter one of *Lumen Gentium*, for example, includes "sheepfold" and "flock" among the biblical images it lists, but these are not good candidates for today's ecclesiological modeling, even though in the document it is very definitely Christ and not the local parish priest who is the shepherd. Unfortunately, they are inescapably reminiscent of Pius X's deplorable declaration that it is the "one duty of the multitude" to "allow themselves to be led and, like a docile flock, to follow the Pastors." It is also increasingly unlikely that models that stress the "nuptial metaphor" of groom (Christ) and bride (church) will reflect the realities of a community that understands the marital commitment very differently from a traditional head/body duality, and may increasingly be questioning the traditional understandings of marriage altogether.

An important model like "communion" could be more useful if it were dislodged from the institutional emphasis on "communion with the head" and focused more on "communion between the parts." It would, moreover, need to be loosened up so that degrees of communion with other Christian churches might be admitted into the model. It would be not so much a tapestry as a quilt, as at least some feminists might suggest. Of all the received images, "people of God" is surely the best candidate for further consideration, since its fuzziness around the edges allows for a greater variety of persons and opinion, and since it reaches out to the whole world, in the vision of *Lumen Gentium*, as a reality to which everyone is somehow related. People of God, in other words, goes beyond church. However, its very imprecision has made it more suspect in the institutional church, so that these days it is more commonly respectfully cast aside in favor of a communion model with a distinctively more conservative spin.

A candidate for consideration as a model more adequate to the emerging reality of American Catholic ecclesiality today is afforded in the concept of "whole-body ecclesiology" that became a focus in 1999 of British ecumenical discussions on conciliarity among Anglican, Methodist, and United Reform Church representatives.[18] The United Reformed Church used the term "whole-body ecclesiality" to denote the particular blend of "representation, constitutionality and consent" primarily expressed in the church meeting, a monthly or quarterly meeting of all the members of a local congregation. The use of this term enabled the United

Reformed Church to come to broad agreement with the Anglicans, who preferred the term "synodical" and naturally saw a role for episcopal oversight that didn't have a place in United Reformed considerations. But the two churches, together with the Methodists, were able to conclude that "conciliarity involving representation, constitutionality and consent could be seen in all three churches. All exercised oversight through councils as well as through personal leadership and all saw their life as in faithful continuity with the apostolic church."

In whole body ecclesiality it is the praxis of the community that determines ecclesiology. The model of American ecclesiality struggling to emerge today is one that is appropriate to a church of adults, one in which the laity—to use the memorable phrase of Bishop Geoffrey Robinson—are citizens, not merely civilians. All we have to do is look at the best of our faith communities. A vibrant parish will include a pastoral council and a finance council that operate to the full extent permitted by canon law and perhaps a little beyond. The care and concern of the parish will extend not only to the active members of the parish and to the wider world, but also to the young and the disaffected who are not present, or not so present, and who yet are a part of the community of faith. The survey data provided by D'Antonio and his colleagues support this view that the church is so much larger than the rolls of registered parish members. While there is no question that the vibrant and perhaps overly optimistic enthusiasm of the immediately post-conciliar years has been supplanted by a more sober awareness that the church is perhaps different from an open and democratic American vision of Catholicism, it remains true that the more enterprising and active voices in the faith community continue to find the personal resources to press for greater voice. The over thirty thousand lay ecclesial ministers are a good case in point. These mostly female full- or part-time church workers in official positions within the parishes are staunchly Vatican II in their ecclesial understanding, while working within a clerical church in rapid decline.[19] They gain enormous job satisfaction working with the people of the parish but are far less comfortable with many other aspects of the still-clerical church.

The beauty of whole-body ecclesiology is that it sees ecclesiology grounded in a polity that takes modern people seriously and that is appropriately adjusted to the cultural expectations of adults. The average American Catholic is no less professionally successful or less well educated than her Protestant counterpart, in fact statistically more so. She is also in all likelihood better educated than her clergy, and quite possibly better adjusted and more experienced in important areas like financial responsibility and ethical discernment. American Catholics are come of age, but they are living their lives of faith in a church that does not show corresponding structural maturity and that wants to keep the laity from all those areas in which their love for the church, their professional expertise, and worldly wisdom could be of enormous value. It is hard to avoid using the word "dysfunctional" in this context.

The continuing infantilization of the laity is not a conspiracy of the higher clergy against the people, but a product of inadequate ecclesiology. The place of the laity in the hierarchical church is an instance of structural oppression, in which everyone is implicated to some degree, and in which villains and victims are identified at our peril. Indeed, in some ways the very perpetuators of the situation are the biggest victims, acting out of their concern for the church while simultaneously hastening its decline. Their attachment to particular ecclesiological models, whether the people of God, communion, sacrament, or some other, is not a matter of choosing a better or worse model, but of misunderstanding the relationship between ecclesiality and the ecclesiological models. That each model might have something to offer is not determined in abstraction from the community of faith but rather in the way in which ecclesiality reveals this or that model to be at work. So, faithful ecclesiality in American Catholicism today has no place for the rigid hierarchical model of institution with its vision of a pyramidal church. An exploration of the sociological evidence suggests that the current situation is very fluid precisely because the older certainties have dissipated. This could be a cause for anxiety or excited anticipation, and there is surely room for both. But the way forward in the context of a mature Catholic laity has to be to let the Spirit work through the faithful sociality of the community. This is so Catholic and, let it be said, so American. Whole-body ecclesiology does not prejudge the outcomes. We are surely subject to the Spirit, to the scriptures, and to our own tradition, but only as living components in the ongoing work of discernment that Vatican II identified as the Spirit-inspired "intimate sense of spiritual realities" of the whole believing community. Might we say, of the "whole body"?

Notes

[1]*Fifty Years of Catholic Theology: Conversations with Yves Congar,* ed. with an introduction by Bernard Lauret (Philadelphia: Fortress Press, 1988), 65.

[2]"Ministères et laïcat dans les recherches actuelles de la théologie catholique romaine," *Verbum Caro* 18 (1964): 127-48; "Ministères et structuration de l'Eglise," *La Maison Dieu* 102 (1970): 7-20; "Quelques problèmes touchant les ministères," *Nouvelle revue théologique* 78 (1956): 5-52.

[3]For recent thorough discussions of these issues see Edward P. Hahnenberg, *Ministries: A Relational Approach* (New York: Crossroad, 2003), and Susan K. Wood, ed., *Ordering the Baptismal Priesthood: Theologies of Lay and Ordained Ministry* (Collegeville, MN: Liturgical Press, 2003).

[4]Pius X, *Vehementer Nos* (1906), 8.

[5]Thomas Jefferson, "A Bill for Establishing Religious Freedom," *Jefferson Papers,* ed. Julian P. Boyd (Princeton: Princeton University Press, 1950), 2, 545-46. See Esdras 4:4.

[6]See Bradford E. Hinze, *Practices of Dialogue in the Roman Catholic Church: Aims and Obstacles, Lessons and Laments* (New York: Continuum, 2006).

[7]*Dei Verbum* 8.

[8]Bernard Lonergan, "Theology in Its New Context," in *Theology of Renewal,* vol. 1 (Montreal: Palm Publishers, 1968), 37-38.

[9]See Paul Lakeland, *Postmodernity: Christian Identity in a Fragmented World* (Minneapolis: Fortress Press, 1997), 58-76 and 101-7.

[10]On this topic see Gerard Mannion, *Ecclesiology and Postmodernity: Questions for the Church in Our Time* (Collegeville, MN: Liturgical Press, 2007), esp. 31-74.

[11]Bellarmine writes: "The Church is one, not twofold, and this one true [Catholic] Church is the assembly of men united in the profession of the same Christian faith and in the communion of the same sacraments, under the rule of legitimate pastors, and in particular, that of the one Vicar of Christ on earth, the Roman Pontiff." *De Controversiis Christianae Fidei adversus Huis Temporis Haereticos,* Tom. 1, (Ingolstadt, 1586). *Quartae Controversia Generlist Liber Terisus, De Ecclesia Militante,* cap. 2, col 1263. English translation cited from "Scholastic Definitions of the Church", Part II, by Msgr. Joseph Clifford Fenton, *American Ecclesiastical Review,* August, 1944.

[12]Jean Daniélou, Henri de Lubac, Yves Congar, and Marie-Dominique Chenu.

[13]John E. Thiel, *Senses of Tradition: Continuity and Development in Catholic Faith* (New York: Oxford University Press, 2000), 129-60.

[14]William V. D'Antonio, James D. Davidson, Mary L. Gauthier, and Dean R. Hoge, *American Catholic Laity in a Changing Church* (Kansas City: Sheed & Ward, 1989); *Laity, American and Catholic: Transforming the Church* (Kansas City: Sheed & Ward, 1996); *American Catholics: Gender, Generation, and Commitment* (Walnut Creek, CA: AltaMira Press, 2001); *American Catholics Today: New Realities of Their Faith and Their Church* (Lanham, MD: Rowman & Littlefield Publishers, 2007).

[15]D'Antonio et al., *American Catholics Today*, 48.

[16]Ibid., 31.

[17]This Boston-based international organization of Catholics was founded in 2002 in response to the sexual abuse scandal, with the objectives of supporting victims, supporting priests and bishops of integrity, and of seeking modest structural reforms in the church.

[18] Available at http://www.urc.org.uk/conversations/conciliarity.htm.

[19] See, for example, the 1992 New Parish Survey of Lay and Religious Parish Ministers at http://www.thearda.com/Archive/Files/Descriptions/NPMLRPM.asp.

Contributors

Thomas F. Burke is a Ph.D. candidate in systematic theology at Boston College and is currently writing his dissertation on conceptions of kenosis in the sacramental theology of Louis-Marie Chauvet. His current research interests include systematic and contemporary sacramental theology, critical theologies of the cross, and the relationship between practical theology and spiritual practices.

William A. Clark, S.J., is an associate professor of religious studies at the College of the Holy Cross in Worcester, Massachusetts. He is the author of *A Voice of Their Own: The Authority of the Local Parish* (Liturgical Press, 2005), and is currently working on a book about the ecclesiological implications of parish reconfiguration.

James T. Cross is an assistant professor in the Department of Theology at Carroll College in Helena, Montana. His research interests include moral theology, especially Catholic social teaching and thought, the relationship between sacraments and the moral life, and the documents of the Second Vatican Council.

Carol J. Dempsey, O.P., a professor of theology (biblical studies) at the University of Portland, is the author of four volumes, the latest of which include *Justice: A Biblical Perspective* (Chalice, 2008) and *Jeremiah: Preacher of Grace, Poet of Truth* (Liturgical Press, 2007). Carol is also the editor of four books and, together with CTS colleagues Anne Clifford and Russell Butkus, Carol is co-editor of and contributor to a new interdisciplinary multivolume series entitled *Theology in Dialogue.*

Zeni Fox is professor of pastoral theology at Immaculate Conception Seminary, Seton Hall University. Author of *New Ecclesial Ministry: Lay Professionals Serving the Church* (Sheed & Ward, 2002) and co-editor of *Called and Chosen: Toward a Spirituality for Lay Leaders* (Rowman & Littlefield, 2005), she served as an advisor to the Subcommittee on Lay Ministry of the Bishops' Conference for over ten years.

Edward P. Hahnenberg is an associate professor of theology at Xavier University in Cincinnati. A past consultant to the U.S. Bishops' Subcommittee on Lay Ministry, he is the author of *Ministries: A Relational Approach* (Crossroad, 2003) and *A Concise Guide to the Documents of Vatican II* (St. Anthony Messenger Press, 2007). He is currently writing a book on the theology of vocation.

Carolyn Weir Herman is a Ph.D. candidate in theology at Boston College. Her dissertation explores the church's sacramentality as it develops in mid-twentieth-century European theology, Latin American liberation theology, and feminist theology in order to argue for greater justice in the contemporary Catholic Church. More broadly, her research interests include contemporary ecclesiology, liberation and feminist theologies, and Catholic social ethics.

Laurie Johnston is an assistant professor of religious studies at Emmanuel College and is a member of the Community of Sant'Egidio. She holds a Ph.D. in theological ethics from Boston College and an M.Div. from Harvard Divinity School.

William H. Johnston, an assistant professor in the Department of Religious Studies at the University of Dayton since 2006, previously served in pastoral ministry in the Diocese of Grand Rapids, the Archdiocese of Baltimore, and the Diocese of Richmond. His teaching and research focus on the areas of lay ecclesial ministry, and liturgy and the sacraments.

Paul Lakeland is the Aloysius P. Kelley S.J. Professor of Catholic Studies and the director of the Center for Catholic Studies at Fairfield University, where he has taught for twenty-seven years. His most recent books are *The Liberation of the Laity: In Search of an Accountable Church* (Continuum, 2003), which received the 2004 U.S. Catholic Press Association Award for the best book in theology, and *Catholicism at the Crossroads: How the Laity Can Save the Church* (Continuum, 2007), which received third place in the social concerns category in 2008 from the Catholic Press Association. He is currently working on an edition of the selected writings of Yves Congar and a book on the theology of the church.

Dolores R. Leckey is a senior fellow at the Woodstock Theological Center. She is the former executive director of the Secretariat for Family, Laity, Women and Youth at the United States Conference of Catholic Bishops, where she served for twenty years. In 1997, she was awarded the *Pro Ecclesia et Pontifice* medal by Bishop Anthony Pilla, then president of the USCCB. She was an official advisor to the American Catholic bishops in 1980 at the Synod on the Family and in 1987 at the Synod on the Laity. Her books include *Laity Stirring the Church: Prophetic Questions* (Fortress/Augsburg, 1987) and the recent *Grieving with Grace* (St. Anthony's Messenger Press, 2008).

Jonathan Malesic is an assistant professor of theology at King's College in Wilkes-Barre, Pennsylvania. His research is in philosophical theology, philosophy of religion, and the relations between Christian thought and modern culture. He is the author of a forthcoming book on Christian identity in political, economic, and cultural life titled *Secret Faith in the Public Square: A Theological Case for Concealing Christian Identity in Contemporary America* (Brazos Press, 2009).

Ann M. Michaud is a doctoral candidate in systematic theology at Fordham University. She has taught courses at Fordham University and at the University of Massachusetts, Boston. Ann was the 2006 recipient of the Elizabeth A. Johnson Fellowship of the Clare Rose Foundation. She is currently writing on the thought of John Haught and ecology and on the ethics of sex and gender. Ann's research interests focus on the intersection of issues in doctrine of God, theological anthropology, and ethics.

Tim Muldoon is assistant to the vice president for University Mission and Ministry at Boston College, where he also is an adjunct associate professor in the Honors Program of the College of Arts and Sciences. He is the author of three books, most recently *Seeds of Hope: Young Adults and the Catholic Church in the United States* (Paulist Press, 2008), and the co-editor of a forthcoming volume on Catholic perspectives on marriage ministry.

Angela Senander is an assistant professor and chair of the Department of Systematic and Moral Theology at Washington Theological Union. She works collaboratively with the Center for Ministry and Public Life at Washington Theological Union on such projects as Ecumenical Advocacy Days for Global Peace with Justice and The Future of Catholic Peacebuilding. Her current research focuses on Catholic identity and public life.

John Sniegocki is an assistant professor in the Department of Theology at Xavier University in Cincinnati. His main areas of interest include Catholic social teaching, globalization, the ethics of war and nonviolence, grassroots social movements, ecology, the impacts of our dietary choices, and contemplative spirituality. His first book, tentatively entitled *Catholic Social Teaching and Globalization: The Quest for Alternatives*, is forthcoming from Marquette University Press.

Tobias Winright is an assistant professor in the Department of Theological Studies at Saint Louis University. His main areas of research include Catholic social teaching, just war theory, criminal justice ethics, and ecology. He is currently working on a book with Mark Allman on post-war justice for Orbis Books, and he is editing a book on Catholic theological ethics and the environment for Saint Mary's Press.